Voting Procedures

Voting Procedures

Michael Dummett

CLARENDON PRESS·OXFORD
1984

Oxford University Press, Walton Street, Oxford OX2 6DP

*London New York Toronto
Delhi Bombay Calcutta Madras Karachi
Kuala Lumpur Singapore Hong Kong Tokyo
Nairobi Dar es Salaam Cape Town
Melbourne Auckland*

*and associates in
Beirut Berlin Ibadan Mexico City Nicosia*

Oxford is a trade mark of Oxford University Press

*Published in the United States
by Oxford University Press, New York*

© Michael Dummett 1984

*All rights reserved. No part of this publication may be reproduced,
stored in a retrieval system, or transmitted, in any form or by any means,
electronic, mechanical, photocopying, recording, or otherwise, without
the prior permission of Oxford University Press*

*This book is sold subject to the condition that it shall not, by way
of trade or otherwise, be lent, re-sold, hire out or otherwise circulated
without the publisher's prior consent in any form of binding or cover
other than that in which it is published and without a similar condition
including this condition being imposed on the subsequent purchaser*

*British Library Cataloguing in Publication Data
Dummett, Michael
Voting procedures.
1. Voting
I. Title
324.6   JF1001
ISBN 0-19-876188-0*

*Library of Congress Cataloging in Publication Data
Dummett, Michael A. E.
Voting procedures.
Bibliography: p.
Includes index.
1. Voting.   I. Title.
JF1001.D86 1984   324.9   84-14859
ISBN 0-19-876188-0*

*Set by Eta Services (Typesetters) Ltd,
Beccles, Suffolk
Printed in Great Britain
at the University Press, Oxford
by David Stanford
Printer to the University*

To my daughter
Susanna

Contents

INTRODUCTION		1
1	Successive Votes	14
2	Fundamental Notions	29
3	Binary Voting Procedures	60
4	Stability	78
5	Degrees of Admissibility	98
6	A Fair Outcome: the Criterion of Majority Preference	114
7	Preference Scores	129
	Appendix to Chapter 7	144
8	The Complete List Mechanism	152
9	The Alternative Vote and other Procedures	168
10	The Preference Score and Majority Number Procedures	176
	Appendix to Chapter 10	195
11	There is no Straightforward Procedure	202
12	Strategic Voting: the Alternative Vote	210
13	Strategic Voting: Preference Score and Majority Number Procedures	231
14	Voting with Many Possible Outcomes	243
15	Electing Representatives	255
16	STV and a New Alternative to it	266
EPILOGUE		294
BIBLIOGRAPHY		301
INDEX		305

Introduction

Voting plays an important part in human affairs, and was doing so long before democracy became a respectable political ideal. Any decision-making body must take votes in order to select its course of action between two or more alternatives proposed by its members. Abraham Lincoln once asked his cabinet for a show of hands on a proposal he had made, and then announced, 'Ayes 1, Noes 6: the Ayes have it.' The Federal cabinet of the United States is not, in the proper sense, a decision-making body, the President being, within the executive, a dictator: but genuine decision-making bodies are, and have long been, manifold—municipal councils, the senates of republics, conclaves of cardinals, cathedral chapters, guilds, boards of governors, appointment committees, and many others. Whenever a decision has to be taken by a number of people collectively, they will have to resort to voting if they cannot attain unanimity by discussion; voting has therefore the most direct practical bearing upon what happens in the world.

There are a number of distinct types of voting procedure. If it seldom made any effective difference to the outcome which of these procedures was adopted, and if, given a particular procedure, it were almost always obvious to every voter how he should best vote to secure an outcome as favourable, from his point of view, as possible, then, despite its practical importance, voting would not deserve much expenditure of thought. Neither of these hypotheses holds good. It is notorious that voters are often in a quandary, not over their own preferences, but over how best to cast their votes in the light of those preferences; and it is probable that many decisions arrived at by voting would have gone differently had a different voting procedure been employed.

This latter fact—that the voting procedure employed often has a critical effect upon the outcome—is one of which most people are largely unconscious; if this book succeeds in nothing else, it may make its readers aware of this important fact. An excellent example of it was provided by the election to the Deputy Leadership of the Labour Party in 1981. The preceding national conference of the Party at Wembley had allocated a 40 per cent share of the vote to the trade unions, and 30 per cent each to MPs and to constituency parties: but it had not laid down how, within each of these allocations, the votes were to be distributed to the rival candidates. The method adopted, by a prior decision of the National Executive of the Party, was to divide the total allocation in the proportion of those within the given category voting for the respective candidates, ignoring abstentions. In the event, on the second ballot, 54.583 per cent of the MPs voted for Mr Healey, 28.287 per cent of them voted for Mr Benn, and 17.13 per cent of them abstained. The 30 per cent of the total vote allocated to MPs was therefore divided between Mr Healey and Mr Benn in the ratio of 54.583 to 28.287, providing 19.759 per cent of the total vote for Mr Healey and 10.241 per cent for Mr Benn; as everyone knows, Mr Healey won by a hair's breadth (50.426 per cent of the total vote as against 49.574 per cent for Mr Benn). Before the election, however, Mr George Cunningham, a Labour MP, had been pointing out to his colleagues the possibility of an alternative method, and emphasizing the potential importance of the choice between it and that actually adopted. On Mr Cunningham's method, the number of votes assigned to any one candidate from any one of the three categories would be in proportion to the percentage of members of that category actually voting for the given candidate. Thus if 60 per cent of MPs had voted for Mr Healey, 30 per cent for Mr Benn, and 10 per cent had abstained, on this method 18 per cent of the total vote would have been assigned to Mr Healey as the contribution of the MPs and 9 per cent to Mr Benn; the remaining 3 per cent of the total vote allocated to MPs would have remained unassigned to either candidate, in accordance with the 10 per cent abstention. On the method actually adopted, on the other hand, the 30 per cent allocation to MPs would have been divided in the ratio 2:1, since twice as many MPs would have voted for Mr Healey as voted for Mr Benn: Mr Healey would therefore have received from MPs 20 per cent of the total vote and Mr Benn 10 per cent, making a difference in favour of Mr Healey 1 per cent greater than on Mr Cunningham's method. As Mr Cunningham explained in a letter published in the *Guardian* on 12 October 1981, he attempted, in advance of the election, to indicate the greater reasonableness of his method by considering an extreme case: if all MPs but one decided to abstain, it would hardly be fair to allocate 30 per cent of the total vote to that one MP, as would happen on the method actually used. The National Executive, however, dismissed the matter as of trifling importance, and refused to modify the method it had laid down. It was not of trifling importance. Had Mr Cunningham's method been adopted, only 16.375 per cent of the total vote would have been assigned to Mr Healey from the MPs, as against 8.486 per cent to Mr Benn: the overall outcome would have been 47.219 per cent of the total vote for Mr Benn and 46.429 per cent for Mr Healey; Mr Benn, rather than Mr Healey, would have won the election by a hair's breadth.

Here we have quite a small difference in voting procedure which, in the event, made a critical difference to the outcome of an election which was surely of immense importance for the future of British politics. If so small a modification would have had a critical effect, it must be conceded that major changes of procedure are more likely yet to make a substantial difference to the outcome of a vote; this will be illustrated in subsequent chapters. It must not be thought that, in the case just discussed, the method of assigning the votes was cynically imposed by people favouring a particular outcome. On the contrary, Mr Cunningham made plain in his letter that it had been a supporter of Mr Benn who impatiently ruled out further discussion of the matter. Such things happen because of a very prevalent prejudice. If you demonstrate, by means of a hypothetical example, that a choice between alternative possible voting procedures could affect the outcome, the reaction of many people is to say that such a case would be very unlikely to occur and that the question is therefore of no practical importance. The fact is that we usually do not have sufficient data to be able to say what, in a particular instance, would have happened had a different voting procedure been employed; it is therefore difficult to cite an actual example, although dispassionate consideration of the possibilities indicates that it must happen very often that a different procedure would have produced a different result. I have discussed the Labour Party election because is it one of the very few instances in which we can say, for certain, what would have happened if a slightly different method had been used.

In view of all this, one would expect that voting procedures and their operation would have been the subject of a considerable amount of intellectual enquiry. One would expect also that the results of such investigations would be well known both to political and social theorists and to all those concerned with practical affairs, and would be applied both by those who have frequently to take part in voting and, above all, by those concerned to devise voting procedures to be as fair and as satisfactory as possible. Of these two natural expectations, the first is indeed satisfied, but the second hardly at all. In the period since the end of the Second World War, a considerable body of theory concerning voting has been built up. This topic was pioneered by Professor Duncan Black, an economist, who published some articles about it in the late 1940s, and a book, *The Theory of Committees and Elections*, in 1958: an important contribution, not expressed specifically in terms of voting, was made by Professor Kenneth Arrow in his book *Social Choice and Individual Values* of 1951.[1] Since then, and especially in the last two decades, the theory initiated by Black and Arrow has been extensively developed, principally in articles published in learned journals. One of the most surprising features of all this is how recent this work is. Duncan Black devoted a section of his book to a historical survey. From this it emerged that almost the only serious work on the theory of voting that had been previously done was carried out in France just before and during the Revolution, by Borda, Condorcet, and Laplace; this work had subsequently been almost entirely forgotten, save by a few British mathematicians of the nineteenth and early twentieth centuries, who made insignificant contributions to it. A minor exception, not noticed by Black, is the unimpressive section devoted to the subject by the German philosopher Hermann Lotze in his *Logik* of 1874. The only exception mentioned by Black is the remarkable intervention by C. L. Dodgson (Lewis Carroll), contained in three pamphlets which he wrote in complete ignorance of the work of his predecessors, and which were directed at the voting

---

[1] See the Bibliography for works by Arrow and Black. Arrow's possibility theorem (more exactly called an impossibility theorem) is so fundamental to the subject that he is often credited with having been the modern initiator of it, especially since his basic notation has become standard. This is unfair to Black, who was the real twentieth-century pioneer of the theory of voting, as well as a diligent researcher into its earlier history; it may be due in part to the fact that, although Black's original papers on the subject appeared in 1948–9, his book was not published until 1958, while Arrow's celebrated monograph came out in 1951. Black was, in particular, the originator of the concept of single-peakedness (not used in the present book), with which Arrow is sometimes credited but which he in fact took over from Black. Single-peakedness is a condition which guarantees the existence of a top. For the case when some preference scales are weak, the condition was weakened by Farquharson and myself in our paper of 1961; alternative though analogous sufficient conditions were later given by Inada, Sen, and Pattanaik.

procedure to be adopted by the governing body of Christ Church, Oxford, to which he belonged.[2]

It is highly surprising that a topic of such evident practical importance, and one in which quite significant discoveries can be made simply by thinking about it systematically without the use of any sophisticated mathematical techniques, should have been so largely neglected until quite recent times. Whatever the explanation, the neglect has been ended: there is now a substantial body of theory in existence. The resulting situation is, however, a greater surprise still. The theory of voting is not worth bothering with unless it is going to be applied: that is, unless those actually concerned with national and local politics, or involved in committees, governing bodies, selection panels, and the like, know something of the theory and use it to devise improved voting procedures. Yet the theory of voting that has been developed appears to be wholly unknown to anyone concerned with its practical applications. It is certainly quite unknown to the politicians, national and local, and to others actually involved in decision-making; it appears to be largely unknown also to experts in political institutions and political theory, to students of psephology (the empirical study of election results), and even to those concerned to advocate schemes of electoral reform. The theory has been developed mainly by theoretical economists, together with a few professional philosophers. Their results are known only to a small circle of people, composed of their academic colleagues in those fields and of some who have studied economics at university. As a result, investigations into the theory of voting have entirely missed the serious point that they might have had and ought to have: those who carry them out talk only to one another, and altogether fail to communicate with those who could put their results to practical use. It is in the hope of remedying this deplorable situation that this book has been written.

To those unacquainted with any of the work to which I am referring, even with Dodgson's masterly pamphlets, these assertions may seem implausible. There is, after all, a considerable literature on electoral reform, advocating or criticizing various systems of

---

[2] See the Bibliography. It is a matter for the deepest regret that Dodgson never completed the book that he planned to write on the subject. Such were his lucidity of exposition and his mastery of the topic that it seems possible that, had he ever published it, the political history of Britain would have been significantly different.

proportional representation, and well known to practical politicians and to students of political institutions. I do not wish to deny that some of this literature contains genuine contributions to the theory of voting; it must nevertheless be classified under a different head from work directly concerned with that theory. The reason is that it does not adopt a systematic approach; and it does not do so because it fails to develop an apparatus of precisely defined fundamental notions. It therefore tends to leave far too much to intuition; and intuition, in this area, is a treacherous guide. Writers on electoral reform rely improperly on intuition when they assert that some system would have a certain effect without attempting to prove that it does; what appears obvious, on such a matter, will very often prove upon investigation to be false. Intuition is an even poorer guarantor of meaning than of truth: works on electoral reform frequently employ terminology whose meaning, though at first glance evident, is exceedingly difficult to state, as when they speak of someone's wasting his vote. The clearest example of this lies at the very heart of the subject of electoral reform. It is agreed on all hands that a parliament should represent the electorate, that is, that its composition should reflect the divisions in public opinion. Proportional representation has the object of making Parliament more representative: rival systems are to be judged, in the first instance, by how effectively they achieve this. It ought, then, to be the first task of any discussion of electoral reform to make precise what is meant by calling a parliament representative; yet the question is virtually never posed. Rather, it is taken for granted that everyone knows what 'representative' means; the assumption appears to be that a parliament is representative if its composition, by political party, corresponds closely to the composition of the electorate, judged by the party which each elector prefers to all the others.

This assumption embodies a possible definition of the word 'representative', as used in this connection; it is far from obvious that it is the right definition to give. Advocates of proportional representation are usually contemptuous of voting procedures which require each elector simply to nominate a single candidate. They ought, therefore, to be suspicious of the definition implicit in the assumption; but they give no appearance of being so. Suppose that the British electorate were divided, in the percentages shown, into groups ranking the four national parties in the following orders:

32%	30%	23%	10%	3%	2%
Lab	Con	SDP	SDP	Lib	Lib
Lib	Lib	Lib	Lib	SDP	SDP
Con	Lab	Lab	Con	Lab	Con
SDP	SDP	Con	Lab	Con	Lab

The table shows, not the voting intentions of the electors, but their personal preferences; it is not, of course, claimed as an accurate diagnosis of the actual division of opinions, only of a possible one. On the assumption under discussion, a fully representative parliament would contain 33 per cent of SDP members, 32 per cent of Labour ones, 30 per cent of Conservatives, and only 5 per cent of Liberals. Yet, by a highly reasonable criterion, the Liberal Party is the most popular: 70 per cent of the electorate prefer it to the Conservative Party, 68 per cent prefer it to the Labour Party, and 67 per cent to the SDP. Conversely, by the same criterion, the SDP is the least popular party: 62 per cent prefer both the Conservative and Labour Parties to it and 67 per cent prefer the Liberal Party. This is not to claim that, in such a case, the Liberals would be the most numerous party, and the SDP the least, in a representative parliament: it is simply to observe that it is far from clear what, in general, a representative parliament is.

Almost everyone's first reaction to such an example is to say that it is highly improbable. So indeed it is: it is very unlikely, for instance, that all Conservatives would rank the other three parties in the same order. A moment's reflection shows, however, that the example could be made much more complex, and hence intrinsically more probable, without affecting its salient features, that to each of the other parties a majority prefers the Liberals, and that every other party is preferred by a majority to the SDP, although the SDP commands the largest number of supporters and the Liberal Party the smallest. In fact, the difficulty will arise when there is only one party which satisfies one, but not the other, criterion for popularity; such a case is quite probable.

In the present connection, this retort is just; but it fails to reach the heart of the matter. The question to be asked is: what is the function of the observation that the difficulty will arise only in rare cases? In the present instance, the observation is not even true: but, if it were true, how would it bear on the problem? The objector might mean one of two things. He might mean, first, that, if we assign each voter to the political party he ranks higher than the others, then we ought not actually to *define* a representative parliament as one whose composition, by political parties, matches that of the electorate; but that, nevertheless, such a match will serve as a generally reliable *sign* that the parliament is representative. On this interpretation of his words, he is therefore claiming that, in the great majority of cases in which is such a match, though perhaps not in absolutely all of them, the parliament will in fact be representative. Now if this is the right way of understanding his claim, this objector has not escaped the duty of explaining what he means by 'representative'. On the contrary, until he has explained that, we are in no position to judge whether his claim is true: we do not know of *what* the match between the composition of parliament and the electorate is supposed to be a reliable sign.

The objector might alternatively be wishing to convey that he is content to leave the meaning of 'representative' unspecified for certain distributions of preferences among the voters: for other distributions, for which he *is* prepared to specify it, he proposes to explain it in terms of a match between the composition of parliament by parties and the distribution of first preferences, as between the parties, among the electorate. In itself, this is not an unreasonable position to adopt: we cannot always demand a definition that will cover every case. It is only reasonable, however, provided that the cases for which the application of 'representative' is left unspecified are truly infrequent; once again, we cannot judge whether they are frequent or infrequent until we have been told which they are. A watertight definition need not be demanded; but some non-circular characterization is required. The mere possibility of a case in which it would be hard to know how to apply a term—in the present instance, the term 'representative'—is enough to show it to be imprecise. It is permissible to decline the task of making it more precise for certain rare cases, if one can explain which cases one is thus setting aside; but one cannot dismiss the difficulty merely by setting aside all those cases in which it arises, without further specifying them.

Because the literature on electoral reform leaves crucial terms undefined and is content with plausible, though unproved, claims, it cannot be reckoned as part of the systematic theory of voting, even though it contains proposals and observations relevant to that theory. The difficulty concerning the representation of the electorate illustrated by the foregoing example closely resembles the difficulty, with which we shall be much concerned in this book, of determining whether or not a collective decision is fair, in the light of the preferences of those participating in it. Suppose that the 100 members of a council have to decide between four possible courses of action. If we reinterpret the labels 'Lab', 'Con', etc., as names for these courses of action, and the table as showing the preferences of the members of the council, what would be the fair decision? The theory of voting as it applies to cases of this kind, namely to votes taken within a decision-making body with a fixed membership, already involves considerable complexity, and we shall be concerned with it until the last two chapters of this book. The topic of electoral systems introduces a great many complications that do not arise in the simpler context. It is rash to tackle the more complex case until one has thoroughly surveyed the problems that arise in the simpler one; one is otherwise building without a secure foundation. It is the lack of such a foundation that, above all, deprives the literature on electoral systems of the status of contributions to a systematic theory.

There are many features that render the theory of electoral systems vastly more complex than that of voting on committees. One of them is the dual significance of a vote in a general election under any system which, unlike that in force in Israel, divides the country into local constituencies: a vote goes to determine both who shall represent the constituency and what the composition of Parliament is to be. In West Germany, each elector casts two distinct votes for the two different purposes; under most systems, including those in use in Britain and the United States, the same vote must serve both ends. Furthermore, an elector's preferences concerning the composition are far from being confined to the wish that his favourite party should do well. He may be anxious that some other party should not be wiped out; he may hope for a coalition; he may want his party to have a decisive, but not overwhelming, majority. Is it possible to devise an electoral system that would allow electors to give expression to such preferences? Perhaps it is not; but the question is seldom posed. Instead, advocates of proportional representation often lose their enthusiasm for the will of the people at this point. Having gauged the probable effect of each rival system on the structure of political parties and the composition of Parliament, they argue in favour of that system most likely, in their judgement, to produce the effects which are most to their own taste.[3] The problem is not, however, to decide in advance what type of result is desirable, and then to impose a system that will make such a result probable: it is to devise a system that will, as nearly as possible, give the electorate what it wants, whatever that may be. To foist on people an electoral system that will make it difficult to elect a parliament in which one party has a majority, even when the bulk of the electorate would prefer any majority to none, is no fairer or more democratic than to compel them to use a system that makes it very hard to achieve a coalition government, even though that might be what most electors wanted. Of course, the phrase 'what the electorate wants' does not always have a clear application: we are back with the problem what constitutes a fair decision, given voters' preferences.

There are two problems: what the outcome ought to be, given what the voters want; and how to devise a voting procedure that will produce that outcome. Both problems are not only hard but messy, in that they have no unique compelling solution. As they relate to electoral systems, they are also enormously complex, which is why I have in this book discussed electoral methods only from a single aspect. As they relate to voting on committees and the like, they are more tractable, though they still demand careful thought; without such thought about this simpler case, one is hardly in a position to tackle the question of electoral systems, which is why I have concentrated largely on the simpler case.

Why does even this simpler case present such difficulty? There is no difficulty in deciding between two possible courses of action, or two candidates for an appointment: one has only to take a straight vote between them, and let the majority decide. The difficulty arises as soon as there are more than two possible decisions open to the voters. Let us suppose that an appointments committee has to decide between three candidates for a post, Miss Abel, Mr Baker, and Mrs Charles. After discussion, it is decided to take a vote; after further discussion, a method of voting is agreed on. The vote is taken, and, in consequence, Mr Baker is appointed. A member of the committee then discovers, after questioning his colleagues, that a majority would have preferred Miss Abel to Mr Baker, although, indeed, a majority preferred Mr Baker to Mrs Charles. Almost

---

[3] A good example of this is the article by Philip Williams cited in the Bibliography.

everyone who has not thought systematically about voting will be inclined to conclude that an injustice has been done, almost certainly due to the adoption of a faulty voting procedure. But it's not necessarily so. The crucial question is whether a majority preferred Miss Abel to Mrs Charles, or a majority preferred Mrs Charles to Miss Abel. If a majority preferred Miss Abel to Mrs Charles, then it is very probable—on some ways of viewing the matter, certain—that an injustice has been done; but that this is so does *not* follow from the fact that a majority preferred Miss Abel to Mr Baker and a majority preferred Mr Baker to Mrs Charles, even though every individual voter who both preferred Miss Abel to Mr Baker and preferred Mr Baker to Mrs Charles naturally also preferred Miss Abel to Mrs Charles. If, as is quite possible, a majority preferred Mrs Charles to Miss Abel, it may well be that Mr Baker was clearly the best candidate, judged from the preferences of the voters. At any rate, the fact that a majority preferred one of the other candidates to him cannot be taken to entail that he was not the best candidate: for the same could be said *whichever* of the candidates had been appointed. If Miss Abel had been appointed, a majority would have preferred Mrs Charles; if Mrs Charles had been appointed, a majority would have preferred Mr Baker. Such facts do *not* prove that a miscarriage of justice has occurred: they may be inescapable.

This is the celebrated 'paradox of voting', which will be discussed in more detail in Chapter 4. It is almost the first thing anyone learns when he begins to study the theory of voting, and it is in no way difficult for anyone to grasp as soon as the very possibility has occurred to him; but that very possibility has not occurred to most people who take part in votes or have to decide what method of voting to adopt. Only when one has not only grasped it but come to terms with it is one really in a position to think clearly about voting procedures. The position of this so-called paradox, which is not a genuine paradox, but merely a surprising fact, as one of the fundamental premisses of the entire theory of voting is perhaps indirectly responsible for the neglect of that theory by those practically concerned with voting. The paradox has the consequence that there are many more negative general theorems to be proved in the theory than there are positive ones: starting with Kenneth Arrow, contributors to the mathematical theory have put out a plethora of such negative theorems, proving the impossibility of any voting procedure having this or that combination of desirable characteristics. It would be natural for anyone with a practical concern with voting to turn in disgust from this literature as incapable of providing any positive guidance.

That would be a mistake. If there are unpalatable facts to be faced, it is useless to blame those who discovered them; harm can only result from refusing to face them, or, perhaps, even to grasp them. The theory of voting provides the concepts that have to be used if voting procedures are to be thought about clearly and fruitfully, the indispensable tools for an important and not altogether easy task. This book is written in the conviction that despair is the wrong reaction to the negative results of the theorists. As we shall see, there is no available, indeed, no conceivable, definition of an ideal voting procedure of which it would not be provable that no such procedure could exist; we can hope for no more than a rough approximation to the ideal. Once this fact has been accepted, however, we can discriminate between rival procedures on a systematic basis, and can try rationally to devise procedures that serve their intended purposes as well as can be hoped for; and, in thus scrutinizing and improving on the procedures in actual use, the conceptual tools supplied by the formal theory can alone provide the necessary intellectual technology.

In the sense that I have left unattempted any comprehensive investigation of the problem of electoral systems, because of its enormous theoretical complexity, my aim in this book is modest. In another respect, it is ambitious: I wish to act as a channel of communication between those who have developed a systematic mathematical theory of voting and those who could put its results to some use. At present the practical politicians are unaware even of the existence of the theorists, whose intellectual effort therefore goes utterly to waste, like water gushing from a disconnected pipe. I have for this reason tried to keep the discussion directed always towards the practical end of selecting a voting procedure to be used for this or that purpose, and have not only expounded the general theory, but applied it to particular procedures. What stands in the way of people's thinking systematically about voting is not the lack of mathematical techniques, but a failure to realize that there is anything which requires much thought. The mechanics of their trade is intrinsically boring to most politicians; they therefore form the prejudice that, as regards voting procedures, intuition is an adequate substitute for thought. It is not: even the simplest facts about the subject are deeply surprising to most people when first grasped. Failure on the part of politicians to understand the possible effects of adopting one or another voting procedure amounts to ignorance of the tools of their trade. In so far as their judgements have positive value, which they must believe to be so, they ought to wish to improve the mechanism they employ for converting their collective wishes into action, which is what voting is. In this context, politicians include all who are involved in any corporate decision-making process: members of boards of governors and of directors as well as of the House of Commons.

1
Successive Votes

A first distinction within the theory of voting might be between a *static* theory and a *dynamic* theory. Suppose that the composition of a committee is fixed for a certain period, during which it has to take a number of decisions. The following proposition, at first glance surprising, belongs to the dynamic theory of voting: a majority of the committee members may be in the minority on a majority of occasions. The simplest possible illustration is the following. The committee has just five members, whom we may label with the numerals from 1 to 5: it votes on just three occasions, each time on a simple motion to be accepted or rejected; each vote is decided by simple majority. Each voter votes 'sincerely', that is, in accordance with his own preferences, and the results are as follows:

	voter 1	voter 2	voter 3	voter 4	voter 5	outcome
motion a	Pro	Con	Con	Pro	Pro	carried
motion b	Con	Pro	Con	Pro	Pro	carried
motion c	Con	Con	Pro	Pro	Pro	carried

Example 1(a)

Voters 1, 2, and 3 constitute between them a majority of the committee members; but each of them has voted with the majority only one time in three, and has therefore been in the minority a majority of times, namely two out of three. Voters 4 and 5, on the other hand, have been in the majority *every* time.

If we allot to each voter a 'satisfaction score' of $+1$ whenever the outcome accords with his wishes, and of -1 whenever it is contrary to them, we can draw up the following satisfaction table for example 1(a):

	voter 1	voter 2	voter 3	voter 4	voter 5	total
motion a	$+1$	-1	-1	$+1$	$+1$	$+1$
motion b	-1	$+1$	-1	$+1$	$+1$	$+1$
motion c	-1	-1	$+1$	$+1$	$+1$	$+1$
total	-1	-1	-1	$+3$	$+3$	$+3$

The grand total of satisfaction, summed over all five voters and all three votes, is thus +3. Such a satisfaction table should not be taken too seriously: but it offers some intuitive indication of how well the voting procedure has realized the conflicting wishes of the voters.

Professor Elizabeth Anscombe is deeply impressed by the proposition illustrated by example 1(a), and has illustrated it by a more complex example with ten voters participating in ten votes; six of her ten voters find themselves in the majority only four times out of ten. From this she argues that 'although (these six voters) have actively exercised their voting rights, their acquiescence' in the decisions 'ought in reason to be called a passive consent'; she comments that 'the appearance that one is not subjected to any authority that exercises power over the individual may be compelling in a case in which one has cast one's vote with the majority, but it is nevertheless an illusion'.[1] To argue in this manner is fallacious, for a fairly obvious reason. Only individuals, not groups, whether a majority or a minority, can be said to give consent, active or passive. If they abide by the decision taken in any one particular vote, those who were in the minority in that vote may be said to give their active consent to it. One cannot argue that the consent of a majority must be passive, not active, on the ground that it is a majority: only the *members* of the majority may be said to consent, and their consent is required only on the occasions on which they were in the minority.

If a procedure is employed under which, in any one vote, a majority in favour of any given outcome is decisive, a majority can always enforce its will. It follows, therefore, that, in example 1, voters 1, 2, and 3 can together secure a series of outcomes more favourable to themselves. If they form a party, and agree always to vote for the outcome preferred by the majority within the party, the results will be as follows:

	voter 1	voter 2	voter 3	voter 4	voter 5	outcome
motion *a*	Con	Con	Con	Pro	Pro	lost
motion *b*	Con	Con	Con	Pro	Pro	lost
motion *c*	Con	Con	Con	Pro	Pro	lost

Example 1(b)

Voters 4 and 5 are now in the minority on every occasion, while voters 1, 2, and 3, because they all vote together, vote with the

[1] See p. 51 of the essay cited in the Bibliography.

majority on every occasion: each of them obtains the outcome he prefers on two out of the three occasions, while voters 4 and 5 fail to do so on any occasion. This is shown by the new satisfaction table:

	voter 1	voter 2	voter 3	voter 4	voter 5	total
motion a	-1	$+1$	$+1$	-1	-1	-1
motion b	$+1$	-1	$+1$	-1	-1	-1
motion c	$+1$	$+1$	-1	-1	-1	-1
total	$+1$	$+1$	$+1$	-3	-3	-3

The grand total of satisfaction is now -3; but voters 1, 2, and 3 have improved their individual totals, bringing them from -1 to $+1$. These three voters are no longer voting sincerely, i.e. in accordance with their personal preferences; each of them votes contrary to his own preference in one of the three votes. None of them, acting alone, could gain any advantage by so voting: by acting in concert, each does so.

Because voters 1, 2, and 3 can form such an alliance, to their mutual benefit, it must be wrong to describe them as merely passively consenting to the committee decisions in the case when they form no such alliance: by refraining from forming the alliance, and voting sincerely, they manifest a very active consent. When all vote sincerely, the three motions are all carried, and the grand total of satisfaction is $+3$. When the alliance is formed, all three motions are lost, and the grand satisfaction total is -3. If one motion were carried, the other two being lost, the grand satisfaction total would be -1; the one voter whose wishes were fulfilled on all three occasions would obtain $+3$ in all, while each of the four other voters would obtain -1. If two of the motions were carried, and the other lost, the grand total would be $+1$: for one voter, all three votes would go the wrong way, so that he would obtain -3 in all, while each of the other four voters would obtain $+1$. It is reasonable to regard these grand totals as representing the degree to which the decisions conform to the wishes of the voters collectively. The four cases mentioned comprise all the distinct possible types of overall outcome: given the preferences of the five voters, the only possible grand totals are $+3$, $+1$, -1, and -3. One motive for refusing to form an alliance might be a social conscience: a voter rightly perceives that he cannot by such a means obtain an advantage for himself without diminishing the total collective satisfaction, that is, without distorting the voting mechanism as a means of realizing the wishes of committee members as nearly as possible. Of course, another reason for not forming the alliance might be that the voters did not foresee that the subsequent motions b and c were going to come up: successful strategic voting always depends upon good information. Once the vote on motion a has been taken, voters 2 and 3 have no motive for forming an alliance: they cannot hit on any pair of voting strategies which will improve the overall result for both.

Since, in any procedure under which a majority is decisive, a majority can always enforce its collective wishes, it will always be to the advantage of a majority to form a party each of whose members are to adopt the voting strategies decided by the party, provided two conditions are fulfilled. These are, first, that the members of the majority can agree upon a set of strategies which will improve the overall result for every member, and, second, that they can trust one another to abide by the decisions of the party. Let us consider the second point first, using our simple example. Assume that, as before, voters 1, 2, and 3 have formed an alliance, agreeing to vote against all three motions, and that the first two motions have been put and duly defeated. Voter 3 has now no personal motive for abiding by the agreement in the vote on motion c. He might of course have one if he believed that further motions were to be put: but if he knows that the vote on motion c is the last one the committee will take, he can greatly improve his own position by reneging on the agreement and voting for motion c, which will then be carried. All three votes will then have gone according to his wishes, so that his satisfaction total will be $+3$; voters 1 and 2 will have satisfaction totals of -1, as they would have done had the voting been sincere, and voters 4 and 5 will also have satisfaction totals of -1, so that the grand total will be -1. If voter 3 refrains from acting in this way, even though he does not expect any further vote to take place, he is acting in accordance with a sense of honour, even if it is honour among thieves, and must be said to be displaying an active consent to the decisions of the party, rather than to those of the committee as a whole.

This consideration about voter 3 may affect the behaviour of voter 2. Suppose that the alliance has been formed, and that motion a has been put and accordingly defeated, but that, before any further vote is taken, voter 2 becomes suspicious of voter 3's integrity. He may then reason as follows. 'If I and voter 3 both abide by the agreement, two of the three votes will go as I want them to and I will obtain a satisfaction total of $+1$. If, on the other hand, I abide by it and voter 3 does not, only one vote, on motion a, will have gone my way and my satisfaction total will be -1. If I renege on the agreement in the vote on motion b, voter 3, even if he is honest, will certainly do the same on the third vote, regarding the agreement as no longer binding: in such a case, I shall again get my way on two of the votes, obtaining a satisfaction total of $+1$. The overall result therefore cannot be worse for me if I break the agreement than if I keep it, and may be better.' So reasoning, he may renege on the second vote, laying the blame on voter 3's suspected intention of doing so on the third: the result will be that voter 1 obtains a satisfaction total of -3, and all the other voters one of $+1$, making a grand total of $+1$.

Even in so simple a case, the complexities of party politics are not yet at an end. Suppose that voter 1, before any vote has been taken, is thinking of forming an alliance with voters 2 and 3. Voters 4 and 5 get wind of his intention, and are naturally alarmed. They therefore approach voter 1 with the proposal that he make an alliance with them instead: they will vote against motion b provided that he votes for motion c (it actually makes no difference whether voter 1 keeps his side of the bargain or not). If voter 1 believes that it is more likely that at least *one* of voters 4 and 5 would stick to such a bargain than that *both* voters 2 and 3 would keep the one he had been proposing to make with them, he should form an alliance with voters 4 and 5. For he may reason in the following way. 'If I form an alliance with voters 2 and 3, and they both keep to their agreement, I shall obtain a satisfaction total of $+1$. If, on the other hand, voter 3 reneges, I shall do no better than if I had formed no alliance, obtaining a total of -1; and if voter 2 reneges, I shall do as badly as I possibly could, obtaining a total of -3, that is, having all three votes go contrary to my wishes. If, on the other hand, I form an alliance with voters 4 and 5, then, if even only one of them keeps to the agreement, motion b will be defeated, and I shall obtain a satisfaction total of $+1$, while, if neither does, I shall obtain -1. Thus, if I join an alliance with voters 4 and 5, I cannot do worse than if no alliance had been formed, and may do better; while, if I join one with voters 2 and 3, I cannot do better than an alliance with 4 and 5, and may do much worse. Besides, if I do not join 4 and 5, there is the danger that they will ally themselves with voter 2 or 3 and agree to vote against motion a: I shall then again be disappointed on all three votes'. So reasoning, he accepts the proposal of voters 4 and 5, who stick to the agreement: the result is that voter 2 obtains a satisfaction total of -3, while, as before, all other voters obtain $+1$, so that the grand total is again $+1$.

The second condition for a successful alliance of a group forming a majority of the voters was that they could agree upon a set of strategies which would benefit every member of the group. Since, being a majority, they have the power to decide the outcome of every vote, it is really only a matter of a single strategy, to be followed by everyone in the group. The easiest means they have for arriving at such a strategy is to vote on it: that is, to vote within the group upon every motion, on the understanding that every member of the group will, when the vote is taken in the committee, vote in accordance with the wishes of the majority within the group. That was how the alliance of voters 1, 2, and 3 proceeded in example 1(b): since, on every motion, a majority within the group was opposed to it, they all voted against each motion in the committee vote. It would be a mistake, however, to suppose that these tactics will always work. To see this, consider an extended example: we have the same five voters as before, but there are now four more motions to be voted on. If all five voted sincerely, the results would be:

	voter 1	voter 2	voter 3	voter 4	voter 5
motion a	Pro	Con	Con	Pro	Pro
motion b	Con	Pro	Con	Pro	Pro
motion c	Con	Con	Pro	Pro	Pro
motion d	Con	Con	Pro	Pro	Pro
motion e	Con	Con	Pro	Pro	Pro
motion f	Pro	Pro	Con	Con	Pro
motion g	Pro	Pro	Con	Pro	Con

Example 2

Under sincere voting, therefore, all seven motions will be carried. Each of the voters 1, 2, and 3 is opposed to four of the motions: thus, once again, every member of a majority of the committee finds himself in the minority on a majority of occasions. When all vote sincerely, each of the voters 1, 2, and 3 will obtain a satisfaction total of -1, since the vote goes his way on three occasions and against him on four. Each of the voters 4 and 5 will obtain a total of $+5$, the vote going his way on six occasions and against him on one: the grand satisfaction total is therefore $+7$.

Suppose that, as in example 1, voters 1, 2, and 3 form an alliance and agree that they all will vote, on each motion, as the majority of members of the alliance wish. Then motions a to e will be defeated, and motions f and g carried. This is highly satisfactory to voters 1 and 2, who each obtain a satisfaction total of $+5$, only one vote going against each of them: but it is disastrous for voter 3, who obtains a satisfaction total of -3, only the votes on motions a and b going his way; he has thus done worse than if the voting had been sincere. He therefore has no motive to make such an agreement with voters 1 and 2, and should refuse to do so.

Obviously, a group within a committee forming a majority of its members cannot come to an agreement to vote in a manner which involves a departure from sincere voting unless, by so doing, they achieve an overall result which benefits every member of the group, or, at the very least, is no worse for any member than the result of sincere voting. Example 2 shows that they cannot always do this by following the rule, which we may call 'rule A', always to vote in accordance with the preferences of a majority within the group. It also shows that they cannot do so, either, by following the rule, which we may call 'rule B', to adopt that strategy which yields the highest possible satisfaction total, summed over the members of the group. In example 2, by voting for motions f and g and against all the rest, voters 1, 2, and 3 together obtained a satisfaction total of $+7$; it will be found that this is higher than the sum of the satisfaction totals of these three voters obtained by adopting any other strategy. Indeed, rules A and B are equivalent. If, on any particular vote, the outcome is *not* that preferred by a majority of members of the group, then the satisfaction obtained from the outcome of that vote by all the members of the group taken together must be less than that which they would have obtained if it had been that which a majority of them preferred. By the same argument, the grand satisfaction total of a committee will always be highest when all its members vote sincerely.

This is not to say that voters 1, 2, and 3, in example 2, cannot hit upon a strategy that will benefit them all. Precisely because each of them was, under sincere voting, in the minority on a majority of the votes, each of them necessarily obtained, under sincere voting, a negative satisfaction total; this is because a voter's satisfaction total is the difference between the number of votes which went his way and the number which went against him. It follows that, by so voting as to produce, in each vote, the opposite outcome to that which would result from sincere voting, each member of the group must obtain a positive satisfaction total. The satisfaction total he will thus obtain will be equal in absolute value to that he would obtain under sincere voting; that is, it can be arrived at from the latter by simply changing the minus sign into a plus sign. This will hold quite generally. Whenever those who under sincere voting would be in the minority on a majority of occasions form a majority of a committee, it will be to the advantage of all of them to agree to follow what we may call 'rule C': namely to vote, on each occasion, contrary to the wishes of the majority of the committee. The resulting overall outcome must be better for each of them, since his satisfaction total will be changed from negative to positive. Correspondingly, the satisfaction totals of the remaining voters will be changed from positive to negative, again with the same absolute values. As a result, the sign of the grand satisfaction total for the whole committee will likewise be reversed from plus to minus. Since, as we saw, the grand satisfaction total is highest when the voting is sincere, it will therefore be lowest when the outcome of each vote is the opposite to that produced by sincere voting, as will happen when a majority agrees to follow rule C.

Thus if, in example 2, voters 1, 2, and 3 agree to follow rule C, they will vote against all seven motions, since each motion is favoured by a majority of the committee and hence would be carried under sincere voting. By this means, the satisfaction total of each of these three voters will be changed from -1 to $+1$; those of the other two voters will correspondingly be changed from $+5$ to -5. The grand satisfaction total, which was necessarily at its maximum of $+7$ under sincere voting, will now drop to its minimum of -7.

The difficulty in following rule C, unlike rule A, lies in discovering in advance the preferences of the voters not in the group; members of the group must, however, have some fairly strong beliefs about the intentions of voters outside it to have thought it worth while to form an alliance at all. Rule C will not always be the best one for the group to follow. It is even possible that, although rule A is not acceptable to the majority group, every member of the group would benefit from a departure from rule C. We can see this from a further extension of example 2, involving fifteen successive motions. When voting is sincere, the results in this example will be as follows; on certain motions, the voting will be the same, as indicated:

SUCCESSIVE VOTES

	voter 1	voter 2	voter 3	voter 4	voter 5
a and j	Pro	Con	Con	Pro	Pro
b and k	Con	Pro	Con	Pro	Pro
c, d, e, l, and m	Con	Con	Pro	Pro	Pro
f and n	Pro	Pro	Con	Con	Pro
g and o	Pro	Pro	Con	Pro	Con
h	Pro	Con	Pro	Pro	Con
i	Con	Pro	Pro	Con	Pro

Example 3

Under sincere voting all the motions are carried by three votes to two. Each of the voters 1, 2, and 3 is opposed to eight of the motions and in favour of seven. If they combine and follow rule C, they will therefore each obtain a satisfaction total of $+1$. They cannot agree on rule A, since that would give voter 3 a satisfaction total of -3, worse for him than if the voting had been sincere. If, however, they agree to vote for motions g, h, and i, or for motions o, h, and i, and against all the others, they will each obtain a satisfaction total of $+3$.

When the decision is determined by simple majority, the whole body of the voters cannot do better for itself, that is, improve its grand satisfaction total, than by sincere voting; nor can it, therefore, by any divergence from sincere voting improve the satisfaction totals of all the voters. When a special majority is required, such as a two-thirds majority, this obviously ceases to be the case. Suppose that a committee is bound by a four-fifths rule: no motion can be passed unless approved by a four-fifths majority. (Four-fifths has been chosen, rather than two-thirds, merely for simplicity of illustration.) Suppose, for simplicity again, that the committee has five members (or can be divided into five equal groups, within each of which opinions coincide). Ten motions are to be put: each is favoured by three members of the committee and opposed by the other two. Moreover, each committee member favours six of the motions and opposes four. If there is no collusion, all ten motions will be lost; each committee member will have a satisfaction total of -2. If, however, the members of the committee meet informally beforehand and vote on the motions, agreeing that, at the formal meetings, each will vote in accordance with the wishes of the (simple) majority, the four-fifths proviso will of course be frustrated: each motion will now be carried unanimously, and each committee member will obtain a satisfaction total of +2. Indeed, it will need only four members of the committee to agree to vote for every motion to achieve this effect; they cannot improve their overall result by voting in any other way. (Failing such an agreement between four of the committee members, there will even be a group of three—not, in general, *any* group of three—who can, by adopting the right strategy, obtain a satisfaction total of at least +1 for each member of the group; the strategy will not always consist, however, in following rule A.)

If the committee's rules require a *unanimous* vote for any motion to be passed, it will of course still be to the advantage of the members if they all agree to vote in accordance with the preferences of the majority; no group of only four members can in this case gain anything by collusion. We now have a representation in terms of voting of a game presented by Robin Farquharson in his book *Theory of Voting*[2] to illustrate Rousseau's political theory. There are five players and a banker. At each round the players are divided into two teams, one of three players and one of two. Each player in turn nominates one of the teams. The banker then chooses one of the nominated teams, and pays £10 to each member of that team; the members of the other team each pay £10 to the banker. There are ten rounds: in each round, the players are differently divided into the two teams. At the outset, there is no collusion between the players. No player can do better, in any round, than to nominate his own team: since the banker will always select the team with only two members, each player will, in the course of the ten rounds, win four times and lose six times, an overall loss to him of £20. This illustrates Rousseau's 'state of nature'. The social contract is illustrated by the players' coming together and agreeing to vote, before each round, on which team to nominate, and then all to nominate that team: this is in effect to adopt rule A. As a result, only the team with three members will be nominated in each round: the banker will therefore be forced to pay that team, and each player will, over ten rounds, make a net profit of £20 (his 'satisfaction total').

The game is evidently equivalent to a voting procedure under which the team with three members will be selected only if it receives unanimous support (a *very* special majority, or a system under which a single black ball is decisive). Farquharson wishes, however, also to use this imaginary game as an example to illustrate, not only

[2] Op. cit., pp. 77–80.

how, according to Rousseau, the social contract improves the position of every member of society as compared with the state of nature, but also his belief in the distorting effect of the formation of political parties: collusion between the members of a party may not only give to those party members an advantage over those who do not belong to it, but may even leave these latter worse off than they would be in the state of nature.[3] As a general belief about the world, this is surely correct: it is highly plausible that those who suffer the most severely from destitution and oppression, in the world as it is now, are much worse off than anyone would be if there were no governments and no commercial firms. We have already seen that, in any voting system in which a simple majority is decisive, it may be possible for a group which forms a majority to manipulate the system to its own advantage by producing that overall outcome which is the worst possible for the voters as a whole. These examples do not, however, clearly show how the power of the majority group depends either upon the active consent of the rest or upon compulsion exercised upon them.

How can a majority group within the set of five players in Farquharson's game gain an advantage to themselves by collusion? Neither a group of three nor even one of four can do so if they leave the remaining player or players free to make nominations as they see fit. However, the agreement between the five players always to nominate the team with three members is vulnerable to breaches of that agreement by individual players seeking a personal advantage. If, for instance, the players all abide by the agreement for the first nine rounds, and in the tenth the team of two is nominated by one or both of its members, those two will have won £40 each over the ten rounds, while the other three will have neither lost nor gained. If the game is to be played again for another ten rounds, therefore, the players may create sanctions in order to enforce the will of the majority.

Once this is done, a group of three players can combine to

---

[3] J.-J. Rousseau, *Du Contrat Social*, Book II, Chapter III. Rousseau's objection is not just to political parties, that is, to associations of voters and of politicians, but to all bodies, of whatever kind, within the state, including churches; this is obviously far too sweeping. It has been argued that Rousseau did not himself perceive the grounds for his objection, so elegantly illustrated by Farquharson's little model. His remarks are indeed terse, so that it is difficult to be sure. Though I am no expert on Rousseau, I nevertheless incline to think that he *did* perceive them, even if, perhaps, a trifle indistinctly; but I leave it to interested readers to judge from his text.

manipulate the system to their own advantage. They can do so by voting strategically in the vote that precedes each round of the game, exploiting the fact that all are compelled then to nominate that team for which the majority has voted. Their strategy is to vote for that team to which two or more of the members of their own group belong: in other words, to follow rule A in the preliminary vote. As a result, the team of two will be nominated in each of the three rounds in which both players who do not belong to the group are in the team of three; but each of those players will be compelled to nominate the team of three whenever he is in the team of two. By this means, each of the three members of the group will, in ten rounds, win seven times and lose three times, making a net gain of £40; the other two players will make a net loss of £40 each, thus losing more than if no agreement had been made between the five players but the 'state of nature' had continued to prevail.

It ought to be noted, as it is not by Farquharson, that this possibility does not depend merely on the fact that each player belongs to the team of two in four of the ten rounds and to the team of three in six of them; it depends specifically on the assumption that, in each ten rounds, the players are divided into the two teams in each of the ten possible ways. If that assumption does not hold good, it may be impossible for any group of three to do better for all its members than when the preliminary voting is sincere, so that the team of two is never nominated.

In this chapter we have had a brief glimpse of the dynamic theory of voting, without attempting any systematic survey of it. This glimpse has introduced us to some important concepts. We have distinguished between sincere and strategic voting; we have looked at different cases in which a specific overall course of voting, over several successive votes, is vulnerable to a change of voting strategy by a single voter or by a group of voters acting in concert. From all this, it has become clear that Rousseau's opposition to political parties was fundamentally sound. Under any procedure in which a simple majority is decisive, the formation of a party within the set of all the voters has one and only one purpose: to benefit the members of the party at the expense, not merely of those outside it, but of the set as a whole. This is so because, as we have seen, in such a case, each vote being between only two alternatives, no outcome other than that which results from sincere voting can yield the maximum total satisfaction summed over all the voters. The intervention of any party whose members vote strategically, that is, in accordance, not with their own wishes, but with the decisions of the party, must, therefore, decrease the total satisfaction of the voters as a whole (the grand satisfaction total), provided that it has any effect at all. It must, in other words, distort the outcome of the voting process as a means of realizing, as far as possible, the wishes of the voters. Political parties, or groups within a decision-making body, are thus, at best, an unavoidable evil.

We saw the fallacy in Professor Anscombe's argument that, in certain cases, a *majority* of voters may be considered as giving only passive consent to, or as being coerced into accepting, decisions arrived at by sincere majority votes. Farquharson's imaginary game, on the other hand, illustrates very clearly how, when there is collusion between the members of a majority group, the resulting decisions can be imposed on a minority only by coercion or by their active consent, mistakenly given. Examples 1, 2, and 3 can all be interpreted in terms of this game. Thus example 1 may be taken as a case in which only three rounds are played, the two-membered team in each case consisting of those opposed to the motion. If the five players agree all to take a vote before each round, and then to nominate the team for which the majority has voted, then, under sincere voting, players 4 and 5 will receive £30 in all and players 1, 2, and 3 will each lose £10: if, further, they make a gentlemen's agreement to share out the winnings equally at the end of play, each will eventually receive £6. If, however, players 1, 2, and 3 conspire to vote in each round for the two-membered team, and not to share out their winnings at the end, each of them will receive £10 in all and players 4 and 5 will each lose £30.

The dynamic theory is to be distinguished from the static theory in that, in the static theory, we consider only a single vote at a time, whereas, in the dynamic theory, we are concerned with a sequence of successive votes. In the static theory, no problem can arise concerning strategy when there are only two possible outcomes to the vote. When there is simply a single motion, to be passed or rejected, then, if we consider only the vote on that motion, prescinding from advantages that a voter may gain from making deals with other voters about how he will vote on subsequent motions, no voter can gain any advantage by not voting sincerely: the static theory therefore has nothing to say about strategy in such a case.

For a vote with only two possible outcomes, there can be little to say about procedure, either. It is useful to distinguish two aspects of any voting process: the mechanism of voting, and the means of determining the outcome from the votes cast. This distinction is not always a clean one, since, in a procedure with several ballots, the outcome of the preceding ballot is usually announced before the next one is taken, and often has to be. The distinction is nevertheless clear enough. When there are only two possible outcomes, there is one obvious mechanism: each voter casts a vote for one or other outcome. In most cases, the successful outcome is then determined as that for which a majority has voted; but there are other means, for example to take the motion as lost unless there was a majority of two-thirds or more in its favour. We may thus distinguish, within the voting procedure, between the *voting mechanism* and the *method of assessment*. A more complicated case in which, although the same mechanism was used, the method of assessment differed from that of a simple majority decision was illustrated, in the Introduction, by the election for the Deputy Leadership of the Labour Party in 1981. Here the voters were divided into three categories, the balance of votes within each category being scaled down by a preassigned ratio. We saw how a minor variation in such a method made the crucial difference to the outcome of that election.

When there are only two possible outcomes, the only serious deviation from the obvious voting mechanism can occur when it is required that a two-thirds or other special majority is needed for a decision in favour of *either* outcome: this of course may necessitate an indefinite sequence of ballots, which, in principle, might not terminate. In such a case, too, no voter has any motive for not voting sincerely in any ballot, except the desire to get away: such a procedure may therefore serve to indicate crudely the strength of feeling on each side. Apart from this, there are only relatively minor questions to be decided concerning the voting mechanism: whether the voting is to be open or secret; what is to happen in case of a tie; and whether voters are to be allowed to abstain. If, as usually happens, and must happen in a secret ballot, abstention is allowed, an absolute majority *of those entitled to vote* becomes another kind of special majority.

Since, in the two-outcome case, there are no problems about strategy and only minor ones about procedure, the static theory is almost entirely concerned with votes between three or more possible outcomes, as when a motion has been proposed, and an amendment to it is introduced but not accepted by the proposer of the motion; or when a selection committee has to choose between three or more candidates (or between only two when it is open to them to make no appointment). Directly there are even three possible outcomes, it ceases to be obvious what should be the best or fairest voting procedure, or, given the voting procedure, how best an individual voter should cast his vote. In the dynamic theory, as the examples in this chapter have illustrated, strategic, though not, of course, procedural, problems arise even when no vote has more than two possible outcomes. This book is directed primarily at the determination of the best voting procedure, rather than at how voters can best make a particular procedure serve their own advantage; its principal intention is to be of practical use to those who have to select a voting procedure. From now on, therefore, we shall be chiefly concerned with the static theory of voting.

2
Fundamental Notions

The serious problems of voting procedure arise only when the voters have to choose between three or more possible outcomes. What motivates a voter to vote in one way or another is his set of preferences between the possible outcomes: if he knew that, by voting differently, he could obtain an outcome that he preferred, he would change his vote accordingly. The most important criterion for a good voting procedure is that it be *fair*; and a voting procedure is fair if it reflects as accurately as possible the preferences of the voters. It is for this reason that empirical studies of voting—detailed records of the actual courses of the voting—can help us little: we cannot deduce from them the preferences of the individual voters as between the alternatives among which they were choosing. We cannot do so for two reasons. First, the voting procedure may provide no opportunity for the voters to express all their preferences. Suppose that there are three possible outcomes, say candidates in an election. Then, if we assume that no voter is wholly indifferent as between any pair of candidates, there are six possible preference scales that any voter can have. It follows that a minimal condition for each voter to be able to express all his preferences is that there be six distinct possible ways for him to vote: in practice, there are usually fewer. The most obvious example is the so-called 'relative majority' procedure: each voter casts a vote for a single candidate or possible outcome, and that candidate or outcome receiving the greatest number of votes is selected. Even if we assume that the voting is sincere, we have no means of knowing, from the course of voting under this procedure, what were the preferences of any voter between the candidates or outcomes other than his first preference.

Suppose, again, that there are three possible outcomes, a, b, and c, and that the procedure is to hold a first ballot between a and b and then a second one between c and the winner of the first ballot; suppose also that b is successful on the first ballot. Then, if we assume sincere voting, one who votes for a on the first ballot and for

b on the second must be presumed to prefer a to b and b to c, while one who votes for b on the first ballot and for c on the second must prefer c to b and b to a. If we have a record only of the number who voted for the relevant alternative outcomes on the two ballots, we cannot make even these deductions. But, even if we have a record of the votes of individual voters, we cannot in all cases determine their preference scales. Of one who voted for b on both ballots, we know only that he preferred b to each of a and c, assuming that he voted sincerely, but not whether he preferred a to c or c to a; likewise, we know of one who voted for a on the first ballot and for c on the second that he preferred each of a and c to b, but not which of them would have been his first choice.

In the second place, we are obviously not entitled to assume that voters always vote sincerely. It is notorious that, in a relative majority procedure, a voter may refrain from casting his vote for his first choice if he thinks that that candidate or outcome has no chance of success, for fear of 'wasting his vote'. The same factor may operate in a procedure with two or more ballots. In the foregoing examples, a voter who preferred a to b and b to c might nevertheless vote for b on the first ballot on the ground that he believed that a could not beat c but that b might. When such a procedure is used, the only thing we can be sure of, concerning any voter, is that he revealed by his vote on the second ballot his preference as between the two possible outcomes then being pitted against each other: his vote on the first ballot depends not only on his preferences but on his estimate of those of other voters.

Empirical studies are thus almost wholly valueless for our purposes, since they cannot supply the relevant evidence. We cannot tell, from the available facts, what the outcome of a given vote would have been if a different voting mechanism had been used; nor, if we could, should we be able to say which outcome would more truly have represented the wishes of the voters. The only case in which we can tell whether a difference of procedure would have affected the outcome is one in which the difference relates solely to the method of assessment, not to the voting mechanism. We therefore have no option but to investigate these questions by a priori methods; that is, by considering the various possible distributions of preferences among the voters, and the consequent effects of different voting procedures.

We have, then, a number of voters, whom we shall designate by numerals, 1, 2, ..., n, and a number of possible outcomes, $a, b, c, \ldots$: we assume that the outcomes are mutually exclusive and jointly exhaustive. Each voter i has preferences between the outcomes: for brevity we shall sometimes write '$xR_i y$' to mean 'voter i considers outcome x to be at least as good as outcome y'. Now, trivially, for every voter i and outcome x, $xR_i x$: in mathematical terminology, R_i, regarded as a relation between outcomes, is reflexive (a relation that everything has to itself). We cannot, however, rule out the possibility that voter i is indifferent between two distinct outcomes x and y. We may symbolize the statement that he is indifferent between them by '$xI_i y$', which is equivalent to '$xR_i y$ and $yR_i x$'. If i positively prefers x to y, we may write '$xP_i y$': this is equivalent to '$xR_i y$ and not $yR_i x$'.

We do wish, however, to insist that, for each voter i, R_i is a *connected* relation between outcomes, that is, that for every x and y, either $xR_i y$ or $yR_i x$ (or, of course, both); hence that i either definitely prefers x to y ($xP_i y$) or definitely prefers y to x ($yP_i x$) or is definitely indifferent between them ($xI_i y$). In other words, each voter must be able to assign to each possible outcome a definite position in his order of preference. It may be objected that he simply need not have decided how he would rate x and y in relation to one another. A misleading answer to this would be to say that it is a question of how voter i *would* choose between x and y if he had to choose between them (for example how he would vote between them if he know that all the other possible outcomes had been eliminated). If this answer were spelled out more exactly, it would have to take the following form. Whether he knows it or not, voter i prefers x to y ($xP_i y$) if, faced with a choice between x and y, he would choose x, and a small inducement would not suffice to make him choose y instead; he is indifferent between x and y ($xI_i y$) if, however he chose between them, any inducement, however small (provided he thought it honourable to accept it), would lead him to choose the other instead.

The fallacy in this answer lies in the assumption that there is already some definite way in which the voter would behave in circumstances that have not arisen and may never arise. If they were to arise, he would reflect and decide which of the two alternatives to choose: but the assumption forces us to view this, not as his adopting a specific policy, but as his becoming aware of the policy he had already unconsciously adopted. On this view, conscious thought and conscious decisions play no role in determining what we do; or, in so far as they do, they do so only as an intermediate link in the chain of causality leading from our unconscious inner states to our actions.

It would be ridiculous, and is unnecessary, to base our theory of voting on a deterministic picture of human action of such a kind, which there is every reason to reject. Rather, we should freely admit that, in assuming that, as between any two possible outcomes, each voter either definitely prefers one to the other or is definitely indifferent between them, we may be going beyond the facts about that voter's mental state, conscious or unconscious, as they stand at the time when he participates in the voting process. The justification for making the assumption lies, rather, in its harmlessness: no voter can possibly suffer by adopting a definite view of the relative merits of each pair of possible outcomes. If, during the course of the voting, he has to take a decision which depends upon his making up his mind which, if either, of the two given outcomes he prefers to the other, then he might as well, or better, have made up his mind on that point at the outset. If, on the other hand, no such decision needs to be made, then, by having so made up his mind, he has suffered nothing worse than some unnecessary thought. In assuming each voter's ordering of the outcomes to be connected in the sense explained, we are not *presupposing* that he has a definite policy, but *making believe* that he has one. It could do him no harm if he did; and the pretence that he has can do no harm to our conclusions. If any reader doubts this last assertion, let him for the moment regard each voter as indifferent between any two possible outcomes for neither of which he has formed or will form a definite preference over the other.

The relation of indifference is by definition *symmetric*: for every voter i and all outcomes x and y, if $xI_i y$, then $yI_i x$. Equally, the relation of strict preference is *asymmetric*: if $xP_i y$, then not $yP_i x$. There is, however, another principle which seems obvious but does *not* follow from anything we have assumed so far. This is that, for every i, R_i is a *transitive* relation: that is to say, for any three outcomes x, y, and z, if $xR_i y$ and $yR_i z$, then $xR_i z$. In words, the principle is that, if voter i thinks x at least as good as y and y at least as good as z, then he must think x at least as good as z. So stated, this seems virtually a logical truth. It is surely a logical truth, at any rate, that if x actually *is* at least as good as y and y at least as good as z, then x is at least as good as z. It seems to follow that, if a voter *thinks* x at least as good as y and y at least as good as z, then he will conclude that x is at least as good as z, provided that he can reason just a little. If he is irrational, he will not draw that conclusion. It therefore does not strictly *follow* that he thinks x at least as good as z: but it seems to be asking too much of a voting procedure that it respond to the preferences of voters when they are irrational.

Unfortunately, the matter is not so simple. What has misled us is our verbal reading of 'xR_iy'. To say that i thinks x at least as good as y gives the appearance that i supposes x to have at least as much of some quantity—desirability, let us say—as does y. If this really is what i supposes, and if he supposes the same about y in relation to z, then indeed he ought to draw the conclusion that x has at least as much of that quantity as z. There is, however, no reason why i should have any such picture of the matter. The fallacious justification of our assumption that R_i is connected was in error in presuming that there need yet be any answer to the question how i would act, faced with a choice between x and y. The objector was quite right, however, in interpreting i's preferences between x and y in terms of such a choice. In deciding whether he prefers x to y, or y to x, or is indifferent between them, *all* that the voter i is directly deciding is which of them he would vote for if all other outcomes were eliminated. Why, then, might he not quite rationally decide that, out of x and y, he would choose x, that, out of y and z, he would choose y, but that, out of x and z, he would choose z?

That *might*, after all be how he would in fact choose: is there anything irrational about it? It might seem so: but it is not so. Here is an example, devised by Professor Keith Lehrer, which shows that it might be quite rational. The example is based on the fact that we cannot always discriminate between things that are in fact different, but that inability to discriminate is not itself transitive. That is, I may be unable directly to tell u from v or v from w, even though I can tell u from w. Suppose you have two tins of paint, red and yellow, and a great many strips of paper. You paint one of the strips red, and then mix a few drops of yellow paint into the red tin, and use the mixture to paint the next strip. You then put a few more drops of yellow paint into the red tin, stir, and paint the third strip, and so on. By the time the red tin contains a mixture of equal amounts of red and yellow paint, the strips are coming out unmistakably orange, and you can easily tell the first, red, strip you painted from the last, orange, one. If, however, you have kept the strips in order, you will certainly not be able to tell any strip from the next one in the sequence: arranged to overlap one another, you cannot see where one ends and the next begins.

Suppose, then, that a customer at a grocery shop is in this position with three kinds of wine: he cannot tell Château Âlève from Château Bèthe, if given a glass of each, nor Château Bèthe from Château Guimelle, although he can tell Château Âlève from Château Guimelle, and prefers the former. One day he goes to the grocery shop: they have Ch. Âlève and Ch. Bèthe on offer, but do not have Ch. Guimelle in stock. The grocer is trying an experiment: he will not sell a bottle of Ch. Bèthe alone, but only together with a bottle of a new type of beer he is trying to popularize, the two at the same price as a bottle of Ch. Âlève. Since the customer drinks beer, and cannot distinguish the two wines from one another, he buys Ch. Bèthe with the beer. The next time he goes to the shop, the grocer has run out of Ch Âlève, but has acquired a new stock of Ch. Guimelle, which he is offering, still at the same price, with two bottles of beer per bottle of wine. The customer, being unable to distinguish the two wines now in stock, takes a bottle of Ch. Guimelle with the two bottles of beer. On the third occasion, the grocer has no more Ch. Bèthe left, but offers a choice between a bottle of Ch. Âlève and a combination of a bottle of Ch. Guimelle with two bottles of beer. Since the customer definitely prefers Ch. Âlève to Ch. Guimelle, despite there being only a subtle difference between them, and since beer is not very important to him, he chooses to have a bottle of Ch. Âlève.

Does the customer behave rationally? It seems at first sight difficult to give any grounds for saying that he does not; for, on each occasion, he chooses that one of the two alternatives available which will give him the greater pleasure. Suppose, however, that he has three neighbours, who have observed his buying habits and are determined to take advantage of them. They have bought a bottle of Ch. Bèthe, together with a bottle of beer, and a bottle of Ch. Guimelle, with two bottles of beer. When, on the third occasion, the customer returns with his bottle of Ch. Âlève, the first neighbour asks him if he will exchange it, for a small compensatory payment, say of 20p, for a bottle of Ch. Bèthe and a bottle of beer: in accordance with his settled policy, the customer agrees, pays his 20p, and makes the exchange. Before he can open the bottles, the second neighbour appears, and offers, for another small payment of 20p, to exchange the bottle of Ch. Bèthe for a bottle of Ch. Guimelle and a bottle of beer: again the customer agrees. Finally, the third neighbour appears, with the bottle of Ch. Âlève that the customer originally bought from the grocer: he offers to exchange it, for a further payment of 20p, for the bottle of Ch. Guimelle and two bottles of beer. If the customer is faithful to his settled policy, he must again agree to this exchange. He is now exactly where he was when he arrived home, with a bottle of Ch. Âlève and no beer, save that he has paid out 60p in the course of the exchanges. While he maintains his policy, the three neighbours can make money from him indefinitely, at no loss to themselves, provided that they do not ask too much at a time.

Suppose that the customer had felt sure, at the outset, before he ever bought any wine, that one of the three wines would be, and would for ever remain, unavailable, without his knowing which. There is then no way of arguing that he would not have been entirely rational to decide in advance to make whichever one of the three choices that he actually made that was relevant to the alternatives offered, in the confidence that only one such choice would ever have to be made. In this sense, it is *not* irrational to maintain intransitive preferences. Directly all three wines come to be available, however, even if they are never all available at precisely the same time, his policy becomes disastrous: he can be induced to pay without, in the end, getting anything whatever for the payment. It is not, therefore, a truth of logic that an individual's preferences must be transitive. It is not even a sign of irrationality in him if they are not. But, whenever three alternatives are, or may come to be, in competition with one another, it is always a bad policy for anyone to maintain intransitive or cyclic preferences between them, and may make for his serious disadvantage. The possible outcomes of a voting process are, by the nature of the case, in competition with one another. It will therefore always be to each voter's interests to decide on a transitive preference-relation between them, of course allowing for the possibility of indifference between two or more: to assume, for any voter i, that R_i is transitive is just to assume that he acts, in this respect, in his own best interests.

It follows at once from the assumption that R_i is transitive that I_i (indifference) and P_i (strict preference) are transitive too: for all x, y, and z, we have that, if xI_iy and yI_iz, then xI_iz, and, if xP_iy and yP_iz, then xP_iz. Furthermore, if xP_iy and yI_iz, or xI_iy and yP_iz, then again xP_iz. For this reason, it is not quite true that, if a voter never makes up his mind as between two outcomes, we may assume him to be indifferent between them: if, for example, he has not thought of comparing x and z, but has decided that he is indifferent between x and y but prefers y to z, we must take him as preferring x to z. Under the assumption of transitivity, a voter's preferences now form an ordering (only what economists call a *weak* ordering, since indifference is allowed). We can therefore arrange the possible outcomes in a sequence, starting with his highest preference. If voter i prefers x to y, y to z, and z to w, we may write '$xP_iyP_izP_iw$' without ambiguity; even more tersely, we may say that i's preference scale is *xyzw*, where by convention we always start with the outcome i prefers to all others. Similarly, when it is convenient to show i's preference scale vertically, it will be written:

$$\begin{array}{c} i \\ x \\ y \\ z \\ w \end{array}$$

with the highest preference always shown at the top. Since preferences have been assumed to be transitive, these notations will always indicate that i prefers x to z and to w, and y to w: if they were allowed to be intransitive, there could be cycles, and we should need a more complicated notation. If voter i is indifferent between, say, y and z, his other preferences being as before, we may write '$xP_iyI_izP_iw$'; we may also represent this by writing his preference scale as '$x(yz)w$', or vertically, as:

$$\begin{array}{c} i \\ x \\ y\ z \\ w \end{array}$$

We have considered the proper reply to be given to the objection that, by presupposing the transitivity of preferences, we were making an unwarranted assumption. Most readers will probably have felt impatient of this objection, though it is to be hoped that something of interest has emerged from considering the correct answer to it. Now a more weighty objection may be launched from the opposite direction, to the effect that we are assuming, not too much, but too little. This is that we are wrong to take as the sole relevant factor relating to a given voter his preferring certain outcomes to others: it is equally important *how strong* his preferences are. We need to know, according to such an objector, not merely in what order a voter places the possible outcomes, but how big a gap he would leave between any of them and the next one in his ordering.

Consider again example 1 of Chapter 1. Suppose that the committee is a subcommittee of a county council, and that motions a, b, and c all concern the building of a bypass around one or another small town: the voters may be individuals, or may represent equal groups within the subcommittee. Voters 4 and 5 are wholly in favour of the project. Voters 1, 2, and 3 are generally against it on grounds of expenditure or of preservation of the countryside; but each comes from one of the three towns concerned, and would prefer a bypass round his town to none at all. The objector urges that it is relevant to their behaviour to ask: how do they weigh the general considerations against their particular interests? *How much* do they care about each? Suppose that vector 1 is principally concerned about the effects on his own town, and only mildly about the general policy. We might then reckon his satisfaction if motion a is carried as $+1\frac{4}{5}$, and as $-1\frac{4}{5}$ if it is defeated; from the defeat of motion b or c, however, he will obtain a satisfaction of only $+\frac{3}{5}$, and of $-\frac{3}{5}$ from its being carried. If then, all vote sincerely, voter 1 will obtain a satisfaction total of $+\frac{3}{5}$; by combining with voters 2 and 3 to defeat all three motions, he will convert this to $-\frac{3}{5}$. Obviously, he has no motive to ally himself with them.

Voter 2, on the other hand, might take quite a different view, placing much more weight on the necessity to avoid expenditure. In such a case, his satisfaction at the success of motion b might be reckoned at only $+\frac{3}{5}$, and at the defeat of motion a or of motion c at $+1\frac{1}{5}$, while the converse results will yield a satisfaction of $-\frac{3}{5}$ and of $-1\frac{1}{5}$ respectively. Under sincere voting, his satisfaction total will be $-1\frac{4}{5}$. By combining with voters 1 and 3 to defeat all three motions, he will convert it to $+1\frac{4}{5}$, which he thus has a strong motive to do. By ignoring *strength* of preferences, and representing each voter as obtaining a satisfaction of $+1$ for each vote that goes as he wishes and of -1 for each that goes against him, the objection runs, we over-simplify the problem.

The argument is compelling: a satisfactory treatment of the

subject appears to require a representation of the strength of preferences. But how is that to be done? The fractions used in the foregoing discussion were a mere device for expressing the intuitive idea that someone may care more about one thing than about another: how can we seriously quantify strength of preference? We can, perhaps, give a clear sense to saying that a particular voter prefers an outcome x to an outcome y by a greater margin than he prefers a third outcome z to a fourth one w, namely by once more considering hypothetical situations. For instance, we could imagine him in an artificial situation in which he was told that only two outcomes, either x and y or z and w, were still in the running, the rest having been eliminated; he knows nothing to make more probable one or other identification of the remaining pair. He is also told that his vote will be decisive: but he can vote in only two possible ways. If he casts his vote in one way, the successful outcome will be either x or w; if he casts it in the other, it will be either y or z. If he votes in the first way, his preference for x over y is greater than his preference for z over w. Even if, by appeal to such bizarre hypotheses, we can give a sense to such a four-termed comparison, that does not yet amount to a means of assigning numerical values to a voter's preferences, still less to regarding such assignments as significant for a comparison of one voter's preferences with another's. There seems to be no way in which we could give sense to comparing the degree of voter i's preference for x over y with the degree of voter j's preference for z over w.

No approach of this kind seems to yield intuitively satisfying results: but it will enormously complicate the theory. Fortunately, we can to some degree represent the strength of preferences by means of mere preference scales. Difficulties about what voting procedure to adopt principally arise when there are more than two possible outcomes: the more there are, the closer we can approximate to a representation of the relative strengths of voters' preferences. Suppose that a family of five is going to the theatre, and is undecided between a play by Beckett and one by Ayckbourn. If we know only that three members of the family prefer Beckett and two Ayckbourn, we shall think that Beckett is the fairest choice: but if we are told that the three have only a slight preference for Beckett, while the two enormously prefer Ayckbourn, we shall alter our opinion. In a family, this will be expressed verbally: it is such feelings that we do not directly represent if we restrict ourselves to the use of preference scales. Suppose now, however, that other possibilities are considered: plays by Stoppard, Pinter, and Ionesco. The three members of the family who prefer Beckett rank the five options in the order. Beckett, Ayckbourn, Stoppard, Pinter, Ionesco. The two who prefer Ayckbourn rank them in the order: Ayckbourn, Pinter, Stoppard, Ionesco, Beckett. It is now obvious from the preference scales alone that Ayckbourn is the fairest choice. The fact that the majority only slightly prefer Beckett to Ayckbourn is sufficiently shown by Ayckbourn's being their second choice. The fact that the minority prefer Ayckbourn by a wide margin is shown by their also preferring three other playwrights to Beckett.

When there are distinct but interrelated issues, the same effect may be obtained by considering, not the outcome of each issue taken separately, but the combined outcome concerning them all. From example 1 of Chapter 1, as originally stated, we learned, about voter 1, only that he was in favour of motion a and against motions b and c. Instead, we may consider the possible overall outcomes taken over the three votes. Let 'A' mean that motion a is passed and '$\bar{A}$' that it is defeated, and likewise for b and c. Then there are eight possible overall outcomes: ABC, AB$\bar{C}$, A$\bar{B}$C, etc. We may now enquire into each voter's ranking of these eight possible overall outcomes: this will give us much more information. Voter 1's preference scale might be:

$$A\bar{B}\bar{C}$$
$$AB\bar{C} \: A\bar{B}C$$
$$ABC$$
$$\bar{A}\bar{B}\bar{C}$$
$$\bar{A}B\bar{C} \: \bar{A}\bar{B}C$$
$$\bar{A}BC$$

Voter 2's might be:

$$\bar{A}B\bar{C}$$
$$\bar{A}\bar{B}\bar{C}$$
$$\bar{A}BC \: AB\bar{C}$$
$$\bar{A}\bar{B}C \: A\bar{B}\bar{C}$$
$$ABC$$
$$A\bar{B}C$$

These would correspond with the weightings imagined above for the preferences of these two voters (voter 1 obtains a satisfaction of $+1\frac{4}{5}$

from the passage of motion a, and of $+\frac{3}{5}$ from the defeat of b or of c, while voter 2 obtains a satisfaction of $+\frac{3}{5}$ from the passage of motion b, but of $+1\frac{1}{5}$ from the defeat of a or of c). The greater weight attached by voter 1 to the passage of motion a is shown by his ranking all four overall outcomes including A over the other four; the greater weight attached by voter 2 to the defeat of a and c is likewise shown by his ranking the two overall outcomes including both $\bar{A}$ and $\bar{C}$ above the others and by his ranking the two including both A and C below the others. From the weightings we inferred that voter 1 had no motive to combine with the other two to defeat all three motions, and that voter 2 had every motive to do so. From the preference scales we can draw just the same conclusion: by joining such an alliance, voter 1 will obtain the overall outcome that he ranks fifth, as against the fourth-ranking outcome which would result from sincere voting; voter 2, by joining the same alliance, will secure his second choice among overall outcomes, as against that which he ranks seventh.

This way of representing example 1 of Chapter 1 was intended to illustrate how, if there are several possible outcomes, preference scales may serve as a surrogate for numerical weightings of the preferences. It will not have escaped the reader's notice that it also illustrates a different point. In representing the example in this way, we in effect converted it from one in which there are three successive votes on distinct issues into one in which there is a single voting process, composed of three ballots, to choose between eight possible overall outcomes. In doing this, we transformed it from an example within the dynamic theory of voting into one in the static theory; the distinction between these two parts of the theory of voting is not in fact so sharp as originally appeared from the discussion at the end of Chapter 1. It is not possible to ignore voting procedures which involve a number of ballots and to treat them always as if each ballot were a distinct complete voting process, since often one ballot will have no effect unless it is followed by another, for instance when it is the vote between a motion and an amendment taken as a preliminary to putting the (original or amended) motion. Since, for this reason, we cannot rule out voting procedures with two or more ballots, it is artificial to insist on treating as a distinct vote any which would have an effect even if not followed, as intended, by further ones. Whether we are concerned with the static or with the dynamic theory will sometimes be a matter of the way we choose to look at the case; as can be seen from the present example, the advantage will often lie with a treatment in terms of the static theory.

We shall revert to this point at the end of the chapter; for the moment, our concern is whether we need some explicit representation of the strengths of voters' preferences. If we could overcome the difficulty of attributing some clear significance to a numerical weighting of preferences, of how much help would it be? That would depend upon the kind of question that we are asking. Suppose that we want to enquire, of a specific example, whether, by voting differently, any one voter could have gained an advantage, provided that the remaining voters voted as before; or whether some group of voters, by all agreeing to vote in some other way, could each have gained an advantage. As is clear from the example just discussed, a weighting of preferences is wholly irrelevant to questions of this sort. All that we need to know is which outcomes a given voter—or each voter in a given group—would have preferred to the actual outcome. We may need to consider the overall outcomes in a sequence of votes, thus assimilating the votes to successive ballots in a single voting process; provided we do this, if necessary, the strengths of the voters' preferences make no difference.

Suppose, now, that we are asking a slightly different question, namely how, given his preference scale, a particular voter ought, in his own best interests, to vote. This is a different question because the voter will not in general know how the others are going to vote: whenever he does, the two questions coincide. We can sometimes answer this question knowing nothing but the voting procedure and the individual voter's preference scale. Suppose, for instance, that we have the standard committee procedure for voting on a motion to which an amendment has been proposed: first a vote is taken for or against the amendment, and then the motion (amended or unamended) is voted on. A voter who approves of the motion in its original form, but would rather see it defeated than passed in the amended form, has no problem how to vote: he must vote against the amendment on the first ballot, and for or against the motion on the second ballot according as the amendment has been defeated or carried. This is, of course, a sincere voting strategy: in each ballot, he votes for that outcome which stands higher on his preference scale. What is more important for the present purpose is that, in the light of his preference scale, it is a *straightforward* strategy: that is to say, whatever the other voters do, there is no other strategy that he could adopt that would in any circumstances yield an outcome that he preferred. The fact that it is a straightforward strategy, and therefore that which he should unhesitatingly adopt, is apparent from his preference scale alone: no weighting of his preferences could affect that in any way.

Unfortunately, a sincere voting strategy is not always straightforward. Consider another of the voters on the same committee: he, too, would best like the motion to be passed in its original form, but would rather see it passed in its amended version than thrown out altogether. His sincere voting strategy is to vote against the amendment on the first ballot, and, on the second, to vote for the motion, whether amended or unamended. Suppose, however, that the amendment is defeated on the first ballot by a single vote, but that the motion is then rejected on the second ballot. If our voter had voted for the amendment on the first ballot, it would have been carried; and it is then possible that the amended motion would have been passed on the second ballot, an outcome that this voter would have preferred to the actual one. Not only is a sincere strategy not straightforward for this voter: there *is* no straightforward strategy for him.

The position, then, is as follows. Let us assume the voting procedure given. Then, first, an individual voter's preference scale is sufficient to determine whether or not he has a straightforward voting strategy: if he has, there is no further question about what his strategy should be. Secondly, if he knows the voting intentions of the other voters, his preference scale is again sufficient to determine the most favourable voting strategy for him: this strategy may of course be one which would not be the best for him if the other voters had different intentions. A third case will be one in which he does not know the intentions of the other voters, but does know their preference scales. In such a case, it may or may not be possible to work out, from this information, what his best strategy is. It will be possible if the other voters' preference scales happen to be such that each of them has a straightforward strategy. It will then be a reasonable assumption that each of them will adopt such a strategy. Even if the voter in question does not himself have a straightforward strategy, he can, on this assumption, work out his own best strategy, which will, as before, depend only on his preference scale.

This may be illustrated by an example. Suppose that it is proposed to co-opt a new member on to a committee of five: the committee has no power to make more than one co-option, and, if any co-option is to be made, some favour Brown and others Conder. The chairman rules that the committee should first vote on whether to make a co-option or not, and then, if it is decided to make one, whether to co-opt Brown or Conder. There are three possible outcomes: *a*—that no co-option is made; *b*—that Brown is co-opted; and *c*—that Conder is co-opted. Voter 5 would like to see Brown co-opted, but detests Conder: his preference scale is therefore *bac*. He is therefore in a quandary over how to vote on the first ballot: he has no straightforward strategy. If, however, he knows that voters 1 and 2 both have the preference scale *acb*, that voter 3 has the preference scale *bca*, and that voter 4 has the preference scale *cba*, he can tell how they will vote, since they all have straightforward strategies. Voters 1 and 2 will vote on the first ballot against making any co-option, and voters 3 and 4 will vote in favour of making one; if there is a second ballot, voters 1, 2, and 4 will all vote for Conder. If voter 5 votes on the first ballot for co-option, the outcome will therefore be the co-option of Conder; he should therefore vote on the first ballot against co-option, and thus produce the outcome *a* (that no co-option is made).

This simple example also illustrates a further point. In order to decide his best strategy, voter 5 did not need to know that the other voters all had straightforward strategies, nor what, in detail, their preference scales were. All he needed to know was what the result of the second ballot would be if one were taken, which is to say how many of the other voters preferred Brown to Conder and how many preferred Conder to Brown. If both voter 1 and voter 4 had had the preference scales *cab*, they would no more have had a straightforward strategy than did voter 5: but voter 5 could still have reasoned in just the same way that his best strategy was to vote against making any co-option on the first ballot, though he would not have known what the outcome would be.

Without, at this stage, attempting any detailed analysis, we may therefore say generally that, even when a voter has no straightforward strategy, it may be possible to determine unequivocally his best strategy, given only his preference scale and some, not necessarily complete, information about the voting intentions or the preference scales of the other voters. Obviously, a voter who has no straightforward strategy often lacks the necessary information about the intentions or preferences of his colleagues to enable him to decide upon his strategy in such a manner. In such a case, he must take a risk. There is a temptation to state the point by saying that he takes a risk by departing from the strategy of voting sincerely. This is misleading, in that it suggests that the sincere voting strategy is safe in some sense in which no other is. On the contrary, if the voter has no straightforward strategy, then, in particular, the sincere strategy is not straightforward for him: this means, by definition, that there is some other strategy which will, if the other voters vote in a particular way, produce an outcome which he prefers to that which would have been produced if he had voted sincerely. Indeed, there would be no motive for his departing from the sincere strategy if this were not so. He therefore takes a risk by voting sincerely, just as he does by adopting any other voting strategy. His problem is whether the particular risk he proposes to take is worth it.

Let us develop some terminology to allow these simple ideas to be expressed more succinctly. Under any given procedure for voting between given possible outcomes, each voter has a certain finite number of voting strategies open to him. For example, under the procedure of the last example, each of the five voters could adopt any one of four possible strategies, which we may label ab, ac, $\bar{a}b$, and $\bar{a}c$. These are: (ab) to vote on the first ballot against co-opting anyone, and, if there is a second ballot, to vote for Brown; (ac) to vote on the first ballot against co-opting anyone, and, if there is a second ballot, to vote for Conder; ($\bar{a}b$) to vote on the first ballot for co-opting someone, and then, if successful, to vote for Brown; and ($\bar{a}c$) to vote on the first ballot for co-opting someone, and then, if successful, to vote for Conder. Suppose, now, that each of the five voters selects a particular strategy: for instance, voters 1 and 2 both select strategy (ac), voter 3 selects ($\bar{a}b$), voter 4 selects ($\bar{a}c$), and voter 5, like voter 3, selects ($\bar{a}b$). Let us call any such selection of a strategy by each voter a *situation*, and refer to it by a letter, r, s, or t. For each voter i, we may refer to the strategy he selects in the situation s as s_i; thus, if s is the particular situation just envisaged, s_1 will be the strategy (ac), s_3 the strategy ($\bar{a}b$), and so on. Obviously, any situation will uniquely determine the actual course of the voting: for instance, our situation s determines that, on the first ballot, voters 1 and 2 vote against co-option and voters 3, 4, and 5 vote for it, while, on the second ballot, voters 1, 2, and 4 vote for Conder and voters 3 and 5 for Brown. When there is only one ballot, a strategy just consists in selecting a particular way of filling in the ballot paper, so

FUNDAMENTAL NOTIONS

that a situation just is a record of the votes cast. When there are two or more ballots, however, distinct situations may determine the same course of the voting, since a strategy involves deciding how to vote in any ballot that may occur. Thus, in our example, if three or more voters decided to vote against co-option on the first ballot, there would be no second ballot, and the course of the voting would be unaffected by what any of the voters proposed to do on the second ballot if one was held. That does not matter for our purpose: all that matters is that the situation determines the course of the voting, which, naturally, in turn determines the successful outcome. We may therefore speak of the outcome produced by any given situation t, and denote it by $|t|$.

Suppose that a voter i is deciding what strategy to adopt. The effect of his choice upon the outcome will depend upon the strategies adopted by the other voters: relative to a voter i, let us call a selection of strategies by each of the other voters a *contingency*. If i's adoption of the strategy τ results in the situation t, so that t_i is τ, the contingency can be labelled $t^{(i)}$, which consists simply in the assignment of the strategy t_j to every voter j other than i. Now it may be that, in that contingency, i would have done better for himself by selecting a different strategy ρ. This means that, if r had been the situation resulting from i's adopting ρ in that contingency, i would have preferred the outcome produced by r to that produced by t, in symbols, $|r|P_i|t|$. Here r is the situation for which r_i is ρ and $r^{(i)}$ is the same as $t^{(i)}$, or, in other words, $r_j = t_j$ for each j other than i. In such a case, we may say that ρ *beats* τ (for i) in the contingency $t^{(i)}$. For instance, if s is the situation envisaged above, and i is voter 5, s_5 is the strategy $(\bar{a}b)$; s produces the outcome c (Conder co-opted). In the contingency $s^{(5)}$, the strategy (ab) beats s_5, because, if voter 5 had adopted it, he would have brought about a situation r producing the outcome a (no co-option), which he prefers to c; here r_5 is (ab) and $r^{(5)} = s^{(5)}$. In general, we may say that a situation t in which there is a strategy open to i which beats t_i in the contingency $t^{(i)}$ is *vulnerable* to the voter i, who, by voting differently, could have obtained an outcome he preferred to $|t|$.

If the voter i knows the contingency, he can calculate the effect of any strategy open to him, and can choose one beaten by no other. Usually, he will not know it. We may say that a strategy σ *rivals* another strategy τ for i if there is a contingency in which σ beats τ. Two strategies may rival one another; but we may say that σ

dominates τ for i if σ rivals τ but τ does not rival σ. We may call a strategy σ *admissible* for i if there is no strategy ρ that dominates it; left to himself, a voter has no motive for considering the adoption of an inadmissible strategy. Finally, a strategy σ is *straightforward* for i if there is no strategy ρ that rivals it.

For any inadmissible strategy τ, there will always be an admissible one that dominates it. Since τ is inadmissible, there will by definition be another strategy σ that dominates it; if σ is not itself admissible, there will be another that dominates *it*. It follows from the transitivity of preference that, if one strategy dominates a second, and that second strategy dominates a third, then the first strategy dominates the third, i.e. that dominance is a transitive relation between strategies. It then follows from the fact that there are only finitely many strategies open to any voter that, starting with τ, and moving always to a strategy that dominates the last, we shall eventually end with an admissible strategy dominating τ.

A voter i who has only himself to think of must choose between admissible strategies; if there is only one, his choice is made. If σ is i's sole admissible strategy, it must be straightforward for him. For suppose that another strategy τ rivalled σ. Since σ was assumed to be the only admissible strategy, τ must be inadmissible; there must therefore be an admissible strategy that dominates τ, and this can only be σ. Thus σ dominates τ, while τ rivals σ, which is a contradiction: so there can be no strategy τ that rivals σ. There may, indeed, be more than one strategy that is straightforward for i, perhaps because two distinct strategies will lead to the same outcome in every contingency, or, more plausibly, because i is indifferent between certain possible outcomes. As we have seen, there may also be *no* strategy that is straightforward for i. In such a case, he will have to choose between different admissible strategies that rival one another: one will beat the other in certain contingencies and be beaten by it in others. Voter i must then take a risk whatever he does.

It would be possible to give an exact means of deciding which, of several rival admissible strategies, a voter would do best to adopt only if he could both assign definite numerical probabilities to the various possible contingencies and definite numerical weightings to his preferences. Let us take as an example a committee of eleven members which has to make an appointment from a short list of three candidates, a, b, and c. The committee has been unable to come to an agreement, and a vote is to be taken. The procedure is by relative majority: each member votes for a single candidate, the candidate receiving the greatest number of votes being successful, with the chairman having a casting vote in case of a tie. X, one of the committee members, not the chairman, rates the candidates in the order *abc*. X has three possible strategies: to vote for *a*, for *b*, or for *c*. Of these, voting for *c* is obviously inadmissible. Voting for *a* is not, however, a straightforward strategy for him: voting for *b* is also an admissible strategy, and rivals voting for *a*, that is, will in certain contingencies produce an outcome X prefers. In many contingencies, X's vote will not affect the outcome: he may therefore ignore these and concentrate upon those contingencies in which it will. These are of three types: (i) those in which, if he votes for *a*, *a* will be successful, and, if he votes for *b*, *b* will be successful; (ii) those in which, if he votes for *a*, *a* will be successful, but, if he votes for *b*, *c* will be successful; and (iii) those in which, if he votes for *a*, *c* will be successful, whereas, if he votes for *b*, *b* will be successful.[1] It is the

---

[1] In detail, we can classify these contingencies according to the numbers of votes cast for the various candidates by the other voters and by the preferences of the chairman. The contingencies of type (i) are then as follows:

votes cast for			
a	*b*	*c*	the chairman prefers
5	5	0	
4	4	2	
5	4	1	*b* to *a*
4	5	1	*a* to *b*
3	4	3	*a* to *b*
3	3	4	*a* to *c* and *b* to *c*

The contingencies of type (ii) are:

votes cast for			
a	*b*	*c*	the chairman prefers
5	0	5	*c* to *a*
4	2	4	*c* to *a*
4	1	5	*a* to *c*
3	3	4	*a* to *c* and *c* to *b*

Those of type (iii) are:

votes cast for			
a	*b*	*c*	the chairman prefers
0	5	5	*c* to *b*
1	4	5	*b* to *c*
2	4	4	*c* to *b*
3	3	4	*b* to *c* and *c* to *a*

Note that a knowledge of the chairman's preferences is crucial to deciding of what type a contingency is, but is in itself no guide at all.

existence of contingencies of type (iii) which makes voting for *b* an admissible strategy for X. Which way he should vote will depend on the probability of a contingency of each type, and the amount of satisfaction X will obtain from the appointment of each of the three candidates.

If X can quantify both of these, he can make an exact calculation. He will have to assign satisfaction values to the appointment of *a*, of *b*, and of *c*; and he will also have to make numerical estimates of the probabilities of each of the three types of contingency, on the assumption that the actual contingency is of one of these three types, that is, that his vote will make a difference to the outcome. For each of the two admissible strategies open to him, he must then calculate what is called his 'expected satisfaction' from adopting it. To arrive at the expected satisfaction derived from voting for *a*, for instance, he must, for each of the three types of contingency, multiply the probability of a contingency of that type by the satisfaction, whether positive or negative, that he will derive from the outcome that will result from his voting for *a* in such a contingency: the sum of the three numbers he thus obtains will be the satisfaction he can expect from voting for *a*. Having calculated his expected satisfaction from voting for *b* in a similar manner, he will now decide to vote for that one of the two possible outcomes that will yield him the greater expected satisfaction. He will not in this way guarantee that he will do better for himself than if he had voted the other way, for he cannot do that unless he knows for certain the contingency that obtains, in which case no calculation will be necessary; but he will be adopting a standard means of making that happy result as likely as possible.[2]

---

[2] Suppose, for example, that, on the assumption that the actual contingency is one in which his vote will affect the outcome, X rates the probability of a contingency of type (i) at $\frac{1}{3}$, that of a contingency of type (ii) at $\frac{2}{9}$, and that of one of type (iii) at $\frac{4}{9}$. If he can view his satisfaction at the appointment of *a* as having the value of $+1$, at the appointment of *b* as 0 and at the appointment of *c* as -1, he should vote for *a*. This may be seen as follows. On the assumption that his vote will make a difference, there is a $\frac{5}{9}$ chance that the contingency is of type (i) or type (ii); if he votes for *a*, *a* will in these contingencies be successful, giving X a satisfaction of $+1$. These two types of contingency therefore contribute $\frac{5}{9} \times (+1) = \frac{5}{9}$ to X's expected satisfaction if he votes for *a*. There is a $\frac{4}{9}$ chance that the contingency is of type (iii), in which case, if he votes for *a*, *c* will be appointed, giving X a satisfaction of -1; this type therefore contributes $\frac{4}{9} \times (-1) = -\frac{4}{9}$ to his expected satisfaction under this strategy. His total expected satisfaction if he votes for *a* is therefore $\frac{5}{9} - \frac{4}{9} = +\frac{1}{9}$. If he votes for *b*, on the other hand, then, in a contingency of type (i) or type (iii), *b* will be appointed, and X will

The result of such a calculation would depend rather sensitively upon the weightings of the preferences (the satisfaction values assigned to the outcomes); quite a small difference in these would have the effect of reversing the order of the expected satisfaction to be gained by adopting the alternative strategies.[3] It is apparent that calculations of this kind are wholly unrealistic. If, by discussion within the committee, a member has obtained precise information about how his colleagues intend to vote, he can decide his own voting strategy by appealing only to his own preferences, independently of their respective strengths. If he has not, he is quite unlikely to be able to assign numerical values to the probabilities of the various types of contingency: even if he could, he has no way of answering the question whether, say, his preference for b over c is three times or only twice as strong as his preference for a over b; and yet it may be the answer to just that question that is needed to determine which strategy will yield the highest expected satisfaction. There is no way in which theory can use weighted preferences to provide a rule that could be applied in practice for choosing between rival admissible voting strategies: although the weighting of preferences has some intuitive significance, it cannot serve any useful theoretical purpose in explaining or in guiding a voter's choice of strategy.

---

receive a satisfaction of 0; contingencies of this type therefore make a zero contribution to his expected satisfaction if he adopts this strategy. There is a $\frac{2}{9}$ chance that the contingency will be of type (ii), in which case, if he votes for b, c will be appointed, giving him a satisfaction of -1. His total expected satisfaction if he votes for b is therefore $\frac{2}{9} \times (-1) = -\frac{2}{9}$. Since his expected satisfaction if he votes for a is $+\frac{1}{9}$, he should obviously vote for a.

[3] Suppose that another voter, Y, has the same preference scale, and, like X, assigns a satisfaction of $+1$ to the appointment of a and of -1 to the appointment of c, but rates his satisfaction at the appointment of b rather higher, say at $+\frac{1}{2}$. If Y is not the chairman, he must consider contingencies of the same kind as those considered by X. Let us suppose that he assigns just the same probabilities as X to the three types of contingency, of course now regarded relatively to Y. Then, on the assumption that Y's vote will make a difference to the outcome, his expected satisfaction if he votes for a will, like that of X, be $+\frac{1}{9}$. His expected satisfaction if he votes for b, on the other hand, will be higher. There is a $\frac{7}{9}$ chance that a contingency of type (i) or type (iii) will occur, in which case, if he votes for b, b will be appointed and he will receive a satisfaction of $+\frac{1}{2}$, yielding a contribution to his expected satisfaction of $\frac{7}{9} \times (+\frac{1}{2}) = +\frac{7}{18}$. His total expected satisfaction if he votes for b is therefore $\frac{7}{18} - \frac{2}{9} = +\frac{1}{6}$, which is higher than his expected satisfaction if he votes for a. Y ought therefore to vote for b. If, on the other hand, Y's satisfaction at the appointment of b had been only $+\frac{1}{3}$ or $+\frac{3}{8}$ (or anything less than $+\frac{3}{7}$), he would do better to vote for a.

The question with which we are principally concerned in this book is neither of those just considered, but, rather, which is the fairest or otherwise best voting procedure. We have, in order to answer this question, both to have a means of judging, from the preferences of the voters, what would be the fairest outcome, and to determine which voting procedure is the most likely to produce that outcome. It is apparent, from the case of family going to the theatre, that, in particular cases, the fairest outcome cannot always be judged from the voters' preference scales alone, but that the strengths of those preferences are relevant. To represent those strengths formally, however, it would be necessary to compare the strength of one voter's preferences with those of another, a difficulty not encountered when the question at issue is the best voting strategy for a particular voter. Since we do not know how to attach more than a vague sense to such comparisons, numerically weighted preferences would be of little use in this context, either. It is therefore best to represent the voters' preferences solely by preference scales, bearing in mind that such a representation is to a certain degree imperfect.

Especially is this so in view of the fact, already noted, that, the greater is the number of possible outcomes to be ranked by each voter in order of preference, the better the position of any one outcome in his preference scale can serve as a surrogate for a weighting of his preference. The point bears upon the significance of a celebrated theorem proved by Kenneth Arrow in his book *Social Choice and Individual Values*. The theorem is not stated specifically in terms of voting: it is best conceived as relating to the question whether there can be a criterion for determining, from the preference scales of a number of individuals as between a set of alternatives, which alternative would be best for them as a whole. When the individuals form a set of voters choosing between those alternatives by means of some voting procedure, the question becomes that stated above: can we devise a criterion for deciding, from the preference scales alone, whether the outcome produced by the voting procedure is the fairest one? Arrow's answer is negative.

Let us refer to the individuals in the set as 'voters', and the alternatives as 'possible outcomes'. Arrow regards each voter i as ordering the possible outcomes on a preference scale R_i, constituting a weak ordering, namely one that is transitive, connected, and reflexive, just as has been done in this chapter; indifference between two or more outcomes is not excluded. Arrow states his theorem in terms of a 'social welfare function'. This is a rule for determining, from the individual orderings $R_1, R_2, \ldots, R_n$, another weak ordering R of the possible outcomes, to be thought of as representing how they are ranked by the set of voters as a whole; we are taking the voters to be labelled by numbers $1, 2, \ldots, n$. It is natural to object that we are not concerned with an ordering R of *all* the possible outcomes, but only with determining which of those outcomes it would be fair to select, on the basis of the individual preference scales, as the best. The answer is that either can be defined in terms of the other. Let ϕ be a social welfare function which, applied to any set $R_1, R_2, \ldots, R_n$ of preference scales upon any set W of possible outcomes, yields a weak ordering R of W; we may write 'xPy' to mean 'xRy & not yRx', and 'xIy' to mean 'xRy & yRx'. Then obviously we can define, in terms of ϕ, a 'social choice function' ψ which, applied to $R_1, R_2, \ldots, R_n$, yields a set of one or more outcomes, understood as those whose selection to be the actual outcome would be fair: we need only take $\psi(R_1, R_2, \ldots, R_n)$ to consist of the outcomes ranking highest in the social ordering R, i.e. those outcomes x such that xRy for every y. Conversely, if we start with such a social choice function ψ, defined on every set of individual orderings of any set of possible outcomes, we can define from it a social ordering R in the following way. Suppose that the set W of possible outcomes has five members, a, b, c, d, and e, and that $\psi(R_1, R_2, \ldots, R_n)$ is the set consisting just of a. We then take a as the highest in the social ordering: aPy when y is any of the other four outcomes. We now consider the set W' consisting of those four remaining outcomes, and let $R'_1, R'_2, \ldots, R'_n$ be the individual orderings of W': each R'_i results from R_i simply by deleting a from the scale, the order of the rest remaining unchanged. Applied to $R'_1, R'_2, \ldots, R'_n$, the social choice function ψ will then yield a subset of W': suppose that it consists of b and c. We shall accordingly set bIc, bPd, cPd, bPe, and cPe. We now remove b and c from W' to form the set W'', consisting of just d and e, and the preferences R''_i of the voters as between these two outcomes, agreeing in that respect with their original preference scales R_i. By applying ψ to the R''_i, we shall obtain a subset of W'', say that consisting of d alone: in this case, we shall finally set dPe. The social ordering, in this example, will thus be $a(bc)de$: the general principle should be evident from the example.

Arrow proves that there can be no social welfare function

satisfying all the conditions he lays down. The generality of his result lies in the weakness of those conditions: he does *not* assume that all voters are equal, nor that all outcomes are. His result therefore still holds good when the preferences of certain voters count more heavily than those of others in determining the social ordering, or when certain outcomes have a better chance of ranking high in it than do others. All but one of his conditions is a minimal requirement for the rule embodied in the social welfare function to be in the least reasonable. One of them, however, is not: Arrow calls it the principle of the 'independence of irrelevant alternatives'. The principle is as follows. Suppose that we consider two sets of individual orderings, $R_1, R_2, \ldots, R_n$ and $R'_1, R'_2, \ldots, R'_n$, of the same set W; and suppose that they agree in respect of a particular pair x and y of outcomes in W, that is, that, for each voter i, $xR'_i y$ just in case $xR_i y$ and $yR'_i x$ just in case $yR_i x$. The principle states that, in such a case, x and y will have the same relative positions in the social orderings R and R': that is, that $xR'y$ just in case xRy and $yR'x$ just in case yRx. In other words, in determining whether x ranks higher than, equal to, or lower than y in the social ordering, the social welfare function takes account only of the preferences of the voters as between x and y: their positions on the preference scales relatively to other possible outcomes are irrelevant.

The significance of Arrow's theorem is best seen if the theorem is stated in the following way. We assume that there are at least three possible outcomes, and that a function is defined that yields, for any possible set of preference scales on the part of a fixed set of voters, a binary relation R between possible outcomes that is reflexive and connected. This function is assumed, further, to satisfy the principle of independence of irrelevant alternatives, and three further principles yet to be stated. On these assumptions, we show that R cannot always be transitive, and hence will not always be a weak ordering: the function is therefore not a social welfare function.

Principle (I), the first of our additional assumptions, states that a voter's preferences do not have a negative effect. Suppose that two sets of individual orderings, $R_1, \ldots, R_n$ and $R'_1, \ldots, R'_n$ are so related that they differ only in the position of a particular possible outcome x, and, further, that x is ranked at least as favourably under the second set as under the first. In other words, if y and z are both distinct from x, then, for any voter i, $yR'_i z$ just in case $yR_i z$; and, for any y and i, if $xR_i y$, then $xR'_i y$, and, if $xP_i y$, then

FUNDAMENTAL NOTIONS 53

xP'_iy. On these assumptions, principle (I) states that, if xRy for any y, then $xR'y$, and, if xPy, then $xP'y$.

From principle (I) and the principle of independence of irrelevant alternatives, we may infer the following. Suppose that two sets of preference scales, $R_1, \ldots, R_n$ and $R'_1, \ldots, R'_n$, are so related that, for two particular possible outcomes, x and y, if xR_iy, then xR'_iy, and if xP_iy, then xP'_iy: in other words, x never has a worse position relatively to y in the second set of preference scales than in the first. It then follows that, if xRy, $xR'y$, and, if xPy, $xP'y$. To state the next two principles, it is convenient to use Arrow's notion of a decisive set of voters. It is plain that the principle of independence of irrelevant alternatives implies that whether xPy, xIy, or yPx depends only on the composition of two sets of voters: those voters who prefer x to y, and those who prefer y to x. A set U of voters is said to be *decisive for x over y* if there is some set of preference scales $R_1, \ldots, R_n$ such that, for every voter i in U, xP_iy, and, for every voter j not in U, yP_jx, and xPy. It follows from the principle of independence of irrelevant alternatives that, if U is decisive for x over y, then xPy for *any* set of preference scales such that all the voters in U prefer x to y, and all those not in U prefer y to x; and it follows from the further assumption of principle (I) that xPy whenever all the voters in U prefer x to y, whatever the preferences of the voters not in U. It is also plain that, when xPy, the set of voters i for whom xR_iy is decisive for x over y.

Principle (II) may be taken as extremely weak, namely that there is some set of preference scales R_i for which xPy, for some x and y. If this assumption failed, then, whatever the voters' preferences, xIy for every x and y, so that all outcomes would rank equal in the social ordering. We may call a set of voters a *decisive set* if it is decisive for x over y for some outcomes x and y. Principle (II) implies that there is a decisive set, namely that comprising those voters i for whom xR_iy when xPy (even in the extreme case that this set is empty!). It follows from principle (I) that, if U is decisive for x over y, so is any set of which U is a subset (any set containing all the members of U); assuming that there are at least three voters, there must be a decisive set with at least two members.

Principle (III) states that there is no decisive set with only one member: that is, for no pair of outcomes x and y is there a single voter i such that xPy whenever i prefers x to y. Now let U be a decisive set such that no set smaller than it is decisive: there must be such a set, and it must have at least two members. Suppose that U is decisive for b over c, and that, as between a, b, and c (which need not be all the possible outcomes), some, but not all, of the voters in U rank them in the order bca, while the remainder rank them in the order abc; suppose also that all voters not in U, if any, rank them in the order cab (we are not ruling it out that U contains all the voters). Since all voters in U prefer b to c, bPc. The set U' of voters i with the ranking bca comprises all those for whom bR_ia: since U is smaller than U, it cannot be decisive for b over a; hence we cannot have bPa, and so, since R is connected, aRb. The set U'' of voters j with the ranking abc likewise comprises all those for whom aR_jc; hence, by similar reasoning, cRa. Thus, in this case, R is not transitive: we have cRa and aRb, but not cRb.

The 'paradox of voting', mentioned in the Introduction, is that the relation of majority preference may not be transitive; we can now see this as a special case of Arrow's theorem. If, with an odd number of voters, we take a set to be decisive (for any outcome x over any other outcome y) just in case it constitutes a majority of the voters, then all four principles are satisfied. In the proof of the theorem, we must then take the set U, consisting of the voters preferring b to c, as a bare majority. Those preferring c to a will then also form a majority, as will those preferring a to b; we have, accordingly, aPb, bPc, and cPa.

Arrow's theorem is rightly considered the fundamental theorem of social choice theory; but it would be a hysterical reaction to interpret it as meaning that there is no rational method of determining the fairest outcome from the preference scales. It shows only that no criterion applicable to every case will always satisfy the principle of independence of irrelevant alternatives; but that principle lacks complete intuitive justification, since it conflicts with the more compelling principle that whether x would be a fairer outcome than y depends not only on how many (or which) voters prefer x to y, and how many prefer y to x, but on how strong their preferences are. We say from the example of the family going to the theatre that, even when the preferences are not explicitly weighted, the specific positions of x and y on a voter's preference scale give a partial indication of the strength of his preference for one over the other: to take this into account is to reject the principle of independence of irrelevant alternatives. If we assume a social welfare function that treats all voters, and all outcomes, as equal, we can illustrate the point with examples. In one closely analogous to the family going to the theatre, the voters' preference scales might be as follows:

1	2	3	4	5	6	7	8	9
a	a	a	a	b	b	c	c	d
b	b	c	d	c	d	b	e	e
c	d	b	b	e	e	e	a	a
d	c	d	c	a	a	a	d	c
e	e	e	e	d	c	d	b	b

Here five voters prefer e to a: but a is the first choice of four of the voters, and is the only outcome regarded as the worst by none, while e is rated worst by the same four voters, and is the only outcome that is the first choice of none. As before, a is strongly preferred to e by four of the five voters, whereas the other five rank e only just above a on their preference scales: there is no intuitive ground for considering e to be as fair an outcome as a.

In the next example, a would plainly be the fairest outcome.

1	2	3	4	5	6	7	8	9
a	a	a	a	b	b	b	c	d
b	e	c	d	a	a	a	e	a
c	b	e	e	c	c	d	b	e
d	d	b	b	d	d	c	a	b
e	c	d	c	e	e	e	d	c

Eight of the voters prefer a to e, so there is no ground for holding e to be as fair an outcome as a. In any reasonable social ordering arrived at by treating all voters and all outcomes equally, a will rank highest: but which will rank second? The claim of b to second place is intuitively stronger than that of e: four voters regard e as the worst possible outcome, whereas none so regards b; three voters regard b as the best, whereas none so regards e. Yet five of the nine voters prefer e to b. It is not reasonable, however, to make this fact a decisive ground for ranking e at least as high as b in the social ordering: for, as before, those who prefer e to b rank it only just above b, whereas voters 5, 6, and 7 strongly prefer b to e, and voter 1's preference for b over e is only slightly less strong.

Since Arrow proved that no social welfare function could conform to the principle of the independence of irrelevant alternatives, provided that it also satisfied a few other very weak principles, it is easy to devise examples to show that insistence on the former principle may have absurd consequences; what is being argued here, however, is that that principle had no plausibility in the first place. We must avoid confusing two distinct propositions. The first, which has been argued for in this chapter, is that it is convenient in the theory of voting to dispense with any overt representation of the strengths of voters' preferences, and to treat only of their preference scales. By definition, a social welfare function determines the social ordering from the voters' preference scales, without appeal to the strengths of the preferences otherwise than as revealed by those scales. It follows from the first proposition that it is worth considering a social welfare function of this kind. The second proposition is that the relative positions of any two outcomes in the social ordering ought to depend solely upon the voters' preferences as between those two alone. This is the principle of the independence of irrelevant alternatives: and it does *not* follow from the first proposition. It is not unreasonable that a social welfare function should take account, as far as it can, of the relative strengths of voters' preferences between any two outcomes; and it can do so to the extent that these are represented, albeit crudely, by their relative positions on the preference scales. In deciding which of two possible outcomes x and y out of several would be the fairer, the voters' preferences between either of them and the remaining outcomes are *not* irrelevant: in deleting another outcome from the preference scales, we should be destroying information relevant to the choice between x and y themselves.

As we saw at the beginning of this chapter, the way someone actually votes may not reveal his preference scale, for two reasons: the voting procedure may not give him the opportunity to reveal it in full, and he may choose not to vote sincerely. Suppose, however, that we could devise some voting procedure that would enable every voter, and indeed require him, to reveal his whole preference scale, and would deprive him of any incentive to depart from sincere voting. We ought then to use a method of assessment—a method of determining the outcome from the votes cast—that would accord with whatever is taken to be the correct rule for determining the fairest outcome from a set of preference scales. Suppose that we had such a procedure; and suppose that the voters were engaged in making an appointment from a short list of five candidates. After the votes have been cast, and before the results have been announced, the tellers learn that one of the candidates has withdrawn. This fact is explained to the voters, who agree that there is no point in their voting again, since their votes already revealed their preferences between the remaining candidates. The tellers nevertheless have more information than they would have had if it had been known in advance of the voting that the candidate in question had withdrawn: they have a more accurate indication of the strengths of the voters' preferences between the remaining candidates. It follows that a perfectly reasonable method of assessment might, on the basis of the actual votes, lead to a different decision between the four remaining candidates than if the voters had voted only between those four candidates, their preferences between them remaining unchanged.

We have considered two ways in which preference scales can serve as a surrogate for an explicit representation of strength of preference. In examples of the second kind, we were from the outset within the static theory of voting: we were concerned with the choice between three or more possible outcomes, and could take the length of the gap between any two of them on any voter's preference scale as indicating the strength of his preference for one over the other. We began, however, with a case involving the transformation of a question within the dynamic theory of voting into one within the static theory. This is possible because there is no sharp distinction between a sequence of separate votes and a sequence of successive ballots within a single voting process: we could therefore reinterpret three votes, each of which had just two possible outcomes, as a procedure for deciding, in three ballots, between eight distinct possible outcomes. By recording each voter's preference scale as between these eight overall outcomes, we could in effect display the different strengths of their preferences between the results of the successive votes or ballots.

Such a transformation has, however, a further advantage: it enables us to display conditional preferences. The preference scales that we gave for voters 1 and 2 between the eight overall outcomes were derived from an assumption about the weightings of their preferences between the components. It is conceivable that a voter has a preference scale that cannot be so derived. Suppose, for instance, that voter 3's preference scale is the following:

$\bar{A}\bar{B}\bar{C}$
$\bar{A}\bar{B}C$
$A\bar{B}C$ $\bar{A}BC$
ABC
$\bar{A}B\bar{C}$ $A\bar{B}\bar{C}$
$AB\bar{C}$

Unlike those of voters 1 and 2, this preference scale has not the right shape to allow of its having been arrived at by assigning satisfaction values to the various components A, $\bar{A}$, B, etc., and summing them to obtain the satisfaction values of the overall outcomes: we could not in this way explain why voter 3 ranks $\bar{A}BC$ lower than $\bar{A}\bar{B}C$, but $A\bar{B}C$ higher than $A\bar{B}\bar{C}$. Voter 3 is generally opposed to the bypass plan, but holds strongly that, if any bypass is built, the third one (C) should be built. That is why, on the third motion, he votes in favour: the first two motions, a and b, having already been passed, the third vote represents a choice between ABC and AB$\bar{C}$. Given the order in which the motions were presented, voter 3's strategy was straightforward, namely to vote against both motions a and b, and then, if either of them was passed, for motion c, but, if both the earlier motions had been defeated, to vote against it. If, however, motion c had been taken first, he would have been in a quandary whether to vote for it or not. In either case, he would have had an incentive to join an alliance to defeat all three motions.

From the standpoint of theory, it is better to treat successive votes statically, that is, as a sequence of ballots in a single voting process, than dynamically, whenever this affords a clearer explanation of voters' behaviour. This will be so in any case in which the voters know, or can guess, the issues that will arise, and in which a subset of them are sufficiently in agreement to contemplate forming an alliance: in such cases the issues themselves may have little intrinsic relevance to one another. The theoretical advantage, in cases of this kind, of a static over a dynamic treatment is that whether a voter does or does not agree to join a proposed alliance can then be explained without recourse to a dubiously meaningful weighting of his preferences. When the issues do have an intrinsic bearing on one another, however, the voters may have conditional preferences concerning the outcomes of different votes; these can be represented by a preference scale between the overall outcomes of the kind just imagined for voter 3 in our example. In such a case, the issues are inextricably linked: the situation cannot be described dynamically, that is, by treating the ballots as distinct votes, even by appeal to weighted preferences. In such a case, to regard them as ballots within a single voting process is no longer a device of theory, but more accurately represents the concrete situation, in which it is, rather, a device of practice to pretend that they are distinct votes. From the standpoint of practice, there is always a temptation, in complex circumstances, to resort to such a device: when there are several different possible courses of action, a chairman who can see a way of deciding between them by taking a number of votes, each of which will have only two possible outcomes, will often propose or rule that such a method is to be adopted, as a means of avoiding having to take a single vote with more than two possible outcomes. If he does, then, if the issues are inherently linked, the proposal ought to be regarded as no more than a particular voting procedure for deciding between the various overall possible courses of action. As such, it is by no means necessarily the best method: if there are voters whose preference scales resemble voter 3's in our example, they will often be perplexed by the fact that such a procedure affords them no straightforward voting strategy.

3
Binary Voting Procedures

An important class of voting procedures consists of those called by Farquharson 'binary procedures': his elegant little book *Theory of Voting* is almost exclusively illustrated by these. A binary procedure comprises a sequence of ballots, each of which has only two possible outcomes: the procedure must therefore allow for more than one successive ballot, save in the trivial case in which the voters have to decide between only two possible courses of action. For most of these procedures there is no generally accepted name, since they are usually presented to the voters as sequences of successive votes; but it will be convenient to introduce names for some of them. We need to distinguish between the final outcome of the entire binary procedure, and what is determined by any one single ballot: we may therefore reserve the word 'outcome' for a possible final outcome of the procedure as a whole, and speak of each individual ballot as having one of two possible 'results'. The result of any one ballot will determine whether or not there is to be a further ballot, and, if not, what is the outcome of the procedure. Farquharson conveniently represents a binary procedure by means of a tree diagram. We may exemplify this for what we may label the 'knock-out procedure'. The possible outcomes are each voted on, in successive ballots, in some predetermined order: if, on any ballot, one of the outcomes is successful, the procedure terminates. We have already considered this procedure as a means of deciding between three possible outcomes: when a is taken first, the tree diagram is as shown in diagram 3.1.

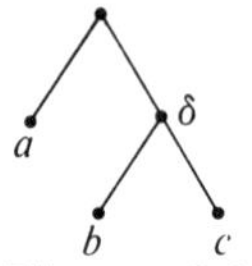

Diagram 3.1

If a is defeated on the first ballot, the second ballot decides between b and c.

BINARY VOTING PROCEDURES

The well-known committee procedure for voting on a motion and an amendment to it has a different form. Where *b* is the passage of the original motion, *c* its passage in its amended form, and *a* the complete rejection of the motion, the tree diagram for the amendment procedure is as in diagram 3.2.

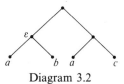

Diagram 3.2

In order to represent a voting procedure, every terminal node of a tree diagram must be shown as determining a final outcome: each such outcome must correspond to at least one terminal node, but, as appears from diagram 3.2, some may correspond to more than one such node. That will happen when the procedure allows the same outcome to be arrived at by more than one route: under the amendment procedure, the status quo may be preserved (outcome *a*) either because first the amendment and then the motion were defeated or because the amendment was carried and the amended motion subsequently defeated. Each non-terminal node represents a ballot: for the diagram to represent a binary procedure, it must have just two branches issuing from it, i.e. two nodes immediately below it. Each node other than the vertex also represents one of the two possible results of the ballot represented by the node immediately above. From any node, it will be possible to reach nodes representing certain of the final outcomes by some (downwards) path or other; we may say that these are the outcomes *live* at that node, or just before the corresponding ballot. For instance, at node δ in diagram 3.1, outcomes *b* and *c* are still live, but not *a*; at node ε in diagram 3.2, *a* and *b* remain live, but *c* does not.

The number of significantly different tree diagrams for a binary voting procedure with three possible outcomes is infinite; but it becomes quite small if we restrict ourselves to what we may call *pure* binary procedures. By a pure voting procedure with successive ballots is meant one under which, whatever the result of any ballot, at least one outcome must have been eliminated: in its tree diagram, therefore, the outcomes live at any node other than the vertex never include all those live at the node immediately above it. There are only six pure binary procedures for selecting one out of three possible outcomes a, b, and c. The knock-out procedure yields three of these, according as a, b, or c is taken first. We may use the name 'amendment procedure' for any binary procedure represented by diagram 3.2, whether or not a in fact constitutes the status quo; the outcome a, whatever its nature, plays a special role under this procedure, and may be called the *residual* outcome. The amendment procedure thus yields the remaining three pure binary procedures for choosing between a, b, and c, according to which of them is residual.

When there are four possible outcomes, the number of pure binary procedures is much greater. In one type, the first ballot is for or against a particular outcome: if it goes in favour of that outcome, the procedure terminates; otherwise, three outcomes remain live, and may be voted on by any one of the six pure binary procedures for deciding between three outcomes. There will be 24 distinct procedures of this type, which will be either a knock-out procedure as in diagram 3.3 or a mixed procedure as in diagram 3.4.

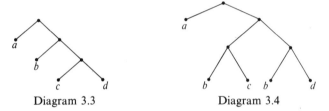

Diagram 3.3   Diagram 3.4

There will be 12 variants of each subtype, obtained by relettering the diagrams.

Quite a different type of procedure is one in which the result of the first ballot will in either case leave three live outcomes: whatever the result of the first ballot, there will then be six possible ways to continue. Since there are six different ways of arranging the first ballot, there are altogether 216 (6 × 6 × 6) distinct procedures of this type. An important subtype comprises 54 distinct procedures: in each of these, just one outcome will be eliminated by the second ballot, so that there will in every case be three ballots. Procedures with successive ballots, each of which results in the elimination of just one outcome, may be called *elimination procedures*: the amendment procedure is a binary elimination procedure with just three possible outcomes. One binary elimination procedure with four possible outcomes is represented by diagram 3.5.

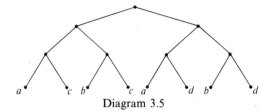
Diagram 3.5

Here there are two distinct routes for arriving at any one of the four outcomes: the first ballot asks the voters whether they wish to eliminate c or d; whatever the result, the second ballot asks them whether they wish to eliminate a or b. Not all binary elimination procedures exhibit such symmetry; the maximum asymmetry is displayed by that represented by diagram 3.6.

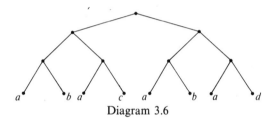
Diagram 3.6

Here there is only one route to either of the outcomes c and d, two routes to b and four to a. The voters are first asked whether to eliminate c or d, and then whether to eliminate b or the survivor of the first ballot. An intermediate form can be obtained by combining the left-hand half of diagram 3.5 with the right-hand half of diagram 3.6.

A completely different type of procedure is one in which the first ballot eliminates two of the outcomes, leaving the other two live: no choice remains how to proceed after that. These may be called *split* procedures; there are only three of them, corresponding to the significantly different possible letterings of diagram 3.7.

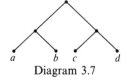
Diagram 3.7

A split procedure often results from a decision to regard the four outcomes as composite choices on two distinguishable issues. For example, someone proposes that there shall be no smoking during transaction of committee business, and another member urges that this should apply only to full committee meetings, not to subcommittees. A third member objects that he would like to see smoking banned at subcommittee meetings, but not at those of the full committee. There are then four possible outcomes: *a*—to ban smoking altogether; *b*—to ban it at full committee meetings only; *c*—to ban it at subcommittee meetings only; and *d*—not to ban it at all. The chairman may rule that there are two separate issues to be considered—whether to ban smoking at full committee meetings (u) or not ($\bar{u}$), and whether to ban it at subcommittee meetings (v) or not ($\bar{v}$), so that two separate votes are to be taken (diagram 3.8).

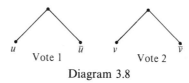

Diagram 3.8

So regarded, *a* is the composite outcome uv, *b* the composite outcome $u\bar{v}$, *c* the composite outcome $\bar{u}v$, and *d* the composite outcome $\bar{u}\bar{v}$. When the vote on u is taken first, as in diagram 3.8, the two votes can equally be viewed as successive ballots in the binary procedure (diagram 3.9).

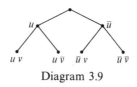

Diagram 3.9

This is, of course, the same procedure as that shown in diagram 3.7 with the labels *a*, *b*, *c*, and *d*.

We have not yet exhausted the possible pure binary procedures for deciding between four possible outcomes. We could also consider those whose first ballot asks the voters to choose between eliminating one particular outcome and eliminating two different ones, leaving three outcomes live under the one result and two under the other: but such a procedure is rather unlikely.

It is particularly easy to decide, for a given binary procedure, whether or not a voter with a particular preference scale has a straightforward voting strategy. Let us first ask whether it is straightforward for him to decide how to vote in any one ballot. The ballot will have one of two possible results: he has no problem in deciding how to vote if he regards each outcome that would remain live under one result as being at least as good as any outcome that would remain live under the other. Suppose that the knock-out procedure, with a first, is used (diagram 3.1). A voter whose preference scale is abc will have no difficulty in deciding how to vote on the first ballot: he must vote for a, since, if his vote makes a difference to the outcome at all, it must do so by producing an outcome that he prefers. The same applies to a voter with the preference scale $(ab)c$: he, too, must vote for a, since, by doing so, he cannot obtain an outcome that he thinks worse than that he would obtain by voting against a, and may obtain one that he thinks better. Likewise, a voter with the preference scale bca or $b(ca)$ must vote against a on the first ballot. There can be no problem how to vote on the final ballot in a binary procedure, when only two outcomes remain live before the ballot is taken: voters with the preference scales mentioned therefore have straightforward strategies under the knock-out procedure with three possible outcomes and a first. There are two, and only two, preference scales for which the procedure does not afford a straightforward strategy, namely bac and cab. It will depend upon the intentions of the other voters whether a voter with one of these preference scales will do worse or better for himself by voting for a on the first ballot. One with the preference scale bac thus has two admissible strategies: to vote for a on the first ballot, and then for b if a second ballot is held; and to vote against a on the first ballot, and then for b if a second ballot is held.

In Chapter 2 we introduced the notation '$xR_i y$' to mean 'voter i thinks outcome x at least as good as outcome y'. In considering binary procedures, we are concerned with ballots in which each voter has, in effect, to choose, not between single outcomes, but between *sets* of outcomes—the set of those which remain live under one result of the ballot and the set of those which remain live under the other. We may therefore extend our notation: where A and B are sets of outcomes, we may write '$AR_i^* B$' to mean that voter i thinks every member of A at least as good as any member of B. Thus, if A contains just two members, x and y, and B contains just two members, z and w, '$AR_i^* B$' will hold just in case $xR_i z$, $xR_i w$, $yR_i z$, and yR_iw. In these terms, our condition that it be straightforward for i to decide how to vote in a particular ballot was that AR_i^*B or BR_i^*A, where A is the set of outcomes remaining live under one result of the ballot, and B the set of those remaining live under the other. In some cases, one or other of the two sets may have only a single member. Thus, under the knockout procedure, the first ballot divides the three outcomes into the set A consisting of a alone and the set B consisting of b and c. The condition that i have a straightforward strategy under this procedure is, then, that:

either $\quad aR_ib$ and $aR_ic \quad$ or $\quad bR_ia$ and cR_ia.

As we saw, only the two preference scales *bac* and *cab* violate this condition. In other cases, the sets A and B may have a common member, though each will always have a member not contained in the other. Thus under the amendment procedure, with a residual, the first ballot divides the three outcomes into the set A consisting of a and b and the set B consisting of a and c. It will be straightforward for i to decide how to vote in this ballot if AR_i^*B or BR_i^*A. When 'AR_i^*B' is spelled out in this case, it comes to:

aR_ia and aR_ic and bR_ia and bR_ic.

It is trivial that aR_ia; by the transitivity of R_i, 'bR_ic' follows from 'aR_ic and bR_ia'. The clause therefore reduces to:

bR_iaR_ic.

Similarly, 'BR_i^*A' reduces to 'cR_iaR_ib', so that the condition for i to have a straightforward strategy under the amendment procedure is that:

$bR_iaR_ic \quad$ or $\quad cR_iaR_ib$.

A voter with the preference scale *abc* cannot vote for the elimination of c on the first ballot with confidence that he will not thereby have had an adverse effect from his own standpoint. If his vote makes a difference, its effect may be to substitute b for a as the final outcome, namely if a majority of voters prefer b to a, but a majority prefer a to c. Among strong preference scales (those not involving indifference between any two outcomes), the amendment procedure therefore affords a straightforward strategy for only two, *bac* and *cab*, out of the six possible ones. Among the seven weak preference scales, there is a straightforward strategy for five of them, $(ab)c$, $(ac)b$, $b(ac)$, $c(ab)$, and, of course, (abc), but not for $a(bc)$ or $(bc)a$.

For which preference scales is a straightforward strategy afforded by the knock-out procedure with four possible outcomes, with a first and b second, represented by diagram 3.3? The first ballot divides the outcomes into the set A_1, consisting of a alone, and B_1, consisting of b, c, and d. Hence, for i to have a straightforward strategy, the following condition must hold:

$(aR_ib$ and aR_ic and $aR_id)$ or $(bR_ia$ and cR_ia and $dR_ia)$.

The second ballot divides the live outcomes b, c, and d into the set A_2, consisting of b alone, and B_2, consisting of c and d. Hence the further condition must also hold:

$(bR_ic$ and $bR_id)$ or $(cR_ib$ and $dR_ib)$.

If i has a strong preference scale, the two conditions will both be satisfied if (i) a is in the first place and b in the second, or (ii) a is in the first place and b in the fourth, or (iii) a is in the fourth place and b in the first, or, finally, (iv) a is in the fourth place and b in the third. Thus, of the 24 possible strong preference scales, i has a straightforward strategy only if he has one of the following eight: *abcd*; *abdc*; *acdb*; *adcb*; *bcda*; *bdca*; *cdba*; *dcba*. The weak preference scales for which there is a straightforward strategy are just those obtainable from any of these by inserting brackets without changing the order of the letters.

Under the split procedure represented by diagram 3.7, the first ballot divides the outcomes into the set A consisting of a and b and the set B consisting of c and d. The condition for i to have a straightforward strategy is therefore that:

$(aR_ic$ and aR_id and bR_ic and $bR_id)$ or
$(cR_ia$ and cR_ib and dR_ia and $dR_ib)$.

Of the 24 strong preference scales, there are again just eight satisfying this condition: *abcd*; *abdc*; *bacd*; *badc*; *cdab*; *cdba*; *dcab*; *dcba*. As before, the weak preference scales satisfying the condition are just those obtainable from the foregoing strong ones by bracketing.

The binary elimination procedures represented by diagrams 3.5 and 3.6 introduce a new feature. In both of these, the first ballot divides the outcomes into the set A consisting of a, b, and c and the set B consisting of a, b, and d: there are thus two outcomes, a and b, common to A and B. If AR_i^*B, then, it will follow both that aR_ib and that bR_ia, i.e. that aI_ib, and the same will follow if BR_i^*A. Thus, for it to be straightforward for i to decide how to vote on the first ballot, he must be indifferent between the two outcomes a and b that will in any event remain live; no voter with a strong preference scale can have a straightforward strategy under either of the two procedures. More precisely, the condition for it to be straightforward for i how to vote on the first ballot is that:

$cR_iaI_ibR_id$ or $dR_iaI_ibR_ic$.

Under the procedure represented by diagram 3.6, this condition will be found to be sufficient for it to be straightforward for i how to vote in any of the subsequent ballots that may occur, and hence to be the condition for i to have a straightforward overall strategy. The procedure thus affords a straightforward strategy for none of the 24 possible strong preference scales, and for only 7 of the 51 possible weak ones, namely $c(ab)d$ and $d(ab)c$, together with those obtainable from them by further bracketing. Under the procedure represented by diagram 3.5, however, the possible later ballots further restrict the condition on i's preference scale, to so great an extent that no voter will have a straightforward strategy unless he is indifferent between all four possible outcomes, in which case, of course, every strategy is straightforward for him under any procedure.

The general principle we have been applying is that, for i to have a straightforward strategy under a binary procedure,

AR_i^*B or BR_i^*A

must hold for every ballot which may occur and which divides the outcomes into the sets A and B. When the sets A and B are disjoint (contain no common members), this means that it is possible to draw a line somewhere in i's preference scale so that every member of A stands on one side of it and every member of B on the other. Thus, if A consists of a and b and B of c and d, this will be possible for such preference scales as:

| a | d | d |
b	c	c
c	b	a
d	a	b

BINARY VOTING PROCEDURES

and so on, but not, for instance, for:

a

c

b

d

When the preference scale is weak, it will be allowable to draw the line *between* two outcomes standing on the same level, i.e. between which the voter is indifferent, as in such a case as:

In the case in which *A* consists of a single outcome, say *a*, the condition requires that *a* either stand at least as high as any of the outcomes in *B* or stand no higher than any of them.

When *A* and *B* are not disjoint, but contain a single common member, say *b*, the condition becomes that it be possible to draw a line *through b* on the voter's preference scale, so that all the other members of *A* stand on one side and all the other members of *B* on the other. Thus, if *A* consists of *a* and *b*, and *B* of *b*, *c*, and *d*, preference scales like this will satisfy the condition:

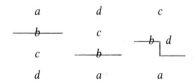

but not:

```
    a              b c
    c
    b              a
    d              d
```

If, however, A and B have two or more common members, the condition for a voter i to have a straightforward way of voting in that ballot requires that he be indifferent between all of those common members, and that it be possible to draw a line through all of them leaving all the other members of A on one side and all the other members of B on the other. If, for instance, A consists of a, b, and c, and B of b, c, and d, then i must be indifferent between b and c; his preference scale will then satisfy the condition if it is like this:

but not if it is like this:

$$a$$
$$d$$
$$b\ c$$

We may thus easily judge, from the diagram for any binary voting procedure, what conditions a voter's preference scale must satisfy if he is to have a straightforward strategy. Consider, as a final example, the mixed procedure represented by diagram 3.4. For i to have a straightforward strategy, a must stand either at the top or at the bottom of his preference scale, possibly level with one or more others, and b must stand between c and d, possibly level with one or both. Just four of the twenty-four strong preference scales satisfy both conditions: $acbd$; $adbc$; $cbda$; and $dbca$.

Armed with this analysis, we may take a closer look at split procedures. In Chapter 1, we considered, as example 1, three successive votes for or against three distinct motions, which we may reletter u, v, and w (diagram 3.10).

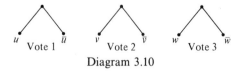

Diagram 3.10

In Chapter 2, we observed that these could be reinterpreted as three successive ballots in a single binary procedure for deciding between eight possible composite outcomes; this will then be represented by diagram 3.11.

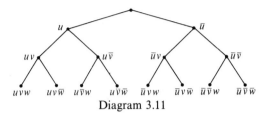

Diagram 3.11

We remarked on the advantage of considering each voter's scale of preferences between the composite outcomes, which could display the different strengths of their preferences between the component outcomes without the need for explicit weightings. We also remarked on the fact that not every scale of preferences between the composite outcomes can be arrived at from a weighting of the components. If a voter has conditional preferences, such as that motion v be passed only if motion w is also passed, his preference scale cannot be so arrived at: for him, the issues are not independent of one another. Voting on them separately, or, equivalently, by the binary procedure represented by diagram 3.11, therefore places him in a quandary how to vote.

There is a further advantage of the static over the dynamic representation, in that it more explicitly displays the strategies open to the voters. In example 1 of Chapter 1, voter 3, who favoured motion w, is unlikely to agree unconditionally with voters 1 and 2 to vote against all three motions: he is more likely to agree to vote against w only if u and v have both been defeated. In terms of diagram 3.11, he has committed himself only to a strategy requiring him, on the third ballot, to vote for $\bar{u}\bar{v}\bar{w}$ against $\bar{u}\bar{v}w$, if that is the choice. The representation in that diagram of the second ballot by two distinct nodes, and of the third by four, according to the results of previous ballots, shows clearly that each voter has, not 8, but 128, distinct strategies that he may adopt.

A static representation may, conversely, be interpreted dynamically: in particular, any split binary procedure can be viewed as the holding of successive votes, each with two possible outcomes. In general, a split procedure will be one under which, as in an elimination procedure, there will in every case be the same number of ballots, but in the diagram of which each terminal node will determine a distinct outcome. The number of possible outcomes must therefore be a power of 2: 4, 8, 16, and so on. Now suppose that a decision has to be taken between eight possible outcomes, not originally presented as composite, and the voting procedure adopted has diagram 3.12.

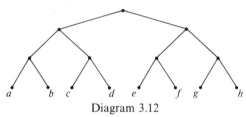

Diagram 3.12

Such a procedure may be interpreted by distinguishing three separate motions u, v, and w, corresponding to the three ballots that occur in the binary procedure, in such a way that each of the eight possible final outcomes is equivalent to one of the possible combinations of outcomes of the votes on these three motions. If, then, a is equivalent to uvw, b to $uv\bar{w}$, c to $u\bar{v}w$, and so on, we have a particular *decomposition* of the original eight outcomes, i.e. a representation of them as composite outcomes with three components. It is very likely that the split procedure of the diagram was arrived at by explicitly proposing such a decomposition: the chairman may actually have formulated three such motions u, v, and w, and ruled that they were to be voted on separately and in succession.

When will it be reasonable to proceed in this way? It can be reasonable only when u, v, and w really represent independent issues in the voters' minds. They may be said to do so just in case each voter's scale of preferences between the eight possible outcomes could be arrived at by assigning suitable satisfaction weightings to the components u, $\bar{u}$, v, $\bar{v}$, w, and $\bar{w}$; the satisfaction obtained by the voter from a given component can then be viewed as independent of the other components.

Let us for simplicity consider the case with only four possible outcomes. It is evident that such decompositions as

$a = u\bar{v}$, $b = uv$, $c = \bar{u}\bar{v}$, $d = \bar{u}v$
$a = \bar{u}\bar{v}$, $b = \bar{u}v$, $c = u\bar{v}$, $d = uv$

are equivalent to one another; it makes no difference which components we take to be affirmative. It is easily seen that every decomposition must be equivalent to one of the following:

(δ) $a = uv,\ b = u\bar{v},\ c = \bar{u}v,\ d = \bar{u}\bar{v}$
(ε) $a = uv,\ b = \bar{u}v,\ c = \bar{u}\bar{v},\ d = u\bar{v}$
(ζ) $a = uv,\ b = \bar{u}\bar{v},\ c = u\bar{v},\ d = \bar{u}v$.

There are three possible split procedures consisting of two ballots, namely those represented by diagram 3.13.

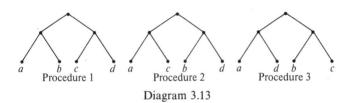

Diagram 3.13

Each of these corresponds to two of the above three decompositions: procedure 1 to (δ) and (ε), procedure 2 to (ζ) and (δ), and procedure 3 to (ε) and (ζ). In the light of decomposition (δ), the first ballot in procedure 1 appears as a vote on the component issue u; in the light of decomposition (ε), it appears as a vote on the issue v.

When is a voter's preference scale consistent with a given decomposition? With only four possible outcomes, this is easy to answer. Any decomposition determines which outcome is to be regarded as the inverse of another, where $\bar{u}\bar{v}$ is the inverse of uv and $\bar{u}v$ is the inverse of $u\bar{v}$. Thus (δ) makes d the inverse of a and c of b; likewise a and c are inverses under (ε) and a and b under (ζ). If a preference scale is to be consistent with a given decomposition, the inverse of any outcome must be in the symmetrically opposite position to it on the scale; when there are only four outcomes, this also suffices for its consistency with it. Thus the scale $abcd$ is consistent with (δ), as are $cdab$ and $b(ad)c$; $abdc$ and $a(cd)b$ are not, however, while $(ab)cd$ is consistent with no decomposition whatever, since it is not symmetrical in form. For instance, under (δ), the scale $cdab$ can be arrived at by assigning satisfaction values of $+2$ to $\bar{u}$ and $+1$ to v and correspondingly -2 to u and -1 to $\bar{v}$. For decompositions of eight outcomes into three components each, the condition that inverses must be in symmetrically opposite positions does not suffice to determine the consistency of a preference scale with a decomposition: for instance, if a, b, c, and d are represented respectively as uvw, $uv\bar{w}$, $u\bar{v}w$, and $u\bar{v}\bar{w}$, we must also require that a voter who prefers a to b should also prefer c to d, and conversely.

If procedure 1 is adopted, this may be viewed as corresponding either to decomposition (δ) or to decomposition (ε). A voter who has a preference scale consistent with neither of these decompositions, such as *acdb*, cannot have a straightforward strategy: he will inevitably be in a quandary how to vote on the first ballot. If there are such voters, the procedure will therefore be inappropriate. It might seem that any voter who has a preference scale consistent with one of the two decompositions will have a straightforward strategy. The procedure is equivalent to two successive votes on the two motions u and v. To say that a voter's scale of preferences between the composite outcomes is consistent with the given decomposition is in effect to say that the components are independent for him, i.e. that he does not have conditional preferences concerning the outcomes of the votes on the two motions. Since, on a single vote with only two possible outcomes, every voter has a straightforward strategy, it would seem that a voter with a scale consistent with, say, decomposition (δ) must have a straightforward strategy under procedure 1.

This is not so, however: a voter with the scale *acbd* has no straightforward strategy, although his scale is consistent with (δ). The reason is that, in the light of the decomposition (δ), procedure 1 involves voting first on the issue u and then on the issue v; but, viewed in terms of (δ), the scale *acbd* indicates that the voter cares more about v than about u, since it can be obtained by assigning a satisfaction value of $+1$ to u and of $+2$ to v. His uncertainty how to vote on the first ballot arises from the possibility that a majority of the voters prefer b to a and a majority of them prefer c to d. This uncertainty will not be resolved by his merely knowing that every voter has a preference scale consistent with one of the decompositions (δ) and (ε) corresponding to procedure 1: for the preference scales *cdba* and *bcad* are consistent with (ε), but involve a preference for b over a and c over d. If he knows, however, that every voter has a scale consistent with (δ), he no longer has anything to fear. In terms of the decomposition (δ), there are only two possible cases: that there is a majority in favour of v, and that there is a majority in favour of $\bar{v}$. In the first case, a majority will prefer a to b, and the same majority will prefer c to d; in the second, a majority will prefer

BINARY VOTING PROCEDURES

d to c, and the same majority will prefer b to a. In either case, he must vote on the first ballot to retain a and b and eliminate c and d, that is, in terms of (δ), in favour of the motion u.

Suppose, then, that it is proposed to adopt procedure 1. For any given voter, there are three possible cases: (1) he has a preference scale, say *dcab*, that affords him a straightforward strategy; (2) he has a preference scale, say *adcb*, that is not consistent with either decomposition corresponding to procedure 1; and (3) that he has a scale, say *acbd* or *adbc*, that is consistent with one of the decompositions corresponding to the procedure, but does not afford him a straightforward strategy. In case (1), he should be willing, in his own interests, to accept the procedure; in case (2), he should certainly object to it. In case (3), he should neither object to it outright nor support it outright. Rather, he should request the formulation of motions u and v which allow the matter to be dealt with as a pair of successive votes on distinct issues. Suppose, for instance, that our voter has the preference scale *acbd*, and makes this request: the motions u and v are so formulated as to yield the decomposition (δ), and it is proposed to vote first on u, so that, in effect, procedure 1 is still followed. Suppose, further, that some other voter has the preference scale *adbc*. This voter was originally in the same position: he had no straightforward strategy, but his scale was consistent with one of the decompositions, in his case (ε), corresponding to procedure 1. This voter ought now to object to the proposed formulation of the motions u and v: he may reasonably point out that he is not unreservedly for or against the motion u, as framed, since he favours it if v is also passed but is opposed to it if v is defeated. If, then, no voter objects to the proposed formulation of the motions u and v, this will be an indication to our original voter, with the scale *acbd*, that all the voters' preference scales are consistent with the decomposition (δ). Hence, although the procedure itself has not been altered, but only redescribed, he has gained an important piece of information that will allow him to vote with confidence for the component outcome u.

Our voter may take a further step. If motions u and v have been framed so as to yield the decomposition (δ), and no one has objected, he may now ask that motion v be voted on before motion u: this will in effect replace procedure 1 by procedure 2, and will afford our voter, whose preference scale is *acbd*, with a straightforward strategy. He could hardly have made this proposal before the motions u and v were formulated; even if it is rejected, he will gain some information about the preferences of the other voters. In sum, then, a voter who has no straightforward strategy under the proposed binary procedure, but has a preference scale consistent with one of the decompositions corresponding to it, should demand a formulation of the component issues. If the suggested formulation does not yield a decomposition with which his scale is consistent, he should object to it. If it does, he should support any voter who objects to it, but accept it if no other voter objects, and may then try to get the order in which the motions are taken altered so as to give himself a straightforward strategy.

Binary procedures offer straightforward strategies to some voters. Of the two types that can be used to decide between three possible outcomes, one afforded a straightforward strategy for four out of the six possible strong preference scales, the other for only two of them. Of those for deciding between four outcomes which we examined in this chapter, two afforded a straightforward strategy for eight out of the twenty-four possible strong preference scales, one for four, and two for none. In general, those who do not have a straightforward strategy are in a considerable quandary under binary procedures: the outcome is thus likely to depend heavily upon their guesses about how others are going to vote. The effect of this will be investigated in more detail in the next chapter.

We have been considering only *pure* binary procedures, namely those under which there are always fewer live outcomes after any ballot than before. If we drop this restriction, many more binary tree diagrams can be drawn, indeed infinitely many, even with only three possible outcomes: for instance diagram 3.14.

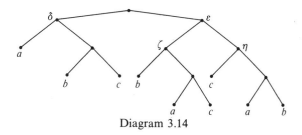
Diagram 3.14

Such a diagram still has a practical interpretation. The ballots corresponding to the vertex and to node ε are, in effect, votes on procedure. It has already been decided that one of the three knock-out procedures in diagram 3.15 is to be used.

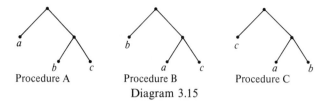

Procedure A   Procedure B   Procedure C

Diagram 3.15

The preliminary procedural vote for deciding between them is again a knock-out procedure, with the form shown in diagram 3.16.

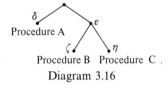

Diagram 3.16

The nodes here labelled by Greek letters correspond to those so labelled in diagram 3.14. Impure voting procedures do thus in fact occur whenever one or more preliminary votes are taken to determine what pure procedure is to be used. A ballot is procedural if, whatever its result, all outcomes live before it is held remain live afterwards. There can be mixed cases, as shown by the diagram:

Diagram 3.17

The procedure so represented is not pure, since all three possible outcomes remain live unless the outcome *a* is selected outright on the first ballot; but that ballot is not merely procedural. The diagram represents a case in which the chairman allows a preliminary motion to decide on *a* outright, without prejudice, if the motion is defeated, to its subsequent consideration as one of three alternatives. It is plain, however, that we lose little by confining our attention to pure procedures.

4
Stability

The concept of sincere voting has, in the course of our discussion, come to be displaced by those of straightforward and of admissible strategies. There is good reason for this. A voting mechanism may be specified by enumerating the strategies open to each voter; a method of assessment by laying down, for each situation, which outcome it produces. It will be recalled that a situation was defined as consisting in a selection of a specific strategy by each voter; we are tacitly assuming that each possible outcome is produced by at least one situation, since otherwise it would not be possible. The voting mechanism and the method of assessment together comprise the voting procedure: which strategies are admissible to a voter under a given procedure, and whether or not he has a straightforward strategy, can be determined from a knowledge of the procedure and of his preference scale. The concept of a sincere vote is not nearly so easy to apply. Consider again the split procedure represented by diagram 3.7: the first ballot asks the voters to choose between eliminating c and d and eliminating a and b. Suppose that voters 2 and 3 have, respectively, the preference scales $acbd$ and $acdb$. Believing that a majority of the voters prefer b to a, both of them vote on the first ballot to eliminate a and b: their votes swing the balance, and the eventual outcome is c. Did they vote insincerely on the first ballot?

Suppose that the procedure had been presented to the voters as two successive votes on the motions u and v, in accordance with the decomposition (δ):

$$a = uv, \quad b = u\bar{v}, \quad c = \bar{u}v, \quad d = \bar{u}\bar{v}.$$

Voter 2's preference scale is consistent with (δ), and he clearly prefers u to $\bar{u}$. He nevertheless voted against u on the first vote: so regarded, we must say that his first vote was insincere. Voter 3's preference scale, on the other hand, is not consistent with (δ): in terms of it, he has the conditional preference that u be passed only if v is also passed. He can therefore hardly be regarded, from this point of view, as having voted insincerely in voting against u on the first vote. Suppose now, however, that different motions u' and v' had been framed, in accordance with the decomposition (ε):

$$a = u'v', \quad b = u'\bar{v}', \quad c = \bar{u}'\bar{v}', \quad d = \bar{u}'v'.$$

If u' were to be voted on first, the actual procedure would be exactly the same as before, namely the split procedure under which, on the first ballot, the voters are asked to choose between eliminating a and b and eliminating c and d. But now the preference scales of both voters would be inconsistent with the decomposition (ε), and conditional preferences would have to be ascribed to both of them: neither voter wants either of the motions u' and v' to be passed unless the other is. Regarded in this way, there is no greater reason to say that voter 2 voted insincerely on the first ballot than to say that voter 3 did.

Our inclination to call a vote sincere or insincere is thus based on more than the preferences of the voter and the actual voting procedure: it depends also on how the vote happens to be described. It is common to regard a vote, or a ballot in the course of a complex procedure, as posing a question to the voters about their preferences: thus a vote between three or more candidates for election under the relative majority procedure is seen as asking each voter to say which one of the candidates he prefers to the others. If a voter then votes for a candidate whom he does not actually think to be the best, we are inclined to call his vote insincere; but if we frame the question put to the voters as 'Which do you think is the best of the candidates you believe to have a chance of winning?', the very same vote no longer appears insincere. The word 'sincere' has moral overtones which actually mislead people into thinking that there is something reprehensible in voting 'insincerely', under a certain description of the significance of the vote: I have actually heard it said, 'Of course, no member of this College would vote insincerely', apropos of a ballot in a complicated voting procedure in which there was plenty of incentive to do what was being described as 'voting insincerely'. A voting paper is not, however, a questionnaire. It is a mechanism in a decision-making procedure which will have whatever effect it has because of the way in which that procedure works. The actual significance of a particular vote is therefore wholly determined by the procedure of which it forms part: it is improper, because unfair to the voters, to attempt to confer on it some different significance by describing it in a particular way, and then to bring moral pressure upon the voters to act as though it had that different meaning. To use the preceding example once more, if a voter believes that the outcome of a vote upon an issue u will have an effect upon the outcome of a subsequent vote upon a further issue v, there can be no justification for asking him to vote on u as if he believed that it would have no such effect. Equally, if his view about whether it is desirable to pass a motion u depends upon his opinion about whether a subsequent motion v will be passed or not, there can be no justification demanding that he vote on u as if no subsequent motion was to be put. The only question that a voter actually answers by casting a particular vote is, 'In which way do you think that you should cast your vote in order to obtain an outcome as agreeable to you as possible?', and this question he inevitably answers sincerely. If one wants to make his vote yield an answer to a specific question about his preferences, there is only one way to do that: to devise the procedure so that it is straightforward for him how to vote, given any possible answer to that question, and so that he will vote in different ways, according to the answer.

The reason why it is desirable that a voting procedure should, as far as possible, afford straightforward strategies for the voters is not, therefore, that otherwise it will tempt them to stray from the path of virtue and submit dishonest voting papers. Voters can be bribed or threatened; so it would be misleading to say that there is no such thing as a dishonest vote. More importantly, voters can join a party or an alliance. In example 1 of Chapter 1, voters 1, 2, and 3 entered into an agreement all to vote against every one of the three motions. This strategy was inadmissible for all of them, but each gained an advantage from it. It will be recalled that we termed a strategy inadmissible for a voter if there was another strategy that dominated it; one strategy dominates another for a voter if, in all contingencies, the first yields an outcome at least as good from his standpoint as that yielded by the second, and, in at least one contingency, it yields a better outcome. We may explain the fact that the voters of example 1 of Chapter 1 gain an advantage by adopting inadmissible strategies by their being concerned, in each vote, not with the outcome of that vote alone, but with those of other, previous or later votes. This explanation is not general enough, however: we could easily represent the three successive votes of the example as ballots in a single split binary procedure. Rather, the advantage depends upon their entering into collusion with one another. The definition of an admissible strategy tacitly presupposed that there was no such collusion: for a contingency was defined as the adoption of specific strategies by all the other voters, and it makes sense for a voter to calculate the effect of his voting one way or another in a given contingency only if the occurrence of that contingency is independent of how he decides to vote.

The objective question, then, is whether an individual's voting strategy is or is not admissible. If it is not, there are only three possibilities: he has made a miscalculation; he has been bribed or threatened, or is otherwise concerned with something other than the outcome of the vote or voting process; or he has joined an alliance for the purpose of that particular vote or process. We should not apply the term 'dishonest' even to the second of these cases, out of respect for our legislators, since almost all Parliamentary votes exemplify it. If an individual's voting strategy is admissible for him, however, no question of dishonesty arises: if the procedure forced him to choose between distinct admissible strategies, his choice was based on his estimate of the probabilities of different contingencies. There is no temptation to dishonesty that he needed to resist.

A good voting procedure should come as close as possible to affording straightforward strategies for the voters. This is not because, if it does not, it will tempt them from the path of virtue, but because its outcome will be partly random: it will reflect, not only the preferences of the voters, but their guesses about what other voters are going to do. It is easy to see that, when there are more than two possible outcomes, no binary procedure can afford a straightforward strategy for every voter, whatever his preference scale. The first ballot will divide the possible outcomes into the sets, A and B, of which at least one must contain more than one member. The condition for it to be straightforward for a voter i how to vote on this ballot is that AR_i^*B: plainly, there will be some possible preference scales that do not satisfy this condition.

A further criterion for a good voting procedure is that it be as fair as possible, that is, should reflect as accurately as possible the preferences of the voters. A principle which it is very natural to adopt is that if, of two possible outcomes a and b, a majority of voters prefer a to b, then, of the two, a would be the fairer outcome. In Chapter 2, the example of the family going to the theatre provided a ground for doubting this principle, namely when a slender majority slightly prefer a to b and a large minority greatly prefer b to a. There is, nevertheless, a particular argument in favour of the principle. Suppose that, of eleven voters, six rank a first and b second out of five possible outcomes, while the remaining five rank b first and a fifth; and suppose that b is the successful outcome in some voting procedure. This outcome will then be *insecure* in the sense that if, before the decision has been implemented, a motion were proposed to substitute a for b, this motion would be successful if all voted according to their personal preferences. The insecurity may, in a given instance, be merely theoretical, in that the rules of procedure or a ruling of the chairman may preclude the putting of a revisionary motion of this sort: in other instances, there may be no way to prevent it. Even in the former case, the idea that the choice of b was unfair, or at least unwise, has strong intuitive appeal.

In discussing majority preferences, we may conveniently introduce the symbol 'R_{maj}': '$xR_{maj}y$' is to mean 'a majority of the voters think x at least as good as y', or, in other words, '$xR_i y$ for a majority of voters i'. It is useful to have a symbol for 'the number of voters i such that ...i...' where '...i...' is to be filled by the statement of some condition true, in general, of some voters and false of others. For this purpose, we may write '$N_i[...i...]$', so that the number of voters who think x at least as good as y is $N_i[xR_i y]$. If we always take the letter n as representing the total number of voters, '$xR_{maj}y$' is then equivalent to:

$$N_i[xR_i y] > \tfrac{1}{2}n.$$

There is, however, a slight awkwardness. If the number n of voters is even, R_{maj} may fail to be connected, that is, may fail to satisfy:

$$xR_{maj}y \quad \text{or} \quad yR_{maj}x$$

for every pair of outcomes x and y. Every voting procedure must include some mechanism for breaking a tie; usually this is done by a casting vote of the chairman. In view of this, it is not unreasonable to understand the term 'majority' to mean 'a set which either contains more than half the voters or contains exactly half of them, including the chairman', and to reinterpret 'R_{maj}' accordingly. Where the voters are denoted by numerals, we may assume that the chairman is always voter 1: hence '$xR_{maj}y$' now becomes equivalent to:

either $\quad N_i[xR_i y] > \tfrac{1}{2}n \quad$ or $\quad N_i[xR_i y] = \tfrac{1}{2}n$ and $xR_1 y$.

This redefinition has the effect of securing the connectedness of R_{maj}, and we shall appeal to it only in assuming R_{maj} to be connected; in specific examples, we shall always take the number n of voters to be odd.

It is useful also to employ the symbol 'P_{maj}', related to 'R_{maj}' as 'P_i' is related to 'R_i'. This remark may seem ambiguous: when n is odd, is '$xP_{maj}y$' to mean:

(i) $N_i[xP_iy] > \frac{1}{2}n$

or:

(ii) $xR_{maj}y$ and not $yR_{maj}x$?

On reflection, it evident that (i) and (ii) are equivalent. Since R_i is connected, 'xP_iy' is equivalent to 'not yR_ix'; hence, if (i) holds, the number of voters i such that not yR_ix must be less than $\frac{1}{2}n$, so that not $yR_{maj}x$. Thus condition (i) implies condition (ii). Conversely, if condition (ii) holds, then yR_ix for only a minority of voters i; since R_i is connected, xP_iy must hold for all the rest, and thus for a majority. Since R_{maj} is itself connected, we may therefore simply define '$xP_{maj}y$' to mean 'not $yR_{maj}x$'. It will also occasionally be helpful to use '$xI_{maj}y$' to mean:

$xR_{maj}y$ and $yR_{maj}x$.

This is emphatically *not* equivalent to:

$N_i[xI_iy] > \frac{1}{2}n$

(even when n is odd): for instance, if $n = 5$, and the preference scales are:

1	2	3	4	5
a	c	c	b	c
b	a		a	b
c	b	a b	c	a

$N_i[aR_ib] = N_i[bR_ia] = 3$, so that $aI_{maj}b$; but only one voter, 3, is actually indifferent between a and b. If $xI_{maj}y$, then there must be at least one voter i such that xI_iy, but need not be more than one.

In these terms, then, the principle that we are considering says that:

(1) if $xP_{maj}y$, then y is not a fair outcome.

From (1) it follows that:

(2) if x is a fair outcome, then $xR_{\text{maj}}y$ for every y.

If, out of a set A of possible outcomes (not necessarily all the possible outcomes), $xR_{\text{maj}}y$ for every outcome y in A, we may say that x *tops* A. If x tops A and is itself a member of A, we may say that x is *a top of A*; and, if A contains *all* the possible outcomes, we may say simply that x is *a top*.[1] Note that we cannot say 'the top' rather than 'a top', since, in view of the possibility that $xI_{\text{maj}}y$, a set may contain more than one top, though not when all preferences are strong. Principle (2) therefore does not in all cases uniquely determine the fairest outcome, given the preference scales, though it greatly restricts those that may be so regarded; it may equivalently be written:

(2′) if x is a fair outcome, x is a top.

It appears natural to assume:

(3) there is always at least one fair outcome.

From (2) and (3) we can easily derive:

(4) if x is the only top, x is the only fair outcome.

Plainly principle (4) does not imply principle (2).

If an outcome is the first choice of a majority of the voters, it is the only top, and hence, according to principle (4), the only fair outcome; this is to be expected under principle (1), which accords an overriding importance to majority preferences. An outcome may, however, be the only top although it is nobody's first choice, as a is in the preference table:

1	2	3	4	5
b	b	c	c	d
a	d	a	a	a
c	a	d	b	b
d	c	b	d	c

---

[1] What is here called a 'top' is often spoken of as a 'Condorcet winner', since, in his *Essai* of 1785 on the subject, Condorcet, one of the great pioneers of the theory of voting, in effect argued for principle (4) below. (For him, there could be at most one top, since he assumed that every individual preference scale was strong.) The greatest honour is of course due to Condorcet for his work, but the phrase is clumsy; I therefore prefer to use the simple term 'top', which can also serve as a verb, introduced by Farquharson and myself in our paper of 1961.

Here $xP_{\text{maj}}y$ just in case y comes later than x in the ordering *abcd*, each majority consisting of three voters; by principle (4), although no single voter prefers *a* to all other outcomes, it would, as the sole top, be the only fair one.

The fundamental fact about voting is that there may be no top at all. It is to this fact that a great part of the difficulty of the subject is due. The fact that there may be no top implies and is implied by what is known as the 'paradox of voting', the fact, namely, that R_{maj} is not always transitive. It is easily inferred from this that, when all preferences are strong, P_{maj} may not be transitive, either. To say that P_{maj} is not transitive is to say that there are three possible outcomes, say *a*, *b*, and *c*, such that a majority of the voters prefer *a* to *b*, a different majority prefer *b* to *c*, and a different majority again prefer *c* to *a*; and this is perfectly possible even though the preference relation R_i of each individual voter *i* is transitive. The paradox of voting implies that there may be no top, because it may well be that there are only three possible outcomes, forming a cyclic triad such that each is preferred by a majority to just one of the others. The fact that there may be no top conversely implies that R_{maj} may not be transitive, since, in any finite set of outcomes on which it is transitive, there must be at least one outcome standing in the relation R_{maj} to all the rest. As we saw in Chapter 2, Arrow's theorem likewise implies that R_{maj} cannot always be transitive: for, if it were, it would itself be a social ordering satisfying the principle of independence of irrelevant alternatives and all the other assumptions of the thorem.

Most people, on learning, after a vote had been taken between several possible outcomes, that a majority would have preferred some other particular outcome to that produced by the vote, would be disposed to regard that as proving that the voting procedure was unfair and had produced the wrong outcome. That cannot always be so, however: for, if there was no top, that would have been bound to happen under any procedure and however the voters cast their votes. To say that there is no top is just to say that, for each possible outcome, there is at least one other possible outcome which a majority prefer to it. Hence, in such a case, whatever the outcome of any vote, there must be come specific other possible outcome which a majority would have preferred. The fact that this can happen, like the fact implied by it and implying it, that the relation of majority preference may be intransitive, comes as a deep surprise to many people when they first become aware of it. Once one has conceived of the possibility, however, it is very easy to show that it may be realized. The simplest possible example occurs when there are three outcomes and three voters:

	1	2	3
	a	b	c
	b	c	a
	c	a	b

In this very simple example, there is complete symmetry between the three outcomes, and hence no ground for holding any of them to be a fairer choice than either of the others; it seems better to say that any of them would be a fair outcome than that there can be no fair outcome in this case. In other examples, however, there need be no such symmetry. Thus in the example:

1	2	3	4	5	6	7
a	a	a	b	b	c	c
b	b	c	c	c	a	a
c	c	b	a	a	b	b

we have $aP_{maj}b$, $bP_{maj}c$, and $cP_{maj}a$, but a has a slightly better claim than either b or c. Three voters think a the best, while b and c are the first choice of two voters apiece; b is rated worst by three voters, a and c by two each. With four possible outcomes, even greater asymmetry is possible with the same number of voters:

1	2	3	4	5	6	7
a	a	a	b	d	c	c
d	d	d	c	b	a	a
b	b	c	a	c	d	d
c	c	b	d	a	b	b

We have: $aP_{maj}d$, $dP_{maj}b$, $bP_{maj}c$, $aP_{maj}b$, $dP_{maj}c$, but $cP_{maj}a$. The claim of a to be selected is clearly the best: a is the first choice of three voters, c of two, and b and d of one each; a and d are regarded as worst by one voter each, c by two, and b by three. R_{maj} cannot be transitive if there is no top, but it may be intransitive even though there is a top: there may be a cycle below the top, as is shown by the example:

STABILITY 87

1	2	3
a	b	c
d	d	d
b	c	a
c	a	b

Here d is the top, but $cP_{maj}a$ although $aP_{maj}b$ and $bP_{maj}c$.

This shows that principle (1), that any fair outcome is a top, is inconsistent with assumption (3), that there is always a fair outcome. We therefore cannot maintain principle (1) in full generality: the closest we can come is a generalization of principle (4), namely:

(5) if a top exists, no outcome can be fair unless it is a top.

Even principle (5) may be doubted; but it has some plausibility.

Part of its force derives from our notion of a *secure* outcome. We may also define, in terms of some one given voting procedure, a closely related notion. We earlier called a situation—a selection of a voting strategy by each voter—*vulnerable* to given voter if, by selecting a different strategy, he could have obtained an outcome that he preferred, provided that the strategies of the other voters remained unchanged. We now extend this concept by laying down that a situation s may be said to be vulnerable to a set A of voters if, by selecting different strategies, the voters in A could have obtained an outcome that they *all* preferred, provided that the other voters' strategies remained unchanged. More formally, s is vulnerable to A if, where s produces the outcome x, there is a situation t producing a different outcome y such that $s_j = t_j$ for every j not in A, and xP_iy for every i in A. We may then call a situation *stable* if it is not vulnerable to any set of voters; and we may call an *outcome* stable if there exists a stable situation that produces it.

If we construe example 1 of Chapter 1 as a single split binary voting procedure for deciding between eight possible composite outcomes, as in diagram 3.11, then the situation in which each voter voted sincerely was not stable: it was vulnerable to the set of voters 1, 2, and 3, who, by adopting a concerted strategy, could obtain an outcome better for all of them, namely the defeat of all three motions instead of the passage of all three. Another example, with only four possible outcomes, occurs when there are three voters using the split binary procedure discussed earlier in this chapter, under which they are asked on the first ballot to choose between (α) eliminating c and d and (β) eliminating a and b. The preference scales are:

1	2	3
b	c	a
d	d	b c
a	a	
c	b	d

Voters 2 and 3 have straightforward strategies: that of 2 is to vote for β on the first ballot and for a or c on the second; that of 3 is to vote for α on the first ballot and for a or c on the second. Voter 1 has two admissible strategies: to vote for α on the first ballot, and for b or d on the second; or to vote for β on the first ballot, and for b or d on the second. Assume that voters 2 and 3 adopt their straightforward strategies, and that voter 1 decides to vote for α on the first ballot. In this situation, the successful outcome is a. The situation is not vulnerable to voter 1 on his own: by voting for β on the first ballot, he would produce the outcome c. It is, however, vulnerable to the set consisting of voters 1 and 2: by agreeing to vote for β on the first ballot and then for d, they will produce the outcome d, which they both prefer to a. Note that this agreement requires voter 2 to adopt an inadmissible strategy; voter 1 therefore runs the risk that voter 2 will renege on the second ballot, thereby producing outcome c. None of the outcomes is a top: we have $aP_{maj}b$, $bI_{maj}c$, $cP_{maj}d$, $aP_{maj}c$, $bP_{maj}d$, but $dP_{maj}a$.

The relevance of majority preferences to stability lies in the fact that most voting procedures are *majority procedures* in the sense that, for any possible outcome x, there exists a situation s such that, for any set A constituting a majority of the voters, if every voter i in A adopts the strategy s_i, then x will be the successful outcome, no matter what strategies are adopted by voters not in A; here the word 'majority' is to be understood in our special sense, as comprising a set of exactly half the voters including the chairman. Formally, a majority procedure is one under which, for any outcome x, there is a situation s such that, for any majority A, if $t_i = s_i$ for every i in A, then t produces x: let us call s the *surest* situation for x. When a majority procedure is used, we can determine whether or not an outcome is stable from the preference scales alone: it will be so just in case it is a top. Suppose that x is a top. Let s be the surest situation for x: it can be seen that s, and therefore x, are stable. s is not vulnerable to any set B not constituting a majority: so long as every voter i not in B follows the strategy s_i, the outcome will still be x. A set C forming a majority can produce a different outcome, say z; but it is not possible that every voter in C should prefer z to x, for then $zP_{\mathrm{maj}}x$, contrary to the assumption that x is a top: so s is not vulnerable to C, either. Conversely, let y be any outcome that is not a top, and t a situation producing y. Suppose that $xP_{\mathrm{maj}}y$, whether or not x is itself a top, and let s, as before, be the surest situation for x. Let A consist of all voters preferring x to y, and let t' be the situation such that $t'_i = s_i$ for each i in A, $t'_j = t_j$ for each j not in A. Since A forms a majority, t' produces x: so t was vulnerable to A, and hence unstable; and y, too, is unstable, since t was *any* situation that produced it.

Thus, under a majority procedure, an outcome is stable just in case it is secure, that is, there is no other outcome y such that a subsequent motion to substitute y for x would be bound to succeed if all voted sincerely. The equivalence of the two notions in this case enhances the importance of both.

A stable outcome is by definition one produced by *some* stable situation. It in no way follows that any situation that produces a stable outcome is itself stable, even when all vote admissibly. Suppose that there are three possible outcomes and three voters, with the preference scales:

1	2	3
a	b	c
b	a	a
c	c	b

The outcome a is the sole top, and is, accordingly, the only stable outcome under any majority procedure. If, then, the knock-out procedure is used with a first, only voter 1 will have a straightforward strategy: he must vote for a on the first ballot. Suppose that voter 2 votes for a on the first ballot, presumably believing that a majority prefer c to b, and that voter 3 votes against a on the first ballot, presumably sharing this belief. The outcome will then be a; but the situation is vulnerable to voter 2, since, if he had voted against a, the outcome would have been b, which he would have preferred. A stable situation would be one in which voters 1 and

3 voted for *a* on the first ballot. Again, suppose that, while the voters retain the same preference scales, the amendment procedure, with *b* residual, is used. Once more, only voter 1 has a straightforward strategy: he must vote, on the first ballot, to eliminate *c*. Suppose that, on the first ballot, voter 2 votes to eliminate *c* and that voter 3 votes to eliminate *a*: the outcome will then be *a*. The situation is again vulnerable to voter 2: if he had voted to eliminate *a* on the first ballot, the outcome would have been *b*, which he prefers to *a*. A stable situation will be one in which voters 1 and 3 both vote on the first ballot to eliminate *c*.

It is often said, of certain electoral or voting procedures, that they are lotteries. This means that they do not respond to the preferences of the voters in a unique way: the outcome depends, not only on those preferences, but also on the guesses of the voters about how others are going to vote. It is therefore of interest to ask, concerning a given voting procedure, for which distributions of preferences among the voters it will not be a lottery: when will the outcome depend only on the voters' preferences, and not upon the particular voting strategies they select?

To make this idea precise, we may assume that every voter adopts an admissible strategy: we may call a situation in which every voter's strategy is admissible for him an *admissible situation*. When, under a given procedure, the preferences of the voters are such that every admissible situation produces the same outcome *a*, we may say that, relatively to those preference scales, the procedure is *fully determinate* and *determines a outright*.

Now does this definition capture the idea we were seeking to clarify? It evidently does if we are justified in assuming that every voter votes admissibly. If so, then, when a procedure is fully determinate, in the sense defined, the actual outcome will always be that which it determines outright; but, if the assumption is not justified, it may not be. Now, if the procedure is fully determinate, no admissible situation can be vulnerable to any *one* voter, since, for any strategy inadmissible for a given voter, there is an admissible strategy that dominates it. If, therefore, in an admissible situation, a single voter could obtain an outcome that he preferred by adopting an inadmissible strategy, he could also do so by adopting an admissible one; and this contradicts the supposition that every admissible situation produces the same outcome. This does not, however, rule out the possibility that an admissible situation may be vulnerable to a set of two or more voters, who, by collusion, can produce an outcome that they all prefer. If so, at least one of them will have to vote inadmissibly. Our assumption that every voter votes admissibly is justified just in case we can be sure either that there will be no collusion or that no collusion will succeed. To say that, in a given situation, no collusion could have succeeded is just to say that the situation is stable. Thus what we need to know is whether, when a procedure is fully determinate, every admissible situation is stable.

If the outcome *a* is not stable, no situation that produces *a* can be stable. Hence, if a procedure determines outright an unstable outcome *a*, there will be a set of voters who, by adopting different, and, at least for some, inadmissible, strategies, would have obtained an outcome that they all preferred. Under a majority procedure, an outcome is stable just in case it is a top. Confining our attention to these, we may therefore ask: (1) If a majority procedure determines *a* outright, must *a* be a top? As we have seen, however, a situation that produces a stable outcome need not itself be stable; so we must ask further: (2) If a majority procedure determines outright a stable outcome, will every admissible situation be stable? We shall be fully justified in assuming admissible voting whenever the procedure is fully determinate if the answers to both questions are affirmative.

Unfortunately, the general answers to both questions are negative: the assumption that the procedure is a majority one is relatively weak, and does not exclude the unwanted possibilities. Counter-examples are nevertheless not easy to find. Little plausibility can be claimed for the following one, which simply serves to show that we cannot hope to prove an affirmative answer to either question without further assumptions. Suppose that there are four possible outcomes, *a*, *b*, *c*, and *d*, and five voters. The voting mechanism is simply that each voter writes on his ballot paper the name of a single outcome. The method of assessment is complex, namely:

(i) if there is an absolute majority of votes in favour of any one outcome, that outcome is successful;

(ii) if no single outcome obtains a majority, but the votes for *b* and *c* together make up a majority, while those for *b* and *d* do not, *c* is successful;

(iii) if no single outcome obtains a majority, but the votes for *b* and d together make up a majority, while those for b and c do not, d is successful;

(iv) if no single outcome obtains a majority, but the votes for b and c together make up a majority, as do those for b and d, then b is successful;

(v) in all other cases a is successful.

Under this procedure, a voter has a straightforward strategy just in case a and b occupy symmetrical positions in his preference scale (first and fourth or second and third), in which case it is straightforward for him to vote for the outcome of his first choice. If, then, the preference scales are:

1	2	3	4	5
a	a	b	c	d
c	d	c	b	b
d	c	d	a	a
b	b	a	d	c

every voter will have a single straightforward strategy. There is therefore only one admissible situation, namely when each voter adopts his straightforward strategy and votes for his first choice. The outcome in this case will be a, so that the procedure determines a outright. In view of clause (i), the procedure is plainly a majority procedure. The outcome a is not stable, however, since $bP_{\text{maj}}a$; there is in fact no top. Thus if voters 4 and 5 agree to follow inadmissible strategies and vote for b, the others voting as before, the outcome will be b. (To be prepared to make such an agreement, voters 4 and 5 must trust each other very well, since if voter 4 keeps the agreement and voter 5 reneges and votes for d, the outcome will be d, and similarly for the converse case.)

The same somewhat bizarre procedure can also be used to answer question (2) in the negative. Suppose that the preference scales are:

1	2	3	4	5
a	a	a	c	d
c	d	b	b	b
d	c	c	a	a
b	b	d	d	c

Here only the scale of voter 3 has changed. As before, then, voters 1, 2, 4, and 5 all have unique straightforward strategies; if they follow them, the outcome will be a, however voter 3 votes. The procedure therefore still determines a outright. Voting for b is, however, an admissible strategy for voter 3, since, if one of the other voters votes for a, two for b, and the fourth for c (or for d), the outcome would be b if he votes for b, but c (or d) if he votes for a. Suppose, then, that voters 1 and 2 vote for a, voter 3 for b, voter 4 for c, and voter 5 for d, as in the preceding example. This is an admissible situation, and produces the outcome a. The outcome a is in this case a top, and therefore stable, being the first choice of a majority of voters; but the situation is not stable, being vulnerable to voters 4 and 5, who, by voting inadmissibly for b, would produce the outcome b. Thus a majority procedure may determine a stable outcome outright, even though not every admissible situation is stable.

We thus cannot hope to obtain as general an answer to questions (1) and (2) as we might have hoped. Let us therefore restrict our attention to binary procedures, all of which are of course majority procedures. With this restriction, both questions can be answered affirmatively. Assume that a binary procedure is being used, and that the preference scales are such that, in every admissible situation, the outcome is a, which is thus determined outright: we have to see why a must be a top. For any given ballot, let us say that its *height* is the greatest possible number of subsequent ballots that could take place. We shall show that, for each possible ballot that could occur in an admissible situation, $aR_{maj}x$ for every outcome x that remained live before that ballot took place; it will follow that a is a top, since, before the first ballot took place, every outcome was live. We shall prove this assertion by induction on the height of the given ballot. This means that we shall first show it to be true for any ballot of height 0, and then show that if, for any positive number h, our assertion holds for every ballot of height less than h, it will also hold for one of height h.

To say that a ballot is of height 0 means that, if it takes place, no further ballot can occur. There must, then, be only two outcomes remaining live before the ballot takes place. If the ballot is assumed to be one that can occur in some admissible situation, one of these two outcomes must be a; let the other be b. Since by hypothesis every admissible situation produces a, the result of this ballot must go in favour of a whenever the voters vote in accordance with their preferences; plainly, this can hold good only if $aP_{maj}b$. Since trivially $aR_{maj}a$, we have proved our assertion for a ballot of height 0.

Now consider any ballot α, of height h, that can occur in an admissible situation, and assume that the assertion holds for any ballot of height less than h. The ballot α will divide the outcomes that remain live before it takes place into two sets A and B (not necessarily disjoint): one result of the ballot will be that the outcomes in A remain live, the other that those in B will remain live. There are now two possible cases: (i) α may have either result when the voters all follow admissible strategies; and (ii) α can have only one result when the voters follow such strategies. In case (i), a must be in both A and B. We want to show that $aR_{\text{maj}}x$ for every x in either A or B; but it is sufficient to show that $aR_{\text{maj}}x$ for every x in A, since the reasoning will be entirely similar for the outcomes x in B. If a is the only member of A, it is trivially true that $aR_{\text{maj}}x$ for each x in A; so suppose that it is not the only member. In this case, when the result of α goes in favour of the set A, there will be a subsequent ballot β: β will be of height less than h, and may occur in an admissible situation. Our assumption thus applies to β: since A is the set of outcomes live before β takes place, $aR_{\text{maj}}x$ for every x in A, as claimed. Since, as remarked, it follows by similar reasoning that $aR_{\text{maj}}x$ for every x in B, we have shown, as we wished, that $aR_{\text{maj}}x$ for every outcome x live before α took place.

In case (ii), suppose that, in an admissible situation, α must go in favour of A. It must therefore be inadmissible, for a majority of the voters, to vote in favour of B in ballot α; hence, for each voter i in that majority, AR_i^*B and not BR_i^*A. Now a must be in A: it therefore follows that $aR_{\text{maj}}x$ for every x in B. If a is the only member of A, that is all we were required to prove. If not, then, as in case (i), a further ballot β will have to take place. Since our assumption must apply to β, it follows, as in case (i), that $aR_{\text{maj}}x$ for every x in A. We have thus shown that $aR_{\text{maj}}x$ for every x in A or B, and so for every x live before α took place.

We have thus proved that, if a binary procedure determines an outcome outright, that outcome must be a top: the converse, of course, is not true. Our second question can now be phrased: if a binary procedure is fully determinate, must every admissible situation be stable? It is easy to see that it must. Suppose that, under a certain binary procedure, every admissible situation produces a. Let D be a set of voters who all prefer some outcome b to a: we wish to show that, so long as the voters not in D vote admissibly, those in D cannot, by adopting certain strategies, which may not be admissible, obtain the outcome b. We may speak of a ballot as having an inadmissible result if it has a result that it could not have had if all had voted admissibly on that ballot. It is plain that, if s is a situation that produces b, some ballot must have an inadmissible result in s. Let α be the first such ballot: the admissible result of α is that the outcomes in the set A remain live, and its inadmissible result is that those in B remain live. A must contain a, and B must contain b. Since α cannot admissibly go in favour of B, it follows that, for a majority of voters i, AR_i^*B; hence, for every voter i in that majority, aR_ib. Consequently, no voter i in that majority can belong to the set D. Thus, if every voter not in D votes admissibly, the ballot α must go in favour of A. This shows that, in any such situation s, some voters not in D must vote inadmissibly, and hence that no admissible situation is vulnerable to D.

The notion of full determinacy is thus indeed the one we need when we are concerned with binary procedures, which we may now look at again in more detail. When is the knock-out procedure, with three possible outcomes and a first, fully determinate? Clearly c cannot be successful if $bP_{\text{maj}}c$, nor b if $cP_{\text{maj}}b$. Voting for a on the first ballot is straightforward for a voter i only if aR_ib and aR_ic. Hence a will be determined outright just in case a majority of voters rank it first, possibly level with one other outcome. It will be determined outright that a will be unsuccessful only if a majority of voters rank a last, possibly level with one other outcome; obviously, given a random distribution of preferences, this will happen just as frequently as that a is determined outright as the successful outcome. The outcome b will be determined outright just in case this condition holds (that a majority of voters rank a last, perhaps level with one other) and, in addition, $bP_{\text{maj}}c$. Since there is a possibility, if at least one voter's preference scale is weak, that $bI_{\text{maj}}c$, it follows that b will be determined outright under less than half as many possible distributions of preferences as those under which a is determined outright; the same, of course, applies to c. For this reason, the outcome taken first under the knock-out procedure has, in general, a better chance of success than does either of the other two.

In all other cases, the outcome will be uncertain under the knock-out procedure, and may be unstable. If the preference scales are:

1	2	3	4	5
a	a	b	b	c
b	c	a	c	b
c	b	c	a	a

b is the sole top, but the outcome may be a. If they are:

1	2	3	4	5
a	b	b	b	c
c	a	a	c	b
b	c	c	a	a

b actually has an absolute majority of first choices, but the outcome may again be a. If they are:

1	2	3	4	5
a	a	b	b	c
b	c	a	c	a
c	b	c	a	b

or:

1	2	3	4	5
a	c	b	c	b
b	a	a	a	a
c	b	c	b	c

a is the sole top, but the outcome may be b. If there is no top, but $aP_{maj}b$, $bP_{maj}c$, and $cP_{maj}a$, then c cannot win, but either a or b may, as in the following example:

1	2	3	4	5
c	b	c	a	b
a	c	a	b	c
b	a	b	c	a

Here c has a slightly better claim to be the best outcome than either a or b, but is the only one certain not to be successful.

When the amendment procedure, with a residual, is used, a will be determined outright just in case it is the sole top: it will then be successful whatever the result of the first ballot. It will be determined that the result of the first ballot will be to exclude c only if voters with the preference scale bac, $b(ac)$, or $(ba)c$ form a majority, since only for them is it straightforward to vote on the first ballot only in that way; if they form a majority, it is then impossible that $aP_{maj}b$, and hence that a be determined outright. The outcome b will, then, be determined outright only when voters with those preference scales form a majority and, in addition, $bP_{maj}a$; similarly for c. Thus, with the preference scales:

1	2	3	4	5
b	b	b	a	c
c	a	a	b	a
a	c	c	c	b

a may win even though b has an absolute majority of first preferences. If there is no top, but the cyclical majorities run in the order $aP_{maj}b$, $bP_{maj}c$, $cP_{maj}a$, the outcome may be either a or c; b cannot win, even though it may, of course, have the best claim.

The split procedure, with four possible outcomes, under which the first ballot divides the outcomes into the set containing a and b and that containing c and d, will determine a outright just in case (i) $aP_{maj}b$ and (ii) the voters i for whom aR_ic, aR_id, bR_ic, and bR_id, but who are not indifferent between all four outcomes, form a majority; similarly, of course, for b, c, and d. Thus, when the preference scales are:

1	2	3	4	5	6	7
a	a	a	a	a	b	c
b	c	d	c	b	a	b
d	b	b	d	d	d	a
c	d	c	b	c	c	d

a large majority make a their first choice, and all seven voters prefer a to d; yet, though the outcome cannot be b or c, it might be d.

5
Degrees of Admissibility

Given only his own preference scale, a voter can decide which of the strategies open to him are admissible, and whether any of them is straightforward. If there is no opportunity, or no incentive, for collusion, the voters may be presumed to select admissible strategies; hence, when every admissible situation produces the same outcome, the procedure, being fully determinate, may be said to be responding only to the voters' preferences. Even in such a case, this cannot be recognized just from a knowledge of the pairs of outcomes x and y for which $xR_{\mathrm{maj}}y$: we need to know the preference scales themselves.

We have seen that the concept of a 'sincere' vote is hardly applicable to binary procedures. We may substitute for it that of a *naïve* vote, explained as follows. Suppose that a given ballot divides the outcomes live before it is taken into the sets A and B. Those outcomes in both A and B will remain live whatever the result of the ballot: let us say of an outcome not in both A and B that it is 'in peril' at that ballot. If a voter prefers one of the outcomes in peril to all others in peril, he may be said to vote naïvely if he votes for that outcome to remain live. For instance, under the amendment procedure the set A may consist of a and b and the set B of a and c: a voter who prefers b to c votes naïvely if he votes for A and against B on the first ballot. We cannot assume that, if the voters have no knowledge of each others' preference scales, they will adopt naïve strategies; but it is the most likely prediction.

Under the amendment procedure, when a is taken as residual, a will be successful whenever it is the sole top. When all voters vote naïvely, it will become true of both b and c, too, that either will be successful whenever it is the sole top; furthermore, in any case in which there is no top, a is certain to be successful. Thus, when the voters have little or no information about each other's preferences, the amendment procedure favours the residual outcome.

Under the knock-out procedure with a first, a will be determined outright only if it has an absolute majority of first preferences; even so, if there are three possible outcomes and all preferences scales are strong, *a* will be determined outright just twice as often as will either *b* or *c*. If we assume naïve voting, however, *a*'s chances of success will become definitely worse than those of *b* and *c*. The outcome will now be *a* only when it has an absolute majority of first preferences; when it does not, *b* will be successful if $bP_{maj}c$, and *c* will be successful if $cP_{maj}b$. When the voters know little of each other's preferences, therefore, a voter who favours *a* should strive to avoid the adoption of the knock-out procedure with *a* taken first: he should propose either that procedure with *b* or *c* taken first, or the amendment procedure with *a* residual.

A voter who knows the preference scales of the other voters has an easier choice of strategy. He can determine, for each of the other voters, what his admissible strategies are. Hence, if he can assume that there will be no collusion, he need not consider the effect of his adopting a particular strategy in every possible contingency, but only in those that are admissible in the sense that each of the other voters adopts a strategy admissible for him. We may thus usefully define a *secondarily admissible*, or, for brevity, a *2-admissible*, strategy in terms of admissible contingencies just as we defined an admissible strategy in terms of all contingencies. We may say that a strategy σ *2-rivals* a strategy τ for a voter *i* if there is some admissible contingency in which, by adopting σ, *i* will obtain an outcome that he prefers to that he would obtain by adopting τ, and that σ *2-dominates* τ for him if σ 2-rivals τ for him, but τ does not 2-rival σ. A strategy may then be called *2-admissible* for *i* if it is admissible and no strategy 2-dominates it for him.

A voter would hardly adopt a strategy inadmissible for him just because, if his information about the intentions of the other voters is correct, it will not actually do him any harm; but we may pause to note why we needed expressly to include in the definition of a 2-admissible strategy the requirement that it be simply admissible. If the knock-out procedure, with *a* first, is used, the only admissible strategy of a voter with the preference scale (*ab*)*c* involves his voting for *a* on the first ballot. If $bP_{maj}c$, however, this strategy will not 2-dominate that of voting against *a* on the first ballot, and for *b* if there is a second ballot, since there is now no fear that *c* will be successful. To guarantee that the latter strategy will not count as 2-admissible, therefore, we had to require every 2-admissible strategy to be simply admissible; the requirement is reasonable, since a voter must take some account of the possibility that his information is incorrect.

We may now say that a situation is 2-admissible if every voter adopts a 2-admissible strategy, that, given the preference scales, a procedure *2-determines* an outcome a if every 2-admissible situation produces a, and that it is *2-determinate* if there is some outcome that it 2-determines. The notion of 2-determinacy is of interest only when all the voters know, or come close to knowing, each other's preference scores, or at least certain critical features of them, for only then can we assume that they will restrict their choices of strategy to 2-admissible ones. Consider, for instance, the amendment procedure with a residual. If all preference scales are strong, then, for any two outcomes x and y, either $xP_{maj}y$ or $yP_{maj}x$. In this case, a voter who knows which P_{maj} relations obtain thereby knows, of each of the possible second ballots, what its result will be if it is held: knowing this, he is no longer in any uncertainty how to vote on the first ballot. The same reasoning evidently applies to any binary procedure of height 1, that is, under which at most two ballots will be held. If all the preference scales are strong, then, under such a procedure, every voter has just one 2-admissible strategy, so that there is only one 2-admissible situation: the procedure will then 2-determine the outcome produced by that situation.

If we continue to assume that all preference scales are strong, the amendment procedure with a residual will 2-determine b whenever b is the top. It will also 2-determine b in one of the two cases when there is no top, namely that shown by diagram 5.1.

Diagram 5.1

Such a diagram will be called an R_{maj} diagram: an arrow from x to y indicates that $xR_{maj}y$. Likewise, c will be 2-determined when it is the top, and in the other cyclic case (diagram 5.2).

Diagram 5.2

DEGREES OF ADMISSIBILITY

The residual outcome a, on the other hand, will be 2-determined only when it is the top, i.e. precisely when it is certain to be successful when the voters are restricted to admissible strategies, but not to 2-admissible ones. Thus, under the amendment procedure, the acquisition by the voters of a knowledge of each other's preferences harms the residual outcome's chances of success.

Such knowledge has quite a different effect under the knock-out procedure with a first. Suppose, as before, that there are just three possible outcomes and that all preference scales are strong. Then a will be 2-determined whenever it is the top, and also whenever there is no top. Either of the other two outcomes will be 2-determined only when it is the top. Thus the outcome of the knock-out procedure, with a first, when all the voters know each other's preferences will be the same as the outcome of the amendment procedure, with a residual, when all vote naïvely: in both cases, a has the best chance of success. When there has been extensive discussion, therefore, so that the voters have a good knowledge of how others are likely to vote, a voter who favours a should object to the use of the amendment procedure with a residual: he should try to persuade his colleagues to use the knock-out procedure with a first, or, failing that, the amendment procedure with b or c residual.

As a final example, consider the split procedure represented by diagram 3.7: there are four possible outcomes, and the first ballot asks the voters to choose between the set containing a and b and that containing c and d. Assume that all preference scales are strong. Then a will be 2-determined whenever it is the top, and also in the two types of cyclic case in diagrams 5.3 and 5.4.

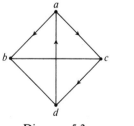
Diagram 5.3

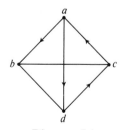
Diagram 5.4

Here it will make no difference how the arrows are placed between b and c or between b and d.

Not every binary procedure is 2-determinate whenever the preference scales are strong. Consider the knock-out procedure with four possible outcomes, with a taken first and b second, represented by diagram 3.3. Suppose that the preference scales are as follows:

1	2	3	4	5	6	7
a	b	a	d	c	d	c
c	a	c	b	d	c	a
b	c	d	a	a	b	b
d	d	b	c	b	a	d

Example 1

These yield the R_{maj} diagram shown in diagram 5.5.

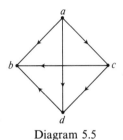

Diagram 5.5

Only voters 3 and 6 have straightforward strategies, which may be written $a\bar{b}c$ and $\bar{a}\bar{b}d$ respectively: voter 3 must vote for a on the first ballot, against b if a second ballot is held, and for c if a third ballot is held, and correspondingly for voter 6. Each voter will have only one 2-admissible way of voting on the second ballot, if held, since, if he knows all the preference scales, he will know that c will beat d on the third ballot if it is held. But, of the five voters who did not have straightforward strategies, only voter 1 finds himself with only one 2-admissible way of voting on the first ballot, namely to vote for a: voters 2, 4, 5, and 7 may all vote 2-admissibly either for or against a. Hence, under 2-admissible voting, the outcome may be either a or c.[1]

---

[1] An amusing example of 2-determinacy occurs when there are five voters and the relative majority procedure is used to decide between three outcomes. In general, a voter with a strong preference scale may admissibly vote for either his first or his second choice: if, for example, his preference scale is abc, and two of the other voters

It is obviously formally possible to define 3-admissible strategies in terms of 2-admissible situations just as we defined 2-admissible strategies in terms of admissible situations. In fact, we may define n-admissible strategies for every number n, according to the following pattern:

an *n-admissible contingency* for a voter i is one in which every voter other than i adopts an n-admissible strategy:

a strategy σ $(n + 1)$-*rivals* a strategy τ for i if, in some n-admissible contingency, i would, by adopting σ, obtain an outcome which he prefers to that he would obtain by adopting τ;

a strategy σ $(n + 1)$-*dominates* τ for i if σ $(n + 1)$-rivals τ for i, but τ does not $(n + 1)$-*rival* σ;

a strategy is $(n + 1)$-admissible for i just in case it is n-admissible and is not $(n + 1)$-dominated by any other strategy;

an *n-admissible situation* is one in which every voter adopts a strategy n-admissible for him;

---

vote for b and two for c, he will secure the outcome b if he votes for it, whereas, if he voted for a, the chairman might give his casting vote in favour of c. For the chairman, on the other hand, it is straightforward to vote for his first choice: if his preference scale is abc, there can be no contingency in which he will do better by voting for b. If three, or all four, of the other voters vote for the same outcome, the chairman's vote cannot prevent it from being successful. If, on the other hand, no outcome receives more than two votes from the other four voters, then either b and c have two each, or a has at least one: having voted for a, the chairman can, in the former case, give his casting vote for b, and, in the latter, give his casting vote for a if necessary. It should be noted that this does not apply when there are six or more voters. Of six voters, two of the others may vote for b and three for c; the chairman will then do best to vote for b and give his casting vote for b.

Suppose, now, that the preference scales of the five voters are:

1	2	3	4	5
a	b	c	c	a
b	c	a	a	c
c	a	b	b	b

Since voter 1 is the chairman, voting for b is not admissible for him. Hence, if every voter knows the preference scales of the others, each knows that b cannot receive more than one vote, and therefore cannot win. Each has therefore only one 2-admissible strategy, namely to vote for c if he prefers c to a and for a if he prefers a to c. In consequence, voters 2, 3, and 4 will all vote for c and voters 1 and 5 for a, and c, which is top, will be successful. The procedure is thus 2-determinate for these preference scales. It would be wrong to draw the general conclusion that, when the other voters are well informed about his preferences, voter 1 is disadvantaged under this procedure by having a casting vote, since the phenomenon occurs only when there are fewer than six voters.

a procedure *n-determines* an outcome a if every n-admissible situation produces a;

a procedure is *n-determinate* if it n-determines some outcome.

If a voter knows the preference scales of all the other voters, he can, for any n, calculate what the n-admissible strategies of any voter are, including, of course, his own. Given that he can rule out the possibility of collusion, he will always be justified in confining his choice of strategy to 2-admissible ones, if he knows what they are. He may find himself with more than one strategy 2-admissible for him, however: when will he be justified in restricting his choice still further to the 3-admissible ones?

A 3-admissible strategy is, in general, to be preferred to a 3-inadmissible one if the other voters can be counted on to adopt 2-admissible strategies. If the other voters do not know the preference scales of their colleagues, they do not know what their own 2-admissible strategies are; if they do know this, they are sure to select such strategies. Thus, in order to have a motive for restricting his choice of strategy to 3-admissible ones, a voter must not only know the preference scales of the other voters (or have a good idea of them), but must also know that each of the other voters knows all the preference scales (or has a good idea of them). If he gained his knowledge of the preferences of the other voters from open discussion before the vote was taken, then each of the other voters will know as much as he does, save that the other voter may not know his preference scale but will certainly know his own. If, on the other hand, he gained his knowledge of the preferences of the others by questioning each of them privately before the meeting, he may have no ground to assume that they have the same knowledge, and hence no motive to adopt a 3-admissible strategy.

A binary procedure of height h is one under which there cannot be more than $h + 1$ ballots, but may be as many as that. If all preference scales are strong, a binary procedure of height h will be $(h + 1)$-determinate, but may not be h-determinate. For instance, the knock-out procedure with four possible outcomes is of height 2: relatively to the preference scales of example 1, it was not 2-determinate, but it is 3-determinate. Voters 2, 4, 5, and 7 each have unique 3-admissible strategies, namely abc, abd, $a\bar{b}c$, and $a\bar{b}c$ respectively: the procedure thus 3-determines the outcome a.

Suppose that a voter not only knows the preference scales of the others, but has reason to believe that they, and his own, are generally known to all. He may then confine himself to 3-admissible strategies: but he may find that he has more than one. Can he go further yet, and confine himself to strategies that are 4-admissible for him? This would be to presuppose that every voter will vote 3-admissibly: and this assumption requires that every voter not only knows everyone else's preference scale, but also knows that everyone else knows that everyone knows all the preference scales. If the given voter's knowledge was derived from open discussion in which he participated, he may assume this. In such a case, indeed, he may confine himself to those strategies that are n-admissible for every n: we may call such strategies *ultimately admissible*, and say that a procedure is *ultimately determinate* if the same outcome is produced by every situation in which every voter adopts an ultimately admissible strategy. Since an $(n + 1)$-admissible strategy must be n-admissible, a procedure is ultimately determinate just in case it is n-determinate for some n. A binary procedure must have some finite height h—there is a limit to the number of ballots that may occur: hence, when all preference scales are strong, every binary procedure will be ultimately determinate.

Open discussion in a sense confers on the voters an infinite amount of knowledge. If every participant revealed his preference scale, then each not merely knows the others' preference scales, but also knows that everyone knows everyone else's preference scale, and knows that they all know that everyone knows everyone else's preference scale, and so on. If, however, our voter acquired his knowledge by private enquiry, the case is different. He may, by such means, have discovered not only the preferences of the others, but the fact that they, too, have discovered them, partly because they have questioned him, and partly by learning of other private conversations. Knowing that every voter knows the preference scales of the others, he has a motive to restrict himself to his 3-admissible strategies; but if he suspects that some voters do not realize that all have been making similar enquiries, he cannot trust them to restrict themselves in the same way, and hence cannot safely confine himself to 4-admissible ones.

Not every procedure is ultimately determinate when all preference scales are strong. Given any procedure, there are only finitely many possible situations. Given, further, a set of preference scales, we may successively determine the admissible situations, the 2-admissible ones, the 3-admissible ones, and so on; if a situation is *n*-inadmissible, it cannot be (*n* + 1)-admissible. We must therefore eventually reach a number *m* for which the (*m* + 1)-admissible situations are the same as the *m*-admissible ones: we may call the smallest number *m* for which this is so the *reduction number* for that set of preference scales and that procedure. For every *n*, any voter must have at least one *n*-admissible strategy, and there will therefore be at least one *n*-admissible situation. If there is only one *m*-admissible situation, and *m* is the smallest number for which this is so, *m* will be the reduction number: the procedure will then be *m*-determinate. It may be, however, that, where *m* is the reduction number, there is more than one *m*-admissible situation: if these produce different outcomes, the procedure will not be ultimately determinate for that set of preference scales.

An ultimately indeterminate procedure must be non-binary. A *symmetrical elimination procedure* consists of a sequence of ballots, each of which results in the elimination of a single outcome; any live outcome can be eliminated at any ballot. Thus, with three possible outcomes, such a procedure has the form of diagram 5.6.

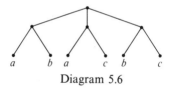

Diagram 5.6

This diagram does not uniquely represent the procedure, since there are different ways of conducting the first ballot. We shall be concerned with two types in particular. In both, in each ballot each voter writes down the name of one of the live outcomes: in one form, that outcome is eliminated whose name appears on the fewest ballot papers; in the other, that one is eliminated whose name appears on the greatest number of them; in either form, the chairman gives a casting vote in case of a tie on any ballot. We shall call these the procedures *with positive voting* and *with negative voting* respectively.

Suppose that, under either procedure, a voter *i* is considering how to vote in any ballot other than the last. Given that the voters other than *i* have decided how to cast their votes, we may say that an outcome is *at risk from i* if he can vote so as to bring about its elimination, and that it is *at acute risk* from him if he has more than one way of voting in that ballot that will result in its elimination; we may say that it is *doomed* if it will be eliminated however i votes. Under either procedure, some outcome may be doomed. Assume that i is not the chairman. Then, under the procedure with positive voting, not more than two outcomes can be at risk from i. If x is at acute risk and y at risk, then x will be eliminated unless i votes for it, in which case y will be. Under the procedure with negative voting, suppose that there are q live outcomes. It is always possible for any number of them up to $q - 1$ to be at risk; if the number n of voters gives remainder 1 when divided by q, it is possible for all of them to be at risk. If all are at risk, each outcome will be eliminated just in case i votes to eliminate it. If there are just three live outcomes, and x is at risk and y at acute risk, then x will be eliminated just in case i votes to eliminate it, while y will be eliminated if he votes to eliminate either it or z.

Let us now ask when the procedure with negative voting and three possible outcomes is 2-determinate. Suppose that R_{maj} yields a strong ordering xyz of the outcomes, i.e. the R_{maj} diagram has the form of diagram 5.7.

Diagram 5.7

A voter who knows the R_{maj} relations knows that z cannot be the final outcome; in deciding how to vote on the first ballot, he will therefore be guided solely by whether he prefers x to y or y to x. If he prefers y to x, his only concern will be that x be eliminated on the first ballot, since, if it is not, it will be the final outcome. He therefore has a unique 2-admissible strategy, which requires him to vote on the first ballot to eliminate x, since this will cause it to be eliminated if it is at risk at all. Such a voter may rank x lowest on his preference scale, or may prefer it to z: it follows that a voter with the strong preference scale *abc* may admissibly vote on the first ballot to eliminate either *b* or *c*. In particular, taking x as *c*, his only 2-admissible vote will be to eliminate *c* if R_{maj} yields either of the strong orderings *cba* and *cab*; taking x as *b*, his only 2-admissible vote will be to eliminate *b* if it yields the strong ordering *bac*.

If the R_{maj} diagram has the form of diagram 5.7, a voter who prefers x to y does not have a unique 2-admissible strategy. His only concern is to prevent the elimination of x. He obviously cannot vote 2-admissibly to eliminate x; but, since the preference scale of no other voter can uniquely determine his admissible strategy, he cannot know whether he can best prevent x's elimination by voting to eliminate y or to eliminate z, either of which is therefore 2-admissible for him. Thus, if R_{maj} yields either of the strong orderings abc and acb, a voter with the preference scale abc can vote 2-admissibly to eliminate either b or c on the first ballot; if it yields the strong ordering bca, he can vote 2-admissibly to eliminate either c or a. This shows that it is admissible for a voter with the scale abc to vote on the first ballot to eliminate a, though he can never have a unique 2-admissible strategy that requires this. In fact, while a voter with a preference scale of the form $x(yz)$ cannot admissibly vote to eliminate x, one with a scale of any other form, including, of course, a strong one, may admissibly vote in any of the three possible ways on the first ballot.

All this is illustrated by the following example:

1	2	3	4	5	6	7	8	9	10	11
a	a	b	b	b	c	c	c	c	b	b
c	b	c	c	c	b	a	a	a	a	a
b	c	a	a	a	a	b	b	b	c	c

Example 2

The R_{maj} diagram is:

Diagram 5.8

so that R_{maj} yields the strong ordering bca. Suppose, first, that the voters do not know each other's preference scales, and that each voter other than voter 2 votes on the first ballot to eliminate the outcome he ranks lowest. Then a is at risk from voter 2, and b at acute risk, since, if he votes to eliminate c, voter 1 as chairman will give his casting vote for the elimination of b. Hence, if voter 2 votes to eliminate either b or c, the final outcome will be c, but, if he votes to eliminate a, it will be b, so that, in this contingency, his best strategy involves his voting to eliminate the outcome he ranks highest.

Now suppose that the voters all know each other's preference scales. The five voters who prefer c to b can vote 2-admissibly only to eliminate b. The six voters who prefer b to c want to prevent b's elimination, but have no way of deciding, without consultation with each other, whether to vote to eliminate a or c: unless all six make the same decision, b will be eliminated.

It follows that the elimination procedure with negative voting can never determine any outcome outright, because the assumption of admissible voting cannot determine the result of any ballot except a final one. Furthermore, when the R_{maj} diagram has the form of diagram 5.7, the procedure will 2-determine the top x only when the number of voters preferring x to y exceeds two-thirds of the number of all those voting. In such a case, if all vote 2-admissibly, more votes will be cast for the elimination of one or other of y or z than for the elimination of x; x will thus not be eliminated on the first ballot, and will become the final outcome. If there are not so many voters who prefer x to y, x may be eliminated on the first ballot under 2-admissible voting, and the final outcome will be y. A voter who has a choice of 2-admissible strategies will not be helped in the least to choose between them by the information that the others are voting 2-admissibly. All 2-admissible strategies therefore remain 3-admissible, so that the reduction number if 2: when the procedure is 2-indeterminate, it is ultimately indeterminate. When majority preferences are cyclic, as in diagram 5.9, the only voters with unique

Diagram 5.9

2-admissible strategies are those with preference scales of the form $x(yz)$: thus, when diagram 5.9 applies, one whose scale is $a(bc)$ can vote 2-admissibly only to eliminate c. In most contingencies, this will be the best strategy of a voter with preference scale abc. If, however, a is at risk from him and b at acute risk, a vote to eliminate c will lead, via b's elimination, to c's being the final outcome; his only way of avoiding this is to vote to eliminate a. Similarly, if the converse cyclic diagram applies, he will usually do best to vote to eliminate b, but, in the corresponding special case, to eliminate c.

The elimination procedure with positive voting is likewise never fully determinate: a voter with a strong preference scale can again vote admissibly in any possible way in any ballot save a final one. The procedure is, however, ultimately determinate whenever all preference scales are strong and P_{maj} is transitive. Suppose that there are only three possible outcomes and that the R_{maj} diagram has the form of diagram 5.7. As before, if the voters know this, their concern on the first ballot will be only to prevent or bring about the elimination of x, according as they prefer x to y or y to x. This time, however, those who prefer x to y have a unique 2-admissible way of voting on the first ballot, namely for x: those who prefer y to x will be in a quandary whether to vote for y or for z. Since the former are by hypothesis in a majority, x will not be eliminated; whether y or z is eliminated, x will be the final outcome, and is thus 2-determined. This shows that, however many possible outcomes there are, if R_{maj} yields a strong ordering of them, the final outcome is 2-determined once the last ballot but one is reached. Now suppose that there are four possible outcomes, and that R_{maj} yields the strong ordering $abcd$. If a is not eliminated on the first ballot, it will then be 2-determined as the final outcome; if a is eliminated, b will be 2-determined. A voter who knows that the others will vote 2-admissibly knows this, and will therefore consider only whether he prefers a to b or b to a in deciding how to vote on the first ballot; if he prefers a to b, he can vote 3-admissibly only for a. Since a majority of voters prefer a to b, a will not be eliminated on the first ballot if all vote 3-admissibly, and hence is 3-determined as the final outcome. If there are r possible outcomes, then, by repetition of the argument, the procedure $(r-1)$-determines the top whenever all preferences are strong and P_{maj} is transitive.

The fact that, when there are three possible outcomes and the R_{maj} diagram has the form of diagram 5.7, any voter who prefers x to y can vote 2-admissibly only for x in the first ballot shows that it is admissible for a voter with the preference scale abc to vote for either a or b in that ballot. When R_{maj} yields the strong ordering abc or acb, he can vote 2-admissibly only for a; when it yields the strong ordering bca, he can vote 2-admissibly only for b. In no other case will he have a unique 2-admissible strategy; but there are contingencies in which his best strategy requires him to vote for c on the first ballot. This will happen when R_{maj} yields the strong ordering bac, b is at risk from him, and c at acute risk. Unless he votes for c on the first ballot, it will be eliminated and b will be the final outcome; if he votes for c, b will be eliminated and the final outcome will be a. This may be illustrated by:

1	2	3	4	5	6	7	8	9	10	11
b	a	a	a	a	a	b	b	c	c	c
a	b	b	b	b	c	a	c	b	b	b
c	c	c	c	c	b	c	a	a	a	a

Example 3

Assume that every voter other than voter 2 votes on the first ballot for the outcome he ranks highest. Then, if voter 2 votes for c on the first ballot, b will be eliminated and a will be the final outcome; if he votes for b, c will be eliminated and b will be the final outcome; and, if he votes for a, c will again be eliminated, by the chairman's casting vote, and hence b will again be the final outcome.

When diagram 5.9 applies, a voter with the preference scale abc may 2-admissibly vote for a or for b on the first ballot; when the converse cyclic diagram applies, he may 2-admissibly vote for a or for c. The procedure is then 2-indeterminate. If all preference scales are strong, every 2-admissible strategy remains 3-admissible, so that it is also ultimately indeterminate.

The notion of higher-order admissibility figures prominently in Farquharson's *Theory of Voting*, and, under different names, has been used by other writers; but its practical importance ought not to be exaggerated. Even 2-admissibility is significant for a voter only if he has a good idea of the preference scales of the other voters, or at least of the R_{maj} relations. When he does, it indeed becomes of dominant importance: we can be sure that such a voter, if he is rational, and can discount the possibility of collusion amongst the others, will confine his choice of strategy to those that are 2-admissible. It would, of course, in every case pay him so to restrict his choice: but he cannot do so unless he knows the other voters' preference scales, or at least a good deal about them, because he cannot otherwise know which his 2-admissible strategies are; and usually he will have at best only a hazy estimate of the preferences of the others. In the same way, ultimate admissibility, or admissibility of any order higher than 2, is relevant only to a voter who knows how much the other voters know; only when he has acquired his knowledge of their preferences by open discussion is he likely to know this. The fact that a given voting procedure, for instance a binary one, has a unique ultimately admissible outcome does not, therefore, constitute any very strong recommendation of it: unless the voters have a near perfect knowledge both of each other's preferences and of each other's knowledge of those preferences, there is no strong likelihood that that outcome will be successful.

Although we ought not to exaggerate the importance of the concept of higher-order admissibility, it would be equally wrong to deny it all value. In some special cases, it is the right concept to apply. More generally, a voter who has no straightforward strategy is forced, in practice, to guess what the other voters are going to do. Sometimes he may be disastrously wrong; but it will be seldom that he is quite ignorant of their intentions: reality usually lies between the extremes of complete ignorance and perfect knowledge. Hence, while, in general, there is far from being any certainty that a voter will select a 2-admissible strategy, let alone an ultimately admissible one, there is a somewhat greater probability of his doing so than of his selecting one that is admissible but not 2-admissible.

Farquharson, unfortunately, belongs among those who have overestimated the importance of higher-order admissibility; indeed, he is guilty of mystification concerning it. He labels a voter who adopts an ultimately admissible strategy 'sophisticated', remarking that 'the assumption that only admissible strategies will be used (by the other voters) is at least a fairly reasonable one'.[2] The assumption in question is of course that underlying a voter's restriction of his choice of strategy to the 2-admissible ones, and Farquharson's comment is an understatement. The assumption is more than 'fairly reasonable': it is wholly evident, given a minimal degree of rationality on the part of the other voters and the absence of collusion between them. What Farquharson skates over is that this assumption, by itself, is of no use if the voter who makes it does not know the other voters' preferences, for, unless he knows them, he does not know what their admissible strategies are. Farquharson then leaps to an account of the successive process of eliminating first 3-inadmissible and then 4-inadmissible strategies, and so on, thus eventually whittling down one's choice to ultimately admissible

---

[2] R. Farquharson, *Theory of Voting*, p. 30.

ones; but he omits to explain the assumptions upon which these iterated eliminations of strategies are based. As we have seen, a voter can reject his 3-inadmissible strategies as pointless only if he can assume that all other voters will adopt 2-admissible ones; and this assumption is not, in general, even 'fairly reasonable': it is wholly unreasonable unless one has grounds to suppose that every voter knows the preferences of all the others. After all this, Farquharson claims that if, by the process of repeatedly narrowing down, a voter is able to arrive at a unique strategy that is ultimately admissible for him, then this 'has a good title to recognition as the unique result of a kind of "hyper-rational" strategy choice';[3] but the claim is unsound. There is no such thing as hyper-rationality: there are only rationality and irrationality. The narrowing down can be done only by a voter who knows the preferences of the others. If he does, and can assume that there is no collusion between them, that it is not hyperrational, but simply rational, for him to select a 2-admissible strategy. Whether or not it is rational in him to confine himself to n-admissible strategies for any n greater than 2 depends on what he is entitled to assume about what the other voters know. In no case is there any room for distinguishing the hyper-rational voter from the merely rational one.

[3] Ibid., p. 42.

6
A Fair Outcome: The Criterion of Majority Preference

Many people, having taken part in a voting procedure to decide between three or more candidates, and discovering that a majority preferred some one of the defeated candidates to the successful one, would take this to demonstrate that the outcome of the voting was unfair. They could think this only if they were unaware that there might be no top, so that such a state of affairs would have obtained whatever the outcome. One reaction to the 'paradox of voting' is to conclude that majority preferences are not decisive for which outcome is the fairest even when there is a top; others may continue to regard them as of overriding importance. They may do so on prudential grounds, believing it unwise, when it can be avoided, to make a decision liable subsequently to be overturned. Alternatively, they may be affected by what may be called the *mystique* of the majority. In either case, they will endorse, not only principle (4) of Chapter 4:

(4) if x is the only top, x is the fairest outcome,

but the stronger principle:

(5) if there is a top, no outcome can be fair unless it is a top.

The purpose of this chapter is to enquire what further criteria, of a kind likely to appeal to those for whom majority preferences are of overriding importance, can be invoked to decide which is the fairest outcome when there is no top, and to discriminate between two or more outcomes all of which are tops. Suppose, then, that, of several possible outcomes, there are two, each of which is preferred by a majority to a certain outcome b, whereas there is only one outcome, which may be b itself or some other, which a majority prefers to a second outcome a. Someone who attaches overriding importance to majority preferences will then surely regard a as a fairer outcome than b. If there is no top, we cannot avoid selecting an outcome to which a majority prefer some other: but an adherent of principle (5) will wish to hold this effect to a minimum.

We may therefore define the *majority number* of any outcome x as the number of other outcomes y for which $xR_{\text{maj}}y$. A natural extension of principle (5) will then be:

(6) no outcome can be fair if it has a lower majority number than some other outcome.

Principle (6) embraces principle (5), since, if there are r outcomes, the majority number of any top will be $r - 1$. Suppose, now, that there are four possible outcomes, and that all preference scales are strong. If P_{maj} is transitive, the majority number of the top will be 3, and the others will have majority numbers 2, 1, and 0 respectively, as shown in diagram 6.1.

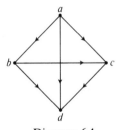

Diagram 6.1

The simplest case in which P_{maj} fails to be transitive is that in which there is a top, say a, and there are cyclic majorities between the remaining three outcomes, as illustrated by diagram 6.2.

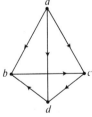

Diagram 6.2

In this case, a's majority number is 3, and those of b, c, and d are each 1. In both these cases, of course, principle (6) requires that the fairest outcome is a. The simplest case in which there is no top is that in which one outcome, say d, is bottom in the sense that $xP_{maj}d$ whenever x is any one of the three other outcomes, but there are cyclic majorities between those three, as shown in diagram 6.3.

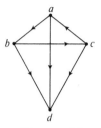

Diagram 6.3

In this case, d will have the majority number 0, and a, b, and c will each have the majority number 2. Principle (6) will rule out d as not being a fair outcome, but will not decide between a, b, and c.

There is, however, yet another kind of case, in which there are two cyclic triads. Let us suppose that a, b, and c form one and a, b, and d another, and, further, that $cP_{maj}d$. Then the R_{maj} relations are as shown in diagram 6.4.

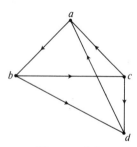

Diagram 6.4

The diagram has been drawn lop-sided in order to bring out the fact that d behaves exactly like c, save that $cP_{maj}d$: b stands in the relation P_{maj} to both of them, and both stand in the relation P_{maj} to a. Here b and c each have the majority number 2, whereas a and d each have the majority number 1. Principle (6) therefore restricts the choice of the fairest outcome to b and c, without deciding between them.

In some instances, principle (6) may select a unique fairest outcome, even though there is no top. This cannot happen with only three or four outcomes, but is possible when there are five, as shown by diagram 6.5.

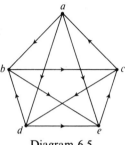

Diagram 6.5

Here there are three cyclic triads: one formed by a, b, and c, a second by b, c, and d, and the third by c, d, and e. The majority numbers can be read off as follows:

a	b	c	d	e
3	2	2	2	1

Principle (6) thus serves to determine a as the fairest outcome, even though it is not a top.

As we have seen, principle (6) will very often fail to select a unique fairest outcome. In some cases, it will not eliminate a single outcome, as when there are only three outcomes and majority preferences are cyclic, as shown in diagram 6.6, or, again, when there are five outcomes, and the majority preferences are as shown by diagram 6.7.

Diagram 6.6   Diagram 6.7

118   A FAIR OUTCOME

In the former case, each outcome has the majority number 1; in the latter, each has the majority number 2. When r is the number of possible outcomes, and I_{maj} does not hold between any two distinct outcomes, the aggregate of the majority numbers must be $\frac{1}{2}r(r-1)$; hence, when all preference scales are strong, it is possible for each outcome to have the same majority number $\frac{1}{2}(r-1)$ when r is odd, but not when r is even.

Is it possible to strengthen principle (6) so as to yield a unique fairest outcome in a greater number of cases, while still appealing to a criterion to do with majority preferences? However complex a criterion we devise, there will still be cases in which, to determine a unique outcome, we have to resort to a criterion of a different kind; conversely, one imbued with the mystique of the majority is in practice likely to be highly satisfied with any voting procedure that can be shown to conform to principle (6) in that it always produces an outcome that (6) does not exclude as unfair. Moreover, a voting procedure ought not to be too complex to explain to the voters: the voting mechanism *must* be easy to understand, but the method of assessment ought also to be comprehensible. It is nevertheless instructive to enquire what elaborations of the criterion of majority preference would be possible before it was necessary to resort to one of a different type.

An R_{maj} diagram is in accord with Arrow's principle of the independence of irrelevant alternatives: if we delete any one outcome, the R_{maj} relations between the rest remain unchanged. For this reason, principle (5) is in partial accord with Arrow's principle in that, if all preferences are strong, and a is the top, deletion of any other outcome can never make a cease to be top or cause any other outcome to become top. Principle (6), on the other hand, is in no sense in accord with Arrow's principle. If we suppress d in diagram 6.4, for example, we obtain diagram 6.6: principle (6) allows a as a fair outcome in diagram 6.6, which it was not in diagram 6.4. Further, if, in diagram 6.6, we suppress a, we obtain diagram 6.8.

Diagram 6.8

THE CRITERION OF MAJORITY PREFERENCE   119

Under principle (6), c has now ceased to be a fair outcome, which it was in diagrams 6.6 and 6.4. Now, for any given criterion, we may consider the result of reiterating it: deleting the outcomes rejected by the criterion as unfair, we apply the criterion again to those it did not reject, in the hope of further narrowing the field. If the criterion were in full accord with Arrow's principle, this would have no effect: when reapplied to the set of outcomes rated fair by it, it would continue to rate them all as fair. Since principle (6) is not in accord with Arrow's principle, we may usefully try the effect of reiterating it.

In diagram 6.4, the outcomes allowed as fair by principle (6) are b and c. In reiterating, we must delete a and d, and consider the resulting R_{maj} diagram, which is diagram 6.8. A reapplication of principle (6) to diagram 6.8 yields b as the only fair outcome; we conclude that b is the unique fairest outcome in diagram 6.4. In effect, we are here arguing that, of the two outcomes b and c allowed as fair by principle (6) in diagram 6.4, b is the fairer because $bP_{maj}c$. Consider a more complex case, with six possible outcomes (diagram 6.9).

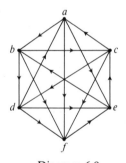

Diagram 6.9

The majority numbers are:

a	b	c	d	e	f
3	3	3	3	2	1

Principle (6) therefore rules out e and f. If we eliminate these two, and consider the majority preferences between the four surviving outcomes, we obtain diagram 6.4. The majority numbers of these four outcomes, calculated over the set consisting only of them, are:

a	b	c	d
1	2	2	1

A second application of principle (6) therefore eliminates a and d; we are here assuming that, having selected a, b, c, and d as candidates for being the fairest outcomes, we are justified in choosing between them just as we should if they were the only possible outcomes. Eliminating a and d, we obtain diagram 6.8, in respect of which the majority numbers are:

$$\begin{array}{cc} b & c \\ 1 & 0 \end{array}$$

Once more reiterating principle (6), we finally conclude that b is the unique fairest outcome in diagram 6.9. We may express this by saying that b *persistently* has the highest majority number; our strengthened principle is, accordingly:

(7) no outcome can be fair unless it persistently has the highest majority number.

Note that here 'having the highest majority number' means 'having one not surpassed by that of any other outcome'.

In diagrams 6.6. and 6.7, principle (7) will no more help us to decide between any of the outcomes than did principle (6): just because principle (6) did not eliminate any of the outcomes, a second application of the principle leaves us just where we were before. In neither of these cases can any appeal to majority preferences rule out any of the outcomes; to determine the fairest outcome, we must resort to a criterion of a different kind. So far, however, we have considered only R_{maj} diagrams in which each line has only one arrow: when $xI_{maj}y$ for certain outcomes x and y, we have further resources. Suppose that there are five outcomes, that some preference scales are weak and that the majority preferences are as shown by diagram 6.10.

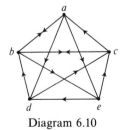

Diagram 6.10

THE CRITERION OF MAJORITY PREFERENCE

The majority number of each outcome is:

a	b	c	d	e
3	3	2	2	2

In accordance with principle (6), therefore, a and b are the only possible fair outcomes. If, applying principle (7), we delete c, d, and e, we obtain diagram 6.11,

$$a \longleftrightarrow b$$

Diagram 6.11

which does not help us to choose between a and b. In the original diagram however, a stood in the relation P_{maj} to two outcomes, and in the relation I_{maj} to only one, where b stood in the relation I_{maj} to two and in the relation P_{maj} to one; and this might serve as a ground for choosing a rather than b. Generalizing this, we may consider the *majority scores* of the outcomes rather than just their majority numbers, where we lay down that the majority score of an outcome is to be calculated by assigning it one point for each outcome to which it stands in the relation P_{maj}, but only half a point for each outcome other than itself to which it stands in the relation I_{maj}. The majority scores of the outcomes in diagram 6.10 are:

a	b	c	d	e
$2\frac{1}{2}$	2	$1\frac{1}{2}$	2	2

so that, by this criterion, a appears as the fairest outcome.

It would be convenient if we could simply substitute the criterion of having the highest majority score for that of having the highest majority number. Unfortunately, we cannot do this without, in some cases, violating even principle (4). Consider a case illustrated by diagram 6.12.

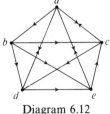

Diagram 6.12

Here the majority numbers are:

a	b	c	d	e
4	3	2	2	2

showing that a is the sole top, and therefore the unique fair outcome according to principle (4). Nevertheless, a does not have the highest majority score, the majority scores being:

a	b	c	d	e
$2\frac{1}{2}$	3	$1\frac{1}{2}$	$1\frac{1}{2}$	$1\frac{1}{2}$

The main concern of an adherent of principle (4) or (5) was, whenever possible, to avoid the selection of an outcome to which a majority preferred some other outcome. He would therefore be more moved by the consideration that, if b were selected, a majority would positively have preferred a, than by the fact that, if a is selected, there will be three outcomes any one of which a majority would be content to have in place of a, without all of them actually preferring it to a. For this reason, we cannot modify principle (7) by substituting 'majority score' for 'majority number', but must treat majority scores as supplying a supplementary criterion, thus arriving at the principle:

(8) no outcome can be fair unless it persistently has the highest majority number; of those that do, no outcome can be fair unless it has the highest majority score, taken over all the possible outcomes.

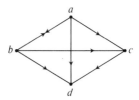

Diagram 6.13

In the case illustrated by diagram 6.13, even principle (8) will not discriminate between a and b. Outcomes a and b are both tops, sharing the majority number 3 and the majority score $2\frac{1}{2}$; since $aI_{\text{maj}}b$, elimination of c and d does not help. Suppose, however, that there are nine voters, of whom three are indifferent between a and b, four prefer a to b, and only two prefer b to a. There will then be a

THE CRITERION OF MAJORITY PREFERENCE

case for saying that a is the fairer outcome of the two, on the basis that a greater number of voters prefer a to b than prefer b to a. We may, in such a case, say that a *preponderance* of voters prefer a to b, and symbolize this by '$aP_{gtr}b$'. How should we define '$xP_{gtr}y$' formally? If we take it simply to mean that the number of voters who prefer x to y is greater than the number who prefer y to x, then '$xP_{gtr}y$' will always imply '$xR_{maj}y$' and '$xP_{maj}y$' will imply '$xP_{gtr}y$' whenever the number n of voters is odd; but there will be one case in which $xP_{maj}y$ but not $xP_{gtr}y$ when n is even, namely when exactly half the voters, including the chairman, prefer x to y, and the other half prefer y to x. To avoid this awkward case, we may add a clause to our definition to exclude it, and so define '$xP_{gtr}y$' to mean:

either $\quad N_i[xP_iy] > N_i[yP_ix]\quad$ or
$\qquad N_i[xP_iy] = N_i[yP_ix] = \frac{1}{2}n$ and xP_1y.

Under this definition, $xP_{gtr}y$ in the awkward case, so that in all circumstances, if $xP_{maj}y$, then $xP_{gtr}y$. We may now define '$xR_{gtr}y$' to mean:

not $yP_{gtr}x$.

'$xR_{gtr}y$' thus says that

$N_i[xP_iy] \geqslant N_i[yP_ix]$

and further that

if $N_i[xP_iy] = N_i[yP_ix] = \frac{1}{2}n$, then xP_1y.

Likewise, we may define '$xI_{gtr}y$' to mean:

$xR_{gtr}y$ and $yR_{gtr}x$.

'$xI_{gtr}y$' is thus equivalent to:

$N_i[xP_iy] = N_i[yP_ix]$ and, for some i, xI_iy.

For any two outcomes x and y, there will now be five exclusive possibilities:

(i) $xP_{maj}y$;
(ii) $xI_{maj}y$ and $xP_{gtr}y$;
(iii) $xI_{gtr}y$;
(iv) $xI_{maj}y$ and $yP_{gtr}x$;
(v) $yP_{maj}x$.

We may represent such relations on what we may call an R_{gtr} diagram, which is just like an R_{maj} diagram save that we put a double arrow from x to y when $xP_{maj}y$ and a single arrow in case (ii), reserving the two arrows in opposite directions for the case when $xI_{gtr}y$: the R_{maj} diagram can therefore be reconstructed from the R_{gtr} diagram by replacing the double arrows by single ones, and putting two arrows in opposite directions in place of single arrows. We may now substitute for the majority score a more refined estimate of the worth of an outcome, to be called its *preponderance score*, calculated as follows: we allot x one point for each y for which case (i) holds, three-quarters of a point for each y for which case (ii) holds, half a point for each y for which case (iii) holds, and one-quarter of a point for each y for which case (iv) holds. It should be noted that, when there are r outcomes, both the majority scores and the preponderance scores must always sum to $\frac{1}{2}r(r-1)$: when all preference scales are strong, the majority number, majority score, and preponderance score of an outcome will coincide.

Consider, then, the R_{gtr} diagram 6.14.

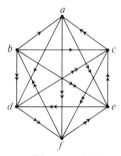

Diagram 6.14

This yields the following figures:

	a	b	c	d	e	f
majority number	4	4	3	3	2	2
majority score	3	3	$2\frac{1}{2}$	$2\frac{1}{2}$	2	2
preponderance score	3	$3\frac{1}{2}$	$2\frac{1}{4}$	$2\frac{1}{4}$	2	2

Principle (6) picks out *a* and *b* as the only possible fair outcomes. Principle (7) does not resolve the issue between them, since $aI_{maj}b$; nor does principle (8), since their majority scores are identical. The preponderance scores, however, allow us to choose b as a fairer outcome than a.

In the R_{gtr} diagram 6.15 the figures are:

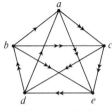

Diagram 6.15

	a	b	c	d	e
majority number	4	3	2	2	1
majority score	3	$2\frac{1}{2}$	2	$1\frac{1}{2}$	1
preponderance score	$2\frac{1}{2}$	$2\frac{3}{4}$	2	$1\frac{3}{4}$	1

By principle (4), a is the only fair outcome, since it is the sole top: but b has a bigger preponderance score than a. This show that, consistently with principle (4), preponderance scores can at most supply a supplementary criterion, and can no more replace majority numbers in principle (6) than majority scores could. It also shows that the preponderance score of one outcome may be greater than that of another when its majority score is smaller. It is not difficult to construct an example where this happens between two outcomes deemed fair by principle (7); it then becomes a delicate matter whether to attach more weight to majority scores or to preponderance scores. We may thus formulate, as an alternative to principle (8), not an extension of it, the principle:

(9) no outcome can be fair unless it persistently has the highest majority number; of those that do, no outcome can be fair unless it has the highest preponderance score, taken over all possible outcomes.

All the criteria here reviewed, from that embodied in principle (4) on, share an important characteristic, namely that they depend upon the preference scales as a whole, and not just on particular features of them such as which outcome stands at the head of each scale: we may express this by saying that they are 'globally sensitive' to the preference scales. We can make this notion precise as follows.

Consider any fixed set of outcomes and any fixed set of voters, and pick any one voter, say voter 2. Let us say that two preference scales 'differ all but minimally' if one can be obtained from the other by inverting the order of two consecutive outcomes: for example, the scales *abcde* and *abdce*. A criterion for a fair outcome may then be said to be *globally sensitive*, for the given numbers of outcomes and of voters, if, for any two preference scales that differ all but minimally and that voter 2 may have, it is possible to assign preference scales to the other voters in such a way that the criterion will select one or another unique outcome according as voter 2 has one or the other preference scale. It is evident that principle (4) is globally sensitive, given at least three voters: for the preference scales of the other voters may be such that, if voter 2 prefers *a* to *b*, *a* will be the unique top, and, if he prefers *b* to *a*, *b* will be.

We may define a *globally hypersensitive* criterion in exactly the same way, save that the two preference scales may differ only minimally: two scales will differ minimally if one can be obtained from the other by bracketing two consecutive outcomes, thus making the voter indifferent between them; for instance, *abcde* and *ab(cd)e*. Principle (4) is not globally hypersensitive, since a shift on the part of a single voter from one preference scale to another differing minimally from it cannot both convert an outcome that was not a top into one that is and convert one that was a top into one that is not. Principles (8) and (9) are globally hypersensitive, given at least three voters. Consider the two preference tables:

1	2	3	1	2	3
a	c	b	a	c	b
b c	a b	a	b c	b	a
		c		a	c

The difference between the two tables lies only in a minimal difference in voter 2's preference scale. The R_{maj} diagrams corresponding to the two tables are diagrams 6.16 and 6.17.

Diagram 6.16

Diagram 6.17

THE CRITERION OF MAJORITY PREFERENCE   127

Since, in both tables, $bI_{gtr}c$, and, in the left-hand table, $aI_{gtr}b$, the majority scores of all outcomes coincide with their preponderance scores. The majority numbers and majority scores are:

	a	b	c	a	b	c
maj. no.	2	2	1	1	2	1
maj. score	$1\frac{1}{2}$	1	$\frac{1}{2}$	1	$1\frac{1}{2}$	1

In diagram 6.17, b is the sole top, and hence the unique fairest outcome by principle (4). In diagram 6.16, a and b are both possible fair outcomes under principle (7); by principle (8) or (9), however, a is the only fair outcome.

When there are at least four possible outcomes, principle (7) itself is globally hypersensitive. Consider the preference tables:

1	2	3	1	2	3
c	d	b	c	d	b
a		a	a	b	a
d	a b	c	d	a	c
b	c	d	b	c	d

These yield the R_{maj} diagrams 6.18 and 6.19.

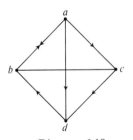 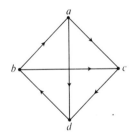

Diagram 6.18   Diagram 6.19

The majority numbers are:

a	b	c	d	a	b	c	d
3	2	1	1	2	2	1	1

In diagram 6.18, a is the only top, and hence, by principle (4), the only fair outcome. In diagram 19, principle (6) allows both a and b as fair outcomes, but principle (7) rules out a and leaves b as the only one, since $bP_{\text{maj}}a$.

The refinements of principle (6) embodied in principles (7) to (9) are of very minor importance. In subsequent chapters, we shall be concerned with how far various procedures conform to principle (6), but not with its extensions. We shall have occasion to mention majority scores again, but not preponderance scores; and we shall revert to using R_{maj} diagrams rather than R_{gtr} ones. Our purpose, in the later part of the chapter, has been to see how long it would be possible to stave off appeal to a criterion not relating to majority preferences: what is more important is that it cannot be staved off indefinitely, as diagrams 6.6, 6.7, and 6.3 illustrate.

7
Preference Scores

A criterion for the fairest outcome based on majority preferences will fail to deliver a definite decision far too often for us to treat it as a matter of indifference which, among the outcomes admitted as fair by that criterion, is successful. A criterion of this type must therefore be supplemented by an ancillary one of another type, which we need now to frame.

A different type of criterion is wanted, moreover, not just as a supplement, but as a rival, to those based on majority preferences. When no particular concern is felt over the danger of a subsequent reversal of the decision, it is far from obvious that majority preferences should be a decisive factor in arriving at it. The end may, rather, be held to be, not to satisfy as many people as possible, but to give the greatest overall satisfaction to all. We saw in Chapter 2 that these two ends are far from being the same: when a bare majority favour a as their first choice and b as their second, while the rest rank b as their first choice and a as their last out of several alternatives, as in the case of the family going to the theatre, b is likely to give more overall satisfaction than a even though a would satisfy most people more.

Suppose that the criteria of Chapter 6 were criticized precisely on the ground of their being globally sensitive. The critic argues that only certain features of a voter's preference scale ought to be treated as relevant to determining which outcome it would be best to select, and the others dismissed as having no bearing on that question. For instance, he might claim that only a voter's first choice is relevant to deciding the fairest outcome. How should we reply to him?

There is a quite general argument in favour of global sensitivity. Under any voting procedure whatever, it is possible, from the standpoint of any particular voter, that a contingency obtains in which, if he adopts any of a certain set of strategies, an outcome x will be successful, while, if he adopts any other strategy, y will be. The voter may well not know that such a contingency obtains, because he does not know how the others are voting; but, if he did know for sure what strategies they were adopting, he would be influenced solely by whether he preferred x to y or y to x, whatever positions x and y occupied on his preference scale relatively to other outcomes. It follows that *any* feature of a voter's preference scale might be decisive in determining which way he would vote, given that he knew what effect his vote would have. A consideration that might rationally motivate a voter to vote in one way rather than another can hardly be irrelevant to the question which would be the fairest outcome: hence any criterion for answering the question should be globally sensitive.

This argument will rule out so absurd a principle as

(10) if a is the first choice of at least as many voters as any one other outcome, a is at least as fair an outcome as any.

It will not, however, defeat a more sophisticated critic, who advances the weaker principle:

(11) if a is the first choice of more voters than b, b is not a fair outcome.

Principles (8) or (9) each invoked an ancillary criterion, that of majority scores or of preponderance scores, to supplement the leading criterion embodied in principle (7). Principle (10) says that the *only* feature of a voter's preference scale relevant to determining the fairest outcome is which outcome he ranks first; principle (11) makes the weaker claim that it is of *overriding* significance. It would be quite consistent for an advocate of principle (11) to supplement it with ancillary criteria to deal with cases when it did not determine a unique fairest outcome; in the process, he might render his complex overall criterion globally sensitive. What this more sophisticated critic objects to is not the use of a globally sensitive overall criterion, but its incorporation of a leading criterion that is globally sensitive, like that embodied in principle (4): against this position the argument given above is impotent.

Against such a principle as (11) one can pit only intuition, by citing a case such as example 1. According to principle (11), g has here a clear title to be the fairest outcome, even though it is regarded as the worst by five of the seven voters; the claim is deeply implausible.

If, in face of this example, the advocate of principle (11) simply

PREFERENCE SCORES

1	2	3	4	5	6	7
a	b	c	d	e	g	g
b	a	a	a	a	a	a
c	c	b	b	f	f	f
d	d	d	c	b	b	b
e	e	e	e	c	c	c
f	f	f	f	d	d	e
g	g	g	g	g	e	d

Example 1

replies that it seems evident to him that g is the fairest outcome, argument peters out: imbued with a mystique of the first choice, his intuitions run counter to ours, and intuitions, because they appear like bedrock, needing no supporting arguments, are hard to dislodge. His intuitions may have been engendered by his familiarity with voting procedures in which each voter is asked to vote for just one possible outcome; however engendered, they now serve for him as axioms.

It is extremely important to distinguish such a response from another that is very frequent, namely that a distribution of preferences as in example 1 is very unlikely. This reply should be dismissed out of hand as beside the point. We are concerned to answer the question: Given the preference scales of the voters, by what criterion should we judge which outcome would be the fairest? It is not being assumed that, once decided on, such a criterion should be incorporated in a voting procedure. If it were so incorporated, then, if we could be sure that the voters had revealed their true preference scales by means of their votes, that procedure would render perfect justice by always selecting the fairest outcome. There are, however, other requirements on a good voting procedure: if the procedure in question were intensely complex for the voters to understand or take part in or for the tellers to operate, there would be good reason to reject it. We should then have to settle for rough justice. To do so, we might need to answer a second question: What simpler test will *usually* pick out that outcome that is fairest by our original criterion? This second question asks for a rough-and-ready test for being the fairest outcome: to answer it, we need to consider which distributions of preferences will be the most frequent and which will be very rare. We cannot even pose the second question, however, until we have answered the first, at least to the extent of deciding upon the leading criterion: we cannot judge whether a rough-and-ready test will usually pick out the fairest outcome until we know how to recognize which *is* the fairest outcome. The reply commends counting only the first choices of the voters as a rough-and-ready test for discerning the fairest outcome. Our critic has thus tacitly abandoned his claim for principle (11) as part of a *criterion* for the fairest outcome; and we cannot judge his claim for it as a rough-and-ready test until we know what his criterion is. We shall later see that first choices are in fact an exceedingly poor guide to the overall pattern of voters' preferences.

There is one ground upon which principle (11) might be defended: a belief that the gap in any voter's preference scale between any outcome other than his first choice and the next outcome on his scale is not merely small, but infinitesimal, in comparison with the gap between his first choice and his second. There is no basis for such a belief. Sometimes, indeed, a voter is overwhelmingly anxious for the success of one particular outcome, and all but indifferent to which of its rivals succeeds if it fails. But this is only one possibility among many. Another is that the voter may find two outcomes almost equally attractive, and both immeasurably more so than the rest; or he may be principally concerned with defeating a certain proposal, and not very strongly concerned about what happens, so long as it is not adopted. 'Negative voting' is notoriously at least as common as 'positive voting', where these phrases refer to the motive of the voter, not to the procedure employed. Principle (11) is therefore no more reasonable than the principle:

(12) if b occurs last on the preference scales of more voters than does a, b cannot be a fair outcome.

Certain gaps between consecutive outcomes on an individual voter's preference scale may be small, others large; but there can be no general rule for determining which: no general proposition such as that the gap between the first outcome and the second on a voter's scale is likely to be greater than that between the third and the fourth, or conversely, has any claim to be believed. We have, for good reasons, restricted ourselves to working from the preference scales, without invoking any explicit weighting of the preferences. No method, based solely on a voter's preference scale, of assessing the satisfaction he will gain from any particular outcome can be more than an approximation. Since we have accepted the restriction,

PREFERENCE SCORES   133

we can only assume, as a general principle, that the gaps between consecutive outcomes on any voter's scale are at least comparable; this assumption suffices to warrant our rejecting principles (11) and (12). Indeed, the only general rule we can reasonably adopt is that all the gaps are not merely comparable, but equal.

These considerations lead directly to the formulation of a criterion for the fairest outcome not dependent on the R_{maj} or R_{gtr} relations, but giving equal weight to every preference of every voter, and thus aimed at picking out that outcome which will give the greatest overall satisfaction to the voters. We shall call this the *preference score* of an outcome.[1] For any one outcome each voter is taken to contribute 1 point to its preference score for each outcome to which he prefers it, and $\frac{1}{2}$ point for each distinct outcome which he regards as equally good. If there are 5 outcomes, a voter with the strong preference scale *abcde* is thus taken to allot 4 points to *a*, 3 points to *b*, 2 points to *c*, 1 point to *d*, and 0 to *e*; when there are *r* outcomes, each voter allots $(r-1)$ points to that of his first choice, and $(r-i)$ points to that which stands in *i*th place on his scale. If a voter is indifferent between two or more outcomes, his contribution to the preference scores of each is the average of those he would have allotted them if his preference scale had been strong. Thus a voter with the scale *ab(cd)e* contributes $1\frac{1}{2}$ points to the preference scores of each of *c* and *d*, since he prefers each of them to one outcome, *e*, and ranks it equal with one other. Likewise one with the preference scale *a(bcd)e* contributes 4 points to the preference score of *a*, 2 points each to those of *b*, *c*, and *d*, and 0 to that of *e*.

The preference scores register, not merely whether one outcome is or is not preferred by a majority to some other, but, if it is, by how large a majority, and, if it is not, by how small a minority. They treat the distance on a voter's preference scale between two outcomes as a rough measure of the strength of his preference for the higher over

---

[1] This is frequently called its 'Borda count' in the technical literature of the subject, after the first of all those who pioneered it, Jean-Charles de Borda. In 1781 Borda wrote a paper proposing what will here be called the preference score procedure (see Chapter 10), without bracketing, for use in elections to the French Académie Royale des Sciences. 'Borda count' is shorter than 'preference score', but the latter is here preferred as being more descriptive and as analogous to expressions for other kinds of score we shall have occasion to consider. This is in line with the use of 'top' in place of 'Condorcet winner', and of course implies no disrespect to Borda. For a very clear account of the work of Borda, Condorcet, and other pioneers, see Part II of Duncan Black's *The Theory of Committees and Elections*, in which the history of the subject was for the first time unearthed.

the lower. His contribution to the preference score of any outcome can therefore be viewed as roughly representing the degree of satisfaction he would obtain if it were successful. One who believes the fairest outcome to be that which would maximize the collective satisfaction of the voters will therefore adopt preference scores as the leading criterion, according to the principle:

(13) if b has a lower preference score than a, b cannot be a fair outcome.

Preference scores can also be appealed to as a last resort, when majority preferences yield no unique decision; thus added to principle (9), we should obtain:

(14) no outcome can be fair unless it persistently has the highest majority number; of those that do, no outcome can be fair unless it has the highest preponderance score; and, of those that pass both tests, none can be fair unless it has the highest preference score.

Of r possible outcomes, the aggregate of their majority scores or of their preponderance scores is $\frac{1}{2}r(r-1)$ points, independently of the number of voters; the average such score is therefore $\frac{1}{2}(r-1)$ points. The preference scores, on the other hand, collectively receive from each voter a contribution of $\frac{1}{2}r(r-1)$ points, so that the aggregate of the preference scores is $\frac{1}{2}nr(r-1)$ points, where n is the number of voters; the average is thus $\frac{1}{2}n(r-1)$ points.

Now if principle (13) only occasionally selected a different outcome from that selected by, say, principle (6), it would not be an important rival to the criteria based on majority preferences. We must therefore enquire how far these principles can diverge from one another. The R_{maj} relations in which an outcome stands to the other possible outcomes set bounds between which its preference score can vary. In reviewing the extent of this variation, we may conveniently make certain simplifying assumptions: (i) that R_{maj} is transitive; (ii) that all preference scales are strong; and (iii) that the number n of voters is odd. We shall take n to be $2m+1$. Now consider any one outcome x: given its majority score q, we want to know between what limits its preference score can vary. By assumptions (i) and (ii), P_{maj} will impose a strong ordering on the outcomes according to their majority scores, which in this case will coincide with their majority numbers. There will thus be one outcome which tops the set and has a majority score of $r - 1$, a second which tops the rest and has a majority score of $r - 2$, and so on down to a single outcome having the majority score 0: the ith outcome in the P_{maj} ordering has the majority score $r - i$.

The preference score of an outcome x will be at a minimum if, for every outcome y for which $xP_{maj}y$, a bare majority of $m + 1$ voters prefer x to y, and, for every outcome z for which $zP_{maj}x$, *every* voter prefers z to x. Since x's majority score was assumed to be q, there are just q outcomes y for which $xP_{maj}y$: x's minimum preference score is accordingly $(m + 1)q$. The preference score of x will be at a maximum when, for each outcome y for which $xP_{maj}y$, every voter prefers x to y, and, for each outcome z for which $zP_{maj}x$, as many as m voters prefer x to z. For each outcome y for which $xP_{maj}y$, x will then receive m points more than when it has its minimum preference score; and, for each outcome z for which $zP_{maj}x$, x will also receive m points more than when it has its minimum score. The difference between x's maximum and minimum preference scores is therefore $m(r - 1)$, independently of its majority score q. Thus, on our assumptions, the preference score of an outcome x with majority score q may vary between:

minimum: $(m + 1)q$ points
maximum: $(m + 1)q + m(r - 1)$ points.

In particular, the majority score of the only top is $r - 1$. Its preference score will therefore range between:

minimum: $(m + 1)(r - 1)$ points
maximum: $(2m + 1)(r - 1)$ points;

it will attain the maximum when it is the first choice of every voter. Conversely, the preference score of the one outcome with majority score 0 will vary between:

minimum: 0 points
maximum: $m(r - 1)$ points;

it will attain the minimum when every voter ranks it last. Thus, if we label the outcomes $a_1, a_2, \ldots, a_r$ according to their P_{maj} order, with a_1 the top, the outcome a_i will have the majority score $r - i$, and its preference score will vary between:

minimum: $(m + 1)(r - i)$ points
maximum: $(m + 1)(r - i) + m(r - 1)$ points.

We may illustrate this for the case that there are thirteen voters and five outcomes, so that $m = 6$ and $r = 5$. Let us assume that P_{maj} orders the outcomes in the order $a\ b\ c\ d\ e$. The maximum and minimum preference scores are then:

	a	b	c	d	e
minimum	28	21	14	7	0
maximum	52	45	38	31	24

Under the given assumptions, it will always be possible for any one outcome to attain its maximum preference score, and for any one other to receive its minimum. It is not possible, however, for two outcomes both to receive their maximum scores or both to receive their minimum scores. If $xP_{maj}y$, then, for x to attain its maximum score, every voter must prefer it to y, whereas, for y to attain *its* maximum, only a bare majority ($m + 1$ voters) can prefer x to it. Conversely, for x to receive its minimum score, only a bare majority can prefer it to y, while, for y to receive *its* minimum, every voter must prefer x to it. If, for example, in the foregoing case, a receives its minimum preference score of 28 points, only seven voters can prefer it to b. For each of the six voters who prefer b to a, therefore, b scores 1 point: it must therefore score at least 6 points above its general minimum of 21 points, and so must score at least 27 points.

If the preference score of the top, a_1, is the lowest possible, then one other outcome may attain its highest possible score. Suppose, then, that a_1 receives its minimum score and that a_i receives its maximum. The condition that a_i's preference score is higher than that of a_1 is then:

$$(m + 1)(r - i) + m(r - 1) > (m + 1)(r - 1)$$

which is equivalent to:

(A) $m(r - i) > i - 1$.

Now principles (4) and (13) will rate different outcomes as the fairest when, for some $i > 1$, a_i has a higher preference score than a_1. For any given value of i, this will have the best chance of happening when a_1 has its minimum score and a_i its maximum, and will then happen if the inequality (A) holds; and (A) is most likely to hold when $i = 2$. As a special case of (A), a_2 will be capable of having a higher preference score than a_1 just in case:

$m(r - 2) > 1.$

When $m > 1$, so that there are five or more voters, this will always hold provided that $r > 2$, i.e. there are three or more possible outcomes. When there are only three voters, so that $m = 1$, it will not be possible when $r = 3$, but will always be possible when $r > 3$, i.e. there are more than three possible outcomes. Thus it is possible for the sole top to fail to have the highest preference score whenever there are at least four outcomes, or at least three and at least five voters.

When $i = r$, (A) cannot hold: thus the bottom outcome a_r, with majority score 0, can never have a higher preference score than a_1. The condition that a_{r-1} be capable of receiving a higher preference score than a_1 is to be found by putting $i = r - 1$ in (A), which yields:

$m > r - 2.$

When there are three outcomes, this is of course the same as the condition for a_2 to be capable of having a higher preference score than a_1, already stated, namely that there should be at least five voters. When there are four outcomes, there must be at least seven voters; when there are five outcomes, it will need at least nine voters, and so on.

We may illustrate these possibilities by some examples with eleven voters and five outcomes: in all cases the P_{maj} ordering is $a\ b\ c\ d\ e$, as before. The preference scores will therefore vary between:

	a	b	c	d	e
minimum	24	18	12	6	0
maximum	44	38	32	26	20

We may begin with an example like that of the family going to the theatre.

1	2	3	4	5	6	7	8	9	10	11
a	a	a	a	a	a	b	b	b	b	b
b	b	b	b	b	b	c	d	e	c	d
c	d	e	c	d	e	d	e	c	e	c
d	e	c	e	c	d	e	c	d	d	e
e	c	d	d	e	c	a	a	a	a	a

Example 2

In this example, the preference scores are:

a	b	c	d	e
24	38	17	16	15

Thus a, the sole top, receives its minimum preference score, while b, the next in the P_{maj} ordering, attains its maximum. By modifying the example, we obtain one in which both b and c receive higher preference scores than a:

1	2	3	4	5	6	7	8	9	10	11
a	a	a	a	a	a	b	b	b	b	b
b	b	b	b	b	b	c	c	c	c	c
c	c	c	c	c	c	d	e	d	e	d
d	e	d	e	d	e	e	d	e	d	e
e	d	e	d	e	d	a	a	a	a	a

Example 3

Here the preference scores are:

a	b	c	d	e
24	38	27	11	10

It will be seen from the table of maximum and minimum preference scores that it is possible for any one of the outcomes b, c, and d to obtain a higher preference score than a. Here are two examples in which c attains its maximum score, and the highest preference score of any outcome:

1	2	3	4	5	6	7	8	9	10	11
b	c	c	b	b	b	c	c	c	b	a
a	d	d	a	a	a	d	d	d	a	b
c	e	e	c	c	c	e	e	e	c	c
d	a	a	d	d	d	a	a	a	d	d
e	b	b	e	e	e	b	b	b	e	e

Example 4

1	2	3	4	5	6	7	8	9	10	11
c	b	b	b	b	a	a	a	a	a	b
d	c	c	c	c	c	c	c	c	b	a
e	d	d	d	d	d	d	d	d	c	c
a	e	e	e	e	e	e	e	e	d	d
b	a	a	a	a	b	b	b	b	e	e

Example 5

In both examples 4 and 5, the preference scores are:

a	b	c	d	e
24	23	32	21	10

The top, *a*, again receives its minimum score, and *c* its maximum; *b* receives its lowest possible score, given that *a* receives its minimum. It will be noticed that the two examples are significantly different. In example 4, although *a* is the top, it is the first choice of only one voter, while *b* and *c* each miss being the first choice of a majority by only one voter. In example 5, although *c* has the highest preference score by a significant margin, it is the first choice of only one voter, while *a* and *b* are now both in the position of missing by a single voter being the first choice of a majority. The two examples agree, however, not only on which majority preferences hold, but on the numbers making up the majorities: in both of them, just six voters prefer *a* to any one other outcome, and just six prefer *b* to any one of *c*, *d*, and *e*, whereas every voter prefers *c* to *d*, *c* to *e*, and *d* to *e*. This illustrates how very far the majority preference relations and the preference scores, even taken together, are from determining uniquely the pattern of preference scales. In particular, it illustrates how poor a guide is the distribution of first choices to the voters' preferences as a whole.

A similar pair of examples will show that even *d* may obtain the highest preference score of any outcome.

1	2	3	4	5	6	7	8	9	10	11
b	b	c	c	c	c	c	a	b	b	b
d	d	d	d	d	a	a	b	a	a	a
e	e	e	e	e	d	d	d	d	d	c
a	a	a	a	a	e	e	e	e	e	d
c	c	b	b	b	b	b	c	c	c	e

Example 6

1	2	3	4	5	6	7	8	9	10	11
d	d	d	d	d	a	a	a	a	a	a
e	e	e	e	e	c	c	c	c	c	b
b	b	b	b	b	b	b	b	b	b	c
c	c	c	c	c	d	d	d	d	d	d
a	a	a	a	a	e	e	e	e	e	e

Example 7

In both examples the preference scores are:

a	b	c	d	e
24	23	22	26	15

In example 6, d, which has the highest preference score, is not the first choice of a single voter; in example 7, it only just misses being the first choice of a majority.

If six voters rank the outcomes in the order $abcde$ and the remaining five in the order $dbcea$, we obtain an example in which a has its minimum preference score of 24, d its maximum of 26 and b the highest preference score of 33. A slight modification yields another example in which b obtains the highest preference score, and d still obtains one higher than a:

1	2	3	4	5	6	7	8	9	10	11
a	a	a	a	a	b	d	d	d	d	d
b	b	b	b	b	c	a	b	b	b	b
c	c	c	c	c	e	b	c	c	c	c
d	d	d	d	d	a	c	e	e	e	e
e	e	e	e	e	d	e	a	a	a	a

Example 8

In this example the preference scores are:

a	b	c	d	e
24	33	22	25	6

It is indeed unlikely in practice that preferences will be distributed as regularly as in some of the foregoing examples. It is nevertheless clear that the margin between the minimum preference score of the top of a set of outcomes and the maximum preference scores of outcomes lower than it in the R_{maj} ordering is sufficiently wide that it will quite frequently happen that principle (13) will rule out, as not being a fair outcome, that which principle (4) selects as the only fair one: the choice between these principles is of genuine practical significance. This fact may be regarded as adequately established by consideration of cases subject to the restrictions embodied in assumptions (i) to (iii), especially as lifting the restrictions makes only a small difference. Since, however, it will prove of importance to us later to know the exact position, the more general case is discussed in the appendix to this chapter.

Taken as a criterion for the fairest outcome, therefore, preference scores cannot be relied on to yield the same result as even the most modest of the criteria based on majority preferences. If preference scores are accepted as supplying the leading criterion, in accordance with principle (13), they will usually select a unique outcome; sometimes, however, two or more outcomes may tie in having the highest preference score. In such a case, it would be senseless to resort to restricted preference scores, i.e. to reiterate the criterion by calculating new preference scores in terms of the scales of preference between those outcomes having the highest overall preference scores. The intuitive idea underlying preference scores is that, the more outcomes are taken into account, the more accurately a voter's preference scale reflects the relative weights of his preferences. Rather, even an adherent of the preference score criterion ought at this point to appeal to majority preferences, adopting as his overall principle:

(15) no outcome can be fair unless it is a top of the set of outcomes having the highest preference score.

Principle (15) might indeed clash with principle (6). It is easy to construct an example in which a and b tie in having the highest preference score, but the R_{maj} diagram is shown in diagram 7.1.

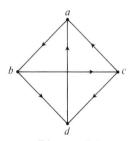

Diagram 7.1

Since b and c have the majority number 2, while a and d each have the majority number 1, principle (6) would rule out a as unfair, while principle (15) selects a as the fairest because $aP_{maj}b$. This divergence is unlikely to trouble anyone to whom principle (15) appears reasonable.

Anyone seeking a criterion that will select a unique fairest outcome in almost every case must have recourse both to the

142   PREFERENCE SCORES

criterion of majority preference and to the preference score criterion: the question at issue is to which to give the priority. The question turns on whether it be thought more important to please as many people as possible or to please everyone collectively as much as possible. The latter is surely more reasonable. The rule to do as the majority wishes does not appear to have any better justification than as a rough-and-ready test for what will secure the maximum total satisfaction: to accord it greater importance is to fall victim to the mystique of the majority, which is only a superstition engendered by familiarity with the use in practice of majority procedures. We have seen in this chapter how inaccurate a test majority preferences may provide for which outcome would yield the maximum overall satisfaction. Failing as a criterion, they thus serve poorly as a test: a concern for justice in general, and for the rights of minorities in particular, must validate the preference score criterion. Many will remain unpersuaded of this. Nothing in what follows will depend upon an acceptance of it. The mere fact that many are imbued with the mystique of the majority bears on what voting procedures they will be disposed to accept as fair. We shall therefore operate henceforward with both criteria in mind: taking principle (6) and principle (13) as of equal validity, we shall consider various procedures in the light of them.[2]

[2] Various as the principles for determining a fair outcome reviewed in Chapters 6 and 7 have been, they do not exhaust all those that have been proposed. The following example was suggested to me, by a political scientist interested in the theory of voting, as showing Arrow's principle of independence of irrelevant alternatives to have greater intuitive merit than I am disposed to accord it.

1	2	3	4	5	6	7
d	a	b	d	a	b	d
a	b	c	a	b	c	a
b	c	d	b	c	d	b
c	d	a	c	d	a	c

The majority numbers and preference scores are as follows:

a	b	c	d
2	2	1	1
12	13	6	11

There are two cyclic triads: a, b, d, and a, c, d. By principle (13), b is the only fair outcome, as having the highest preference score; by principle (7), a is the only fair outcome, since a majority prefer it to b, the only other outcome to have a majority score of 2. The objection made by the proposer of this example is that c is genuinely an irrelevant alternative, since every voter prefers b to it, and ought therefore to be eliminated at the outset: when c is eliminated, we are left with a cyclic triad; if preference scores are calculated over these three outcomes, d obtains the highest (8), and b the lowest (6).

A preference table like this might occur if b and c were very similar proposals, and b had an obvious advantage over c. The rule that is in effect being proposed is that, before applying any criterion for a fair outcome, one should first eliminate from consideration (and from the calculation of preference scores and majority numbers) any outcome y such that, for some other outcome x, every voter thinks x at least as good as y and some prefer x to y. Adoption of this rule would of course yield a variant on all the principles considered in this chapter and the preceding one.

Now, of course, there can be no proof that any of these principles is sounder than the others. The principal difficulty of estimating the merits of rival voting procedures lies in the fact that there is no unique criterion for a fair outcome that must command universal assent. Nevertheless I do not think that any strong argument can be made for applying the proposed rule. Of course, an outcome eliminated under that rule, such as c in the above example, could not possibly be fair; but that does not show it wrong to take it into account in calculating the preference scores of other outcomes. The rationale for using preference scores at all is that they give an indication, though of necessity an imperfect one, of the strengths of voters' preferences; this indication becomes more accurate the more outcomes are taken into account. Even if, in the example, b and c are highly similar proposals, it says something about the strength of voter 2's preference for a over d that he would rather have even c than d. Although c could not conceivably be a candidate for being considered a fair outcome, there is no reason to ignore the information yielded by its inclusion in the preference scales about the relative strengths of the voters' preferences between the other outcomes.

Appendix to Chapter 7

If we drop assumption (ii), that all preference scales are strong, we may suppose, for any one possible outcome x, that there are just q_1 outcomes y for which $xP_{\text{maj}}y$, and just q_2 outcomes w distinct from x for which $xI_{\text{maj}}w$. With $2m + 1$ voters, x's minimum possible preference score will then be

$$(m + 1)q_1 + \tfrac{1}{2}(m + 1)q_2.$$

Since x's majority score is $q_1 + \tfrac{1}{2}q_2$, the formula given for an outcome's minimum preference score under assumptions (i) to (iii), namely

$$(m + 1)q$$

remains valid, provided that q is taken as x's majority *score* (not its majority number). This minimum score will be obtained when, for q_1 outcomes y, $m + 1$ voters prefer x to y, and m prefer y to x, for q_2 outcomes w, $m + 1$ voters are indifferent between x and w, and m prefer w to x, and, for the remaining $r - q_1 - q_2 - 1$ outcomes z, every voter prefers z to x. Conversely, x will attain its maximum preference score when, for q_1 outcomes y, every voter prefers x to y, for q_2 outcomes w, m voters prefer x to w and $m + 1$ are indifferent between them, and, for the remaining $r - q_1 - q_2 - 1$ outcomes z, $m + 1$ prefer z to x and m prefer x to z. The difference between x's maximum and minimum possible preference scores is therefore

$$mq_1 + \tfrac{1}{2}mq_2 + \tfrac{1}{2}mq_2 + m(r - q_1 - q_2 - 1),$$

which is simply $m(r - 1)$ as before. Hence the formulae for the maximum and minimum preference scores of an outcome x with majority score q remain valid, namely

minimum: $(m + 1)q$
maximum: $(m + 1)q + m(r - 1)$.

When some preference scales are weak, the lowest possible positive majority score is $\tfrac{1}{2}$; if any outcome obtains a majority score of $\tfrac{1}{2}$, then none can obtain one of 0. With $2m + 1$ voters, if x has the majority score $\frac{1}{2}$, its maximum possible preference score is

$$\tfrac{1}{2}(m + 1) + m(r - 1).$$

If there is an outcome a with a majority score of $r - 1$, it will be the sole top, and its minimum possible preference score will be

$$(m + 1)(r - 1).$$

The condition for x to be capable of having a higher preference score than a is therefore:

$$\tfrac{1}{2}(m + 1) + m(r - 1) > (m + 1)(r - 1)$$

which is equivalent to:

(B) $m + 3 > 2r$.

Hence, if there are three possible outcomes, this can happen if there are nine or more voters; if there are four outcomes, there must be thirteen or more voters; in general, with r outcomes, there must be at least $4r - 3$ voters. The case when there are nine voters and three outcomes is illustrated by the example:

```
   1    2    3    4    5    6    7    8    9
   a    a    a    a    a    b    b    b
   b                                  c    c    c    b c
   c    b c  b c  b c  b c  a    a    a    a
```

Example 9

The preference scores are:

$$\begin{array}{ccc} a & b & c \\ 10 & 10\tfrac{1}{2} & 6\tfrac{1}{2} \end{array}$$

Let us now drop assumption (iii), that the number n of voters is odd, and suppose that $n = 2m$. A bare majority will now consist of m voters, including the chairman, while the largest possible minority is still of m voters. When all preference scales are strong, the minimum possible preference score of an outcome x with majority score q is therefore mq, while the difference between its maximum and minimum scores is still $m(r - 1)$: the formulae now become

minimum: mq
maximum: $m(q + r - 1)$.

The majority score of the ith outcome, a_i, in the P_{maj} ordering is $r - i$, so that its maximum preference score is $m(2r - i - 1)$. The minimum preference score of the top, a_1, is $m(r - 1)$. The condition for a_i to be capable of having a higher preference score than a_1 is therefore

$$m(2r - i - 1) > m(r - 1),$$

which is equivalent to

(C) $r > i$.

Hence it will always be impossible, as before, for the lowest outcome a_r in the P_{maj} ordering to have a higher preference score than a_1, but it will always be possible for any other outcome to do so, whatever the number of voters. By the same reasoning as before, the above formulae remain valid, with $2m$ voters, when there are weak preference scales, so long as R_{maj} is transitive. If a has a majority score of $r - 1$, and x one of $\frac{1}{2}$, x's maximum preference score will be $m(r - \frac{1}{2})$, while a's minimum score is $m(r - 1)$: the condition for x to be capable of having a higher preference score than a is thus

$$m(r - \tfrac{1}{2}) > m(r - 1)$$

which of course always holds. The upshot is that, when the number of voters is even, and R_{maj} is transitive, any outcome may have the highest preference score provided that its majority score is greater than 0.

If, now, we drop assumption (i), that R_{maj} is transitive, the situation becomes more complicated. When there are cyclic majorities, the range of possible variation in preference score is slightly diminished. If an outcome belongs to a cyclic triad, it cannot attain either the maximum or minimum preference score, given by the foregoing formulae, relatively to its majority score. Suppose that $xP_{\text{maj}}y$, $yP_{\text{maj}}z$, and $zP_{\text{maj}}x$. For x to attain its maximum preference score, every voter would have to prefer it to y. In that case, any voter who preferred y to z would also prefer x to z; and so, since by hypothesis a majority prefer y to z, that same majority would prefer x to z, which is contrary to the assumption that $zP_{\text{maj}}x$.

A voter who preferred y to z and was indifferent between x and y would also prefer x to z. The reasoning shows, therefore, that the least one voter must actually prefer y to x: in fact, this must be a voter who prefers y to z and z to x. It is not necessary, however, that

APPENDIX TO CHAPTER 7

this be true of more than one voter. If, of $2m + 1$ voters, one ranks these three outcomes in the order yzx, while m voters rank them in the order xyz, and m rank them in the order zxy, the required majority preferences will hold. Hence, if this is the only cyclic triad to which x belongs, its greatest possible preference score will be diminished by one; and thus, if its majority score is q, and there are $2m + 1$ voters, its highest possible preference score will be

$(m + 1)q + m(r - 1) - 1$.

It is not necessary to assume strong preference scales to reach this result: the same conclusion follows, by exactly similar reasoning, whenever $xR_{\text{maj}}y$, $yR_{\text{maj}}z$, but not $xR_{\text{maj}}z$. Likewise, when there are $2m$ voters, x's highest possible preference score will, under the same assumptions, be

$m(q + r - 1) - 1$.

In just the same way, x cannot have a preference score as low as the minimum consistent with its majority score q. Suppose again that $xP_{\text{maj}}y$, $yP_{\text{maj}}z$, and $zP_{\text{maj}}x$. For x to obtain its minimum preference score, every voter would have to prefer z to x. In that case, however, any voter who preferred y to z would also prefer y to x, contrary to the assumption that $xP_{\text{maj}}y$. As before, there must be at least one voter who actually prefers x to z, but it is not necessary that there be more than one: the required majority preferences will hold if one voter ranks these three outcomes in the order xyz, and m each in the orders yzx and zxy. Hence, if this is the only cyclic triad to which x belongs, its lowest possible preference score will be increased by one. If there are $2m + 1$ voters, its lowest possible score will therefore be

$(m + 1)q + 1$;

if there are $2m$ voters, it will be

$mq + 1$.

As before, the same holds good whenever $xR_{\text{maj}}y$, $yR_{\text{maj}}z$, but not $xR_{\text{maj}}z$.

It should be noted that it follows from the foregoing discussion that, when x, y, and z form a cyclic triad, in that cyclic order, then, if m is greater than 1, it will be possible for x to have its highest possible preference score and y its lowest, but not for x to have its highest and

z its lowest. For x to have its highest possible score, there must be no more than one voter who ranks the three outcomes in the order yzx. The same condition holds for y to have its lowest possible score: but, for z to have its lowest possible score, there must be m voters ranking them in the order yzx. Thus, if a member of cyclic triad has its highest possible score, its immediate successor in the cyclic order may have its lowest score, but its immediate predecessor cannot.

An outcome may belong to two or more cyclic triads, as in diagram 7A.1.

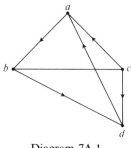

Diagram 7A.1

The number r of outcomes is 4. The values of q, i.e. the majority scores, are:

a	b	c	d
1	2	2	1

There are two cyclic triads (diagrams 7A.2 and 7A.3).

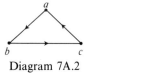

Diagram 7A.2   Diagram 7A.3

In both triads, a's immediate successor in the cyclic order is b. The only limitation on a's highest possible preference score is therefore that at least one voter must prefer b to a, so that, if there are $2m + 1$ voters, a's highest possible score is $(m + 1) + 3m - 1 = 4m$ points. In one triad, a's immediate predecessor is c, in the other it is d: hence there must be at least one voter who prefers a to c and at least one who prefers a to d. Accordingly, a's lowest possible preference score is $(m + 1) + 2 = m + 3$ points. By similar reasoning, we obtain the table:

	a	b	c	d
lowest possible score	$m + 3$	$2m + 3$	$2m + 3$	$m + 2$
highest possible score	$4m$	$5m$	$5m + 1$	$4m$

There are restrictions on possible combinations: if a has its highest possible preference score, and there are more than three voters, then b can have its lowest score, but neither c nor d can do so.

Suppose that there are five voters ($m = 2$), and that the R_{maj} relations are as in diagram 7A.1. The highest and lowest possible preference scores are:

	a	b	c	d
lowest	5	7	7	4
highest	8	10	11	8

When c has its highest possible score, b cannot have its lowest, but must have a lower score than c, as in the example:

1	2	3	4	5
a	b	b	c	c
b	c	c	d	d
c	d	d	a	a
d	a	a	b	b

Example 1

Here the preference scores are:

a	b	c	d
5	8	11	6

Principle (6) demands that, when the R_{maj} diagram is 7A.1, b and c be considered the only possible fair outcomes; principle (7) selects b. When there are only five voters, neither a nor d can have a preference score higher than any other outcome, since neither can attain a score higher than 8, and either b or c must have a score of at least 8. With seven voters, the highest and lowest possible preference scores are:

	a	b	c	d
lowest	6	9	9	5
highest	12	15	16	12

In this case, either a or d can have the highest score. An example in which a has the highest score is:

1	2	3	4	5	6	7
a	a	a	b	c	c	d
b	b	b	c	d	d	c
c	d	d	d	a	a	a
d	c	c	a	b	b	b

Example 2

The preference scores are:

a	b	c	d
12	9	11	10

One in which d has the highest score is:

1	2	3	4	5	6	7
a	b	b	b	d	d	d
b	c	c	c	a	a	c
c	d	d	d	c	c	a
d	a	a	a	b	b	b

Example 3

In this case the preference scores are:

a	b	c	d
8	11	11	12

Thus, when principle (5) fails to give a decision, principle (13) may flout even principle (6).

Principle (13) can also run counter to principle (6) when the latter principle selects a unique outcome, as when the R_{maj} relations are as in diagram 7A.4 (the same as diagram 6.5).

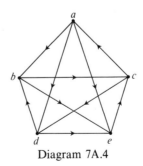

Diagram 7A.4

APPENDIX TO CHAPTER 7

Here the majority scores are:

a	b	c	d	e
3	2	2	2	1

so that, by principle (6), a is the only fair outcome. There are three cyclic triads, diagrams 7A.5, 7A.6, and 7A.7,

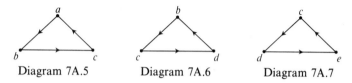

Diagram 7A.5   Diagram 7A.6   Diagram 7A.7

so that, with $2m + 1$ voters, the preference scores range between:

	a	b	c	d	e
lowest	$3m + 4$	$2m + 4$	$2m + 4$	$2m + 3$	$m + 2$
highest	$7m + 2$	$6m + 1$	$6m$	$6m$	$5m$

When there are five voters ($m = 2$), these become:

	a	b	c	d	e
lowest	10	8	8	7	4
highest	16	13	12	12	10

An example in which b has the highest preference score is given by:

1	2	3	4	5
a	b	b	c	d
d	c	e	a	a
b	e	c	d	b
e	d	a	b	e
c	a	d	e	c

Example 4

Here the preference scores are:

a	b	c	d	e
11	13	9	10	7

8
The Complete List Mechanism

Having studied the criteria that may be used to judge, from the voters' preference scales, which of several possible outcomes would be the fairest, we can now approach the question which is the best voting procedure to employ. It proves to be possible to answer half of this question with fair certainty in advance of the other half. A distinction was made in Chapter 1 between two aspects of any voting procedure: the voting mechanism and the method of assessment. The voting mechanism concerns what the voters are required to do: how many ballots there will be and what the voters have to write on their ballot papers. The method of assessment concerns what the tellers have to do: how, from the ballot papers returned by the voters, the successful outcome is to be determined. It is possible to say what, in general, must be the best possible voting mechanism before deciding on the best method of assessment.

We have seen in the previous two chapters that any preference any voter may feel for any one outcome over any other may be relevant to determining which is the fairest outcome. It follows that, in order to have a chance of being better than other procedures at producing the fairest outcome, a voting procedure must give each voter the opportunity to express any preference that he may feel. This puts a lower bound upon the number of distinct voting strategies that the procedure should allow any voter to adopt: they must be at least as many as the distinct possible strong preference scales that he may have. If there are fewer possible strategies than possible strong preference scales, there must be distinct preference scales which would elicit from a voter just the same votes in all ballots, even when he knows the voting intentions of all the other voters. This will mean, in turn, that there are certain preferences which the voters are unable to express by means of their votes, and hence to which the voting procedure is incapable of being responsive. For instance, a knock-out procedure with r possible outcomes will allow each voter a choice between only 2^{r-1} strategies, according to the way he

THE COMPLETE LIST MECHANISM

decides to vote in each of the $r - 1$ possible ballots, whereas he may have any one of $r!$ different strong preference scales (where $r!$ is the product of all the whole numbers from 2 to r). Thus, when $r = 3$, the knock-out procedure affords each voter a choice between four possible strategies, while there are six possible strong preference scales. If a is taken first, two voters, both of whom know that $bP_{maj}c$, and whose preference scales are bca and bac respectively, will then both vote in the same way, namely against a on the first ballot and for b on the second. The voting procedure thus fails to distinguish between these two preference scales, except in so far as it leaves it open for a voter with the scale bac, who does not know whether or not $bP_{maj}c$, to vote for a on the first ballot and for b on the second, in which case it fails to distinguish him from a voter with the scale abc.

It is a demerit in a voting procedure that it should afford to the voters too restricted a choice of strategies: it is also a demerit that it should afford them too wide a choice. In certain cases, an excessively wide choice is harmless. These occur when some strategies are superfluous, and also when some are equivalent. A *superfluous* voting strategy is one which is in principle open to the voters, but which they will never adopt, because it is inadmissible under every preference scale save that involving complete indifference between all the outcomes. The amendment procedure provides an example of a superfluous strategy: for instance, when a is the residual outcome, to vote on the first ballot to eliminate c, and, on the second ballot, for a if c has been eliminated and for c if b has. For this strategy to be admissible for a voter i, it must be the case that cR_iaR_ib, in view of the voting intentions on the second ballot which it comprises. In this case, however, if voter i actually preferred c to a or a to b, it would not be admissible for him to vote on the first ballot to eliminate c: it thus follows that the strategy can be admissible only for a voter who is indifferent between all three outcomes. It would make no effective difference to any voting procedure if a way were found of modifying it so as to make some superfluous strategy unavailable.

Two voting strategies may be called *equivalent* if, in every contingency, each produces the same outcome as the other. The existence of distinct equivalent strategies points only to a certain redundancy in the voting procedure, and does not constitute a serious defect in it. What is a serious demerit is the existence of too many non-equivalent, non-superfluous strategies. If, given his preference scale, a voter has two or more non-equivalent admissible strategies open to him, the choice between them will depend upon strategic considerations, that is, upon his assessment of the probabilities of the various possible contingencies. When there are more non-equivalent, non-superfluous strategies than strong preference scales, this is certain to happen for some possible strong scales: the greater the excess of strategies over preference scales, the more often it will happen. To the extent that it happens, the outcome of the procedure will be random. At least, it will be random except when, in the terminology of Chapter 5, the procedure is ultimately determinate under all possible distributions of preferences, and the voters all in fact know each other's preference scales, know that they all know them, know that they all know that they all know them, and so on. When there is not such perfect information, or when there is, but the procedure is not ultimately determinate, some voters may guess rightly how the others are going to vote, and some may guess wrongly. The outcome will then depend upon whose guesses are right: it will therefore be to that degree random, and so will not depend solely upon the voters' preferences.

A voting procedure can respond directly only to the actual votes. Hence, if it is to be responsive to the preferences of the voters, the adoption of a particular voting strategy by any voter ought to indicate, with certainty or with high probability, what his preference scale is. The ideal would be that, to every strong preference scale, there should correspond a straightforward strategy. Two non-equivalent strategies cannot both be straightforward for the same strong preference scale; hence, in these ideal circumstances, each voter's preference scale would be uniquely determinable from the strategy he adopted (at least on the assumption that it was strong). If the ideal is unattainable, then, for each voting strategy, there ought to be only one strong preference scale that would give the voter a strong incentive to adopt that strategy if he did not know how the others were going to vote: the voter's strategy would then determine his preference scale with a high degree of probability. In ideal circumstances, then, there would be a one-to-one correspondence between possible voting strategies and possible strong preference scales. Even in non-ideal circumstances, each voting strategy would correspond, in the way indicated, to just one strong preference scale. By the argument of the preceding paragraph, however, it follows that there ought to be no more than one strategy corresponding in this way to a given strong preference scale, and hence that there should again be a one-to-one correspondence between them. For, if there were two non-equivalent strategies corresponding to the same preference scale, the voter's choice between them would, as before, depend only upon his estimate of the likelihood of the various possible contingencies; and the existence of such choices must impair the extent to which the outcome of the procedure reflects the preferences of the voters.

The number of distinct possible strong preference scales thus not only imposes a lower bound upon the number of voting strategies open under the best possible voting procedure, but also something like an upper bound. It is not an absolute upper bound, because the voting procedure may reasonably afford strategies which are optimal only for a voter with a weak preference scale, whereas, if there is a one-to-one correspondence between strong preference scales and voting strategies, a voter with a weak preference scale will have to choose between those strategies which are optimal for the strong scales between which his own scale is in an obvious sense intermediate. At any rate, it is clear that the number of distinct possible preference scales, strong or weak, imposes an absolute upper bound on the desirable number of possible voting strategies.

These general considerations prompt a conclusion that can equally be arrived at by more intuitive reflections. We wish the outcome of the voting procedure to depend as closely as possible upon the preferences of the voters. We therefore wish each voter's strategy to reveal his preference scale, and his preference scale to determine his strategy. The simplest and most natural method of doing this is to adopt a voting mechanism consisting of a single ballot in which each voter is required to write down all the outcomes in order. Such a mechanism guarantees him the opportunity to reveal all the preferences he may have between pairs of outcomes, and excludes his having to choose between distinct ways of casting his vote that do not correspond to any difference between possible preference scales. A voting mechanism of this kind may take one of two forms: it may require any voter to impose a strong (linear) ordering upon the outcomes, or it may permit him to bracket any two or more outcomes as equal. In the former case, it allows as many possible ways of voting as there are strong preference scales; in the latter case, it allows as many as there are preference scales together, strong or weak. We do not need at present to decide between these two forms. Under the former, a voting paper that does not include the name of every outcome must be treated as spoiled; under the latter, any outcomes not listed may be treated as bracketed equal and ranked below those whose names appear on the paper.

The mere adoption of such a voting mechanism will not, of course, guarantee that the order in which a voter lists the outcomes represents his actual order of preference. Whether it does or not, or, more realistically, how probable it will be that the two orders coincide, will depend upon the method of assessment. We shall have arrived at a satisfactory voting procedure if we can devise a method of assessment that will both render it probable that the voters will list the outcomes in order of preference and, given that they do, will usually produce the fairest outcome.

We need a name for the voting mechanism here advocated: let us call it the 'complete list' mechanism.

The adoption of the complete list mechanism in no way prejudges the method of assessment. This fact of itself supplies a further argument in favour of that mechanism. The argument rests on the possibility of adopting a method of assessment that mimics any one of a large range of voting procedures. For any such procedure, there can be only a slender basis for arguing in favour of it as against the method that consists in using the complete list mechanism and then applying a method of assessment corresponding to the given procedure. To illustrate this, consider the two types of symmetrical elimination procedures, with positive and negative voting, discussed in Chapter 5. Given the complete list mechanism, these procedures can be mimicked by adopting suitable methods of assessment. The assessment will then proceed in successive stages, corresponding to the successive ballots in the procedure being imitated. When the procedure with positive voting is being mimicked, that outcome will be eliminated at the first stage which stands at the head of the list on the fewest ballot papers. At any subsequent stage, the lists are considered as they would appear after deletion of the names of those outcomes which have already been eliminated: that one is now eliminated which stands at the head of the fewest lists after such deletion. The same method will be used when it is the procedure with negative voting that is to be mimicked, save that the outcome eliminated at any stage is that which most frequently stands at the bottom of a list (after the names of all previously eliminated outcomes have been deleted). If a tie occurs at any stage, that outcome will be eliminated, under either procedure, which, of those that are candidates for elimination, stands lowest on the chairman's list.

Of these two procedures using the complete list mechanism, and mimicking the two symmetrical elimination procedures with successive ballots, that corresponding to the procedure with positive voting is well known in its own right, under the name of the *alternative vote* procedure.

As we shall see, it would be untrue to say that it is a mere matter of convenience, not affecting the final outcome, whether either of the procedures with successive ballots be used or, instead, the corresponding procedure with the complete list mechanism. Nevertheless, there would not be a great difference; for this reason, there cannot be any very strong objection to the complete list mechanism on the part of anyone who would favour a procedure that can, in the manner illustrated, be mimicked by a suitable method of assessment applied to complete lists.

Are there voting procedures that cannot be mimicked in this way? At first glance, one may be inclined so to categorize all binary procedures. The reason for this is that it is not immediately obvious how, in the method of assessment that simulates a given binary procedure, every possible listing of the outcomes is to be interpreted. Suppose the binary procedure is the amendment procedure with a residual: how should the tellers interpret a ballot paper on which the outcomes are listed in the order abc? The ground of uncertainty is that a voter with the preference scale abc does not have a straightforward strategy: if he feels fairly sure that $bP_{maj}a$ but $aP_{maj}c$, he will prefer to vote on the first ballot to eliminate b. To argue in this manner is, however, to adopt a faulty way of looking at the matter. The question is not whether we can tell from a voter's preference scale how he would vote under the amendment procedure: it is whether we can code instructions for voting under that procedure by means of a list of outcomes. It might seem that we cannot do so unless bracketing is allowed, since there are eight possible strategies and only six linear orderings of three outcomes. This is not so, however, because two of the strategies are superfluous. No ballot requires the voter to vote directly between b and c: we can therefore lay down that a ballot paper on which b is listed higher than c instructs the tellers to treat the voter as voting on the first ballot to eliminate c, and conversely: this coding is extremely natural, since the first ballot under the amendment procedure is often described as 'voting on the amendment'. Likewise, if a voter lists *a* higher than *b*, he may be taken as instructing the tellers to treat him as voting for *a* on the second ballot if *c* was eliminated on the first, and so on. To each non-superfluous strategy there will then correspond one of the six possible listings of the outcomes without bracketing. Use of the complete list mechanism thus amounts to a means of ruling out the superfluous strategies as unavilable even in principle: with this exception, it constitutes an exact simulation of the amendment procedure.

Under this coding, a ballot paper on which the outcomes are listed in the order *abc* codes the instruction to vote on the first ballot to eliminate *c* and for *a* on the second ballot, whatever the result of the first. Someone who votes in this manner cannot be assumed to have the preference scale *abc*: he may well have the scale *acb*. He should resist any exhortation to list the outcomes on his ballot paper in his order of preference, and, in particular, any suggestion that he is being dishonest if he does not. He is not being asked what his preference scale is: he is being asked what instructions he wishes to give the tellers under a coding known to him and them. It is indeed true that the method of assessment corresponding to the amendment procedure does not enable us to determine a voter's preference scale with any high degree of probability, except when he has placed *a* between *b* and *c*: that is a feature of the procedure, not a reflection on the integrity of the voters.

So far from its being impossible to mimic the amendment procedure by the use of the complete list mechanism, then, it can be simulated *exactly*. The same applies, under some coding or other, to any voting procedure which affords no more non-superfluous, non-equivalent strategies than there are possible preference scales, strong or weak—though this observation offers no guarantee that the coding will not be highly conventional and unnatural. If there are fewer strategies than strong preference scales, then either some possible listings of outcomes will have to be prohibited, or certain listings must be treated as equivalent. Thus if, under the knock-out procedure with three possible outcomes and *a* first, the listing *abc* is interpreted as an instruction to vote for *a* on the first ballot and for *b* on the second ballot, if it is held, and the listing *bca* as one to vote against *a* on the first ballot and for *b* on the second ballot, if it is held, then either the listing *bac* must be disallowed, or it must be understood as equivalent to *abc*, or, by a different convention, to *bca*.

It might occur to the reader to propose a very different way of assessing the ballot papers returned under the complete list mechanism in a simulation of the knock-out procedure with *a* first. As before, the relative positions of *b* and *c* in a voter's listing will be taken as indicating his vote in the (simulated) second ballot; and, as before, the listing *abc* or *acb* will be taken as indicating a vote for *a* on the first ballot, and *bca* or *cba* a vote against *a*. Since, however, there is in fact only one ballot, the tellers can compute the result of the simulated second ballot in advance of determining that of the simulated first ballot. They can accordingly handle ballot papers with the listings *bac* and *cab* as follows. They first determine the result of the second ballot: if it goes in favour of *b*, they take any voter who returns the list *bac* as voting against *a* on the first ballot, and any who returns the list *cab* as voting for *a*; conversely if the second ballot goes in favour of *c*. If every voter lists the outcomes according to his true preference scale, the effect will be to produce the outcome 2-determined by the knock-out procedure with *a* first, namely that produced by every voter's adopting his unique 2-admissible strategy.

It might appear at first sight that we have achieved, by this modified method of assessment, a procedure affording a straightforward strategy to every voter, for it is certainly now straightforward for a voter with the preference scale *bac* or *cab* to list the outcomes in order of preference. This would be a mistake; for a voter with any other strong preference scale than these two no longer has a straightforward strategy, and cannot be counted on to vote 'sincerely'. A voter with the preference scale *abc* may admissibly return the list *acb*: for it may be that, if the simulated second ballot goes in favour of *b*, the simulated first ballot will go against *a*, but, if the simulated second ballot goes in favour of *c*, the simulated first one will go in favour of *a*. This method of assessment does *not*, therefore, exactly simulate the knock-out procedure as used when every voter knows the others' preference scales: it differs from it precisely in that a voter can affect the result of the simulated first ballot by manifesting an intention to vote in one or other way in the simulated second ballot. In effect, the modified method of assessment simulates, not the knock-out procedure, but the amendment procedure: by working out the result of the second ballot first, the tellers transform it into the first ballot under the amendment procedure; what had been the first ballot under the knock-out procedure now splits into the two distinct possible second ballots under the amendment procedure, according to the result of the ballot between b and c.

Looked at in this way, the previously suggested simulations of the two symmetrical elimination procedures are imperfect. Suppose that there are only three possible outcomes. Then, under either of the symmetrical procedures, there are twenty-four possible strategies: three ways of voting on the first ballot, and two ways of voting on each of the three possible second ballots. Of these, six are superfluous, namely the three committing the voter to vote on the second ballot for a against b, c against a, and b against c, and the three involving the converse cycle. None of the remaining eighteen strategies is superfluous, however: under either procedure, it is admissible for a voter with any strong preference scale to nominate any one of the three outcomes on the first ballot. There are only six strong orderings of three items, and seven more weak ones; it is therefore not possible to code instructions for each of the eighteen non-superfluous strategies by listing the outcomes, with or without bracketing. In fact, each voter must list them without bracketing if he is to give determinate instructions how he is to be taken as voting in each of the three possible second ballots; he has then no latitude to indicate how he wishes to vote on the first ballot. In simulating the procedure with positive voting, we took each voter as voting on the first ballot for the outcome heading his list; in simulating that with negative voting, we took him as voting on the first ballot for the elimination of that standing last on his list. In both cases the simulation was imperfect, since it might force a voter to choose between voting otherwise than he would wish on the first ballot and risking voting contrary to his true preference on the second ballot.

The defectiveness of the simulation is illustrated by the way we described the procedures. The alternative vote procedure simulates the symmetrical elimination procedure with positive voting. It is, however, usual to describe it by laying down that the assessment process terminates at any stage at which some outcome is found to have an absolute majority of first preferences among those not hitherto eliminated; as it was described above, on the other hand, it continues until every outcome but one has been eliminated. It is clear that the difference cannot affect the final outcome. If, at some stage, a has an absolute majority of first preferences, it will continue to do so as other outcomes are successively eliminated; the modification therefore only simplifies the work of the tellers. By contrast, to introduce an analogous rule into the elimination procedure, with its successive ballots, would modify that procedure in substance.

The reason for this is that, when there are successive ballots, the voters are under no constraint to vote in any ballot in accordance with their votes on previous ballots. Suppose that there are fifty-nine voters and four possible outcomes. Voter 2 has the preference scale *abcd*, and votes for *a* on the first ballot, which results in the following numbers of votes for the various outcomes:

a	*b*	*c*	*d*
14	18	13	14

As a result, *c* is eliminated. Voter 2 has formed the impression, we may suppose rightly, that $dP_{maj}a$. He is therefore anxious, above all, that *b* should not be eliminated on the second ballot, which might happen if not more than one of *c*'s supporters transferred his vote to *b* and the rest were evenly divided between *a* and *d*. To avert this calamity, voter 2 transfers his vote to *b* on the second ballot. As it happens, so far from being eliminated, *b* now obtains an absolute majority, since two of *c*'s supporters now vote for *a* and the rest for *b*, with the result:

a	*b*	*c*	*d*
15	30	—	14

If the absolute majority rule is in force, *b* now wins outright without any further ballot. If not, however, *d* is eliminated and there is a third ballot between *a* and *b*. Voter 2 transfers his vote back to *a*: if all of *d*'s supporters vote for *a*, *a* will win by 30 votes to 29. Thus, with successive ballots, the imposition of the absolute majority rule may, though rarely, affect the outcome, and will make a voting strategy such as that of voter 2 more dangerous.

Since the procedures using the complete list mechanism are not exact simulations of the two symmetrical elimination procedures, we cannot in this case argue in favour of that mechanism that its use would make no effective difference to the outcome or to the voters' choice of strategies. We may instead argue for it from the kind of difference that it would make. Someone who favours one or other elimination procedure presumably believes that it by and large produces a fair outcome. From the discussion of these procedures in Chapter 5, it is apparent that a successful choice of voting strategy may depend very delicately upon a correct estimate, not only of the other voters' preferences, but also, very often, of their voting intentions. It is improbable that all will estimate these correctly; false estimates will introduce virtually random perturbations in the working of the procedure. It follows that anyone who favours either procedure will almost certainly base his view that it will usually produce a fair outcome on the supposition that the voters are likely to vote naïvely in the following sense: that, under the procedure with positive voting, each voter will vote in any ballot for the outcome which, of those that remain live, stands highest on his preference scale; and that, under the procedure with negative voting, he will vote for the elimination of that which stands lowest on his scale.

If the supposition of naïve voting forms the basis for anyone's recommendation of either of these procedures, he must welcome any modification of them that reduces the opportunity for departing from a naïve voting strategy. That, however, is precisely the effect of adopting the complete list mechanism, just because it cuts down the number of possible strategies. Suppose that the elimination procedure with positive voting is employed, and that the voters' preference scales are as follows:

1	2	3	4	5	6	7	8	9	10	11
c	a	a	a	a	a	b	b	b	c	c
a	b	b	b	b	c	c	c	c	b	b
b	c	c	c	c	b	a	a	a	a	a

Example 1

The majority preferences are cyclic (diagram 8.1).

Diagram 8.1

If all but voter 2 vote naïvely, c will be at risk from voter 2 and b at acute risk. It he votes naïvely for a, b will be eliminated by voter 1's casting vote, and c will be the final outcome: if he votes for c, b will

THE COMPLETE LIST MECHANISM 163

again be eliminated; but, if he votes for *b*, *c* will be eliminated and when, in the final ballot, he transfers his vote back to *a*, *a* will be the final outcome. Under the alternative vote procedure, on the other hand, voter 2 would have no corresponding strategy open to him, since it involves his voting on the second ballot against the outcome for which he had voted on the first. He can still gain an advantage, if all the others vote naïvely, by departing from his naïve strategy of listing the outcomes in his true order of preference, but not such a substantial one: if he lists them in the order *bac*, *c* will be eliminated at the first stage and *b* will be successful at the second, whereas, if he had listed them *abc*, the final outcome would have been *c*.

The replacement of the elimination procedure with positive voting by its simulation, the alternative vote procedure, may deprive a voter of any chance of doing better for himself by not voting naïvely, as in the following example:

1	2	3	4	5	6	7	8	9	10	11
b	a	a	a	a	a	b	b	c	c	c
a	b	b	b	b	c	c	c	b	b	b
c	c	c	c	c	b	a	a	a	a	a

Example 2

Here *b* is top, the R_{maj} diagram being as in diagram 8.2.

Diagram 8.2

If all but voter 2 vote naïvely under the elimination procedure with positive voting, *b* will be at risk from voter 2 and *c* at acute risk. Hence, if he votes for *c* on the first ballot, *b* will be eliminated; when he switches to *a* on the second ballot, it will become the final outcome. If all the others vote naïvely under the alternative vote procedure, on the other hand, voter 2 can gain no advantage by listing the outcomes in any order than *abc*: if he lists them in the order *cab*, *b* will indeed be eliminated at the first stage, but *c* will then beat *a* at the second stage, whereas, if he votes naïvely, *b* will be the final outcome.

The alternative vote procedure thus deprives the voters of any equivalent of a type of strategy open to them under the elimination procedure with positive voting, that of voting for an outcome on one ballot and against it on a subsequent one. Similarly, when the elimination procedure with negative voting is replaced by the simulated version with the complete list mechanism, voters are deprived of the equivalent of any strategy that involves voting to eliminate an outcome x on one ballot and, if it is not eliminated, to eliminate some other outcome on the next ballot. The complete list mechanism will therefore discourage departure from a naïve strategy in three ways: it will deprive some voters of any strategy more advantageous to them than the naïve one; it will leave others with a strategy more advantageous than the naïve strategy, but less so than a strategy open to them under the procedure with successive ballots; and it will make any departure from a naïve strategy more risky. A naïve strategy, under the complete list mechanism, consists in writing down the outcomes in the voter's true order of preference. Since it is undeniably an objective of any good voting procedure to provide an incentive for the voters to reveal their true preferences, it cannot but be a merit in the complete list mechanism that it diminishes the motive for departing from a naïve strategy.

This conclusion is quite general. Either a voting procedure can be exactly simulated by applying a suitable method of assessment to the complete list mechanism, or it cannot. If it can, there can be no objection to that mechanism in favour of the given one on the ground that it will produce a less satisfactory outcome, since the outcome will be exactly the same. If it cannot, this must be because it allows either fewer non-equivalent, non-superfluous voting strategies than possible strong preference scales, as does the knock-out procedure, or more such strategies than possible scales, strong or weak, as do the two symmetrical elimination procedures. Any procedure that does the latter must give an avoidably great opportunity for strategic voting. This is very glaring in the elimination procedures. A voter's preference scale, if strong, uniquely determines and is determined by his voting intentions in all of the possible final ballots under either procedure; his latitude of choice in all the other ballots therefore represents a space within which he is wholly free to engage in strategic manœuvres. The opportunity for strategic voting will certainly be reduced by the adoption of the complete list mechanism, which allows no more distinct ways of voting than there are distinct preference scales.

THE COMPLETE LIST MECHANISM

Someone who favours a voting procedure requiring only a single ballot, in which the voters are not required to list all the possible outcomes, might object to the complete list mechanism on the score of severe inconvenience. The best known of such procedures is the relative majority procedure, under which each voter writes the name of a single outcome on his ballot paper, the successful outcome being that whose name appears on the greatest number of ballot papers. Under the negative version of this procedure, each voter is again asked to write the name of only one outcome on his ballot paper, and that outcome is declared successful which has been nominated by the fewest voters. There can, of course, be no difficulty in simulating such procedures by means of the complete list mechanism: the relative majority procedure can be simulated by declaring successful an outcome which is the first preference of more voters than any other, and its negative mirror image by declaring successful any that figures last on the lists of fewer voters than any other. It would be very natural for anyone who favoured either of these procedures to object that only an extensive waste of time could result from asking the voters to list all the outcomes in order, and then applying such a method of assessment, since no feature of a voter's list would count save, in the one case, which outcome he placed at the head of his list, and, in the other, which he ranked last.

Even to this objection, however, there is a compelling reply. It is that, unless the voters are required to list all the outcomes, any procedure which allows no possibility of more than a single ballot is subject to a grave disadvantage. Under either the relative majority procedure or its mirror image, if these are strictly understood as single-ballot procedures, it will be necessary, in case of a tie, to resort either to the casting vote of the chairman or to drawing lots. Because the possibility of complete symmetry can never be ruled out, every determinate procedure must provide for some such arbitrary method of resolving ties; but it is obviously desirable to restrict its use to a minimum. For this reason, even the most passionate supporter of the relative majority procedure must concede that, whenever the number of voters is sufficiently small to make a tie more than a negligible possibility, the procedure would be improved by providing for a further ballot in case of a tie. The most natural method of doing this, consistently with the spirit of the relative majority procedure, would be to eliminate all the outcomes other than those tying for the largest number of votes on the first ballot, and to hold a second ballot in which each voter could vote for just one of the outcomes so tying; if there was still a tie between some, but not all, of these outcomes, the others could be eliminated and a third ballot held, and so on. This modified relative majority procedure is obviously an improvement upon immediate resort, in case of a tie, to a casting vote; but it is no longer, strictly speaking, a single-ballot procedure.

As against this modified relative majority procedure, it is by no means any longer apparent that the complete list mechanism is more cumbersome in practice. It would be easy to employ a method of assessment that closely simulated the modified procedure. If, at the first stage, any outcome had a great number of first preferences than any other, it would be declared successful. If not, then, at the second stage, all the outcomes which, at the first stage, had fewer first preferences than some other would be eliminated, and the lists with these outcomes deleted would be compared: any outcome receiving more first preferences than any other on the lists so culled would be declared successful at the second stage, and so on. If preferred, some other method might be used to resolve ties arising at the first stage; so long as this method depended upon the ballot papers submitted by all the voters, this would correspond to some other way of taking second and possibly later ballots. Exactly similar considerations apply to the negative procedure which is the mirror image of the relative majority procedure. It is by no means evident that it is more trouble to the voters to write down the names of all the outcomes in order than to have to wait until the votes on the first ballot have been counted to see if a second ballot is to be held, and then perhaps to have to do the same thing for a second ballot.

There is therefore no voting procedure that could not just as well, and in some cases distinctly better, be replaced by one using the complete list mechanism and some suitable method of assessment. This conclusion is almost obvious: it could certainly have been arrived at without the detailed analysis given in this chapter. We are considering the preference scales of the voters to be the sole basis on which an outcome is to be judged fairer than other possible ones. We therefore want a voting procedure which will respond to the voters' preferences as sensitively as possible, and which will therefore respond as little as possible to anything else. This entails that every voter ought to be able, by the way he votes, to express all the preferences that he feels; it also entails that it should not be open to

THE COMPLETE LIST MECHANISM

him to choose between different ways of voting that may affect the outcome but do not reflect any feature of his preference scale, but only his estimate of the probable ways in which the others will cast their votes. All this has been illustrated in detail in this chapter; but many will find it evident without illustration. Now the simplest way of eliciting from each voter a vote that will reveal his preference scale is simply to ask him to record his preference scale; and the simplest way of ensuring that he has not available to him an excess of voting strategies over possible preference scales is to ask him to record nothing but his preference scale, and to hold no other ballot save that in which he does so. This is simply the complete list mechanism.

As already remarked, the mere adoption of the complete list mechanism will not guarantee that the voters actually list the outcomes in order of preference; if it is not in fact advantageous to them to do so, it is illegitimate to bring pressure to bear on them to do so. Now that we have determined what the voting mechanism ought to be, we shall have to select the best possible method of assessment; and one criterion for the best method is, plainly, that it should offer as strong an incentive as possible for the voters to vote sincerely in the sense of listing the outcomes in an order corresponding to their true preference scales.

9
The Alternative Vote and other Procedures

Provided that there are few enough possible outcomes—say, up to about eight or nine—to make it practically feasible, the best possible voting procedure will employ the complete list mechanism, with or without bracketing. We need to give the voters the opportunity to reveal their complete preference scales; we must avoid giving them a wider choice of strategy than this opportunity demands: the simplest way to achieve both ends is to ask them to list the outcomes in order of preference. That was the argument of the last chapter: we have now to decide on the best method of assessment.

The method of assessment must be simple enough to explain to the voters. With that proviso, it must satisfy two further requirements. When the voters vote sincerely, that is, when they list the outcomes in their true order of preference, it must, as far as the requirement of simplicity allows, produce the fairest outcome according to whatever criterion we favour. Secondly, it must provide as little incentive as possible for departing from a sincere voting strategy. The means of satisfying the first requirement lies to hand: we have simply to adopt a method of assessment in direct accord with our favoured criterion for the fairest outcome. Unless it should prove that such a method more grossly violates the second requirement than some quite different method which is still in reasonable accord with the first, there can be no ground for refusing to acknowledge it as the best. We shall indeed conclude that a method of assessment modelled on the criterion for the fairest outcome will come as close to satisfying the second requirement as any rival method, and is therefore to be adopted. We might accordingly proceed immediately to an investigation of opportunities for strategic voting under various procedures; but, in this chapter, we shall briefly pause to consider how far other procedures fall short of satisfying the first requirement.

We may legitimately confine ourselves to procedures employing the complete list mechanism. Given any procedure employing some other mechanism, we may take its simulation to be that procedure using the complete list mechanism and interpreting the voters as voting naïvely, on the assumption that they have listed the outcomes on their ballot papers in their true order of preference. For example, under the amendment procedure, where b is the original motion and c the amended one, a voter votes naïvely in the first ballot if he votes to eliminate c when he prefers b to c and to eliminate b when he prefers c to b. In the simulated procedure, each voter lists all three possible outcomes in order of preference, and the assessment proceeds in two stages: first, b is eliminated if a majority of voters have listed c higher than it, and conversely; secondly, a is declared the final outcome if a majority have listed it higher than the survivor of the first stage, while, if a majority have listed it lower, that survivor is declared successful. There will be two variants, according as bracketing is or is not allowed.

How often a given procedure will produce the fairest outcome is a statistical matter; and this introduces a considerable difficulty into the question. 'I am quite prepared to be told', wrote C. L. Dodgson (Lewis Carroll), 'with regard to the cases I have here proposed, as I have already been told with regard to others, "Oh, *that* is an extreme case: it could never really happen!" Now I have observed that this answer is always given instantly, with perfect confidence, and without any examination of the details of the proposed case. It must therefore rest on some general principle: the mental process being probably something like this—"I have formed a theory. This case contradicts my theory. *Therefore* this is an extreme case, and would never occur in practice."'[1] Dodgson here accurately characterized the irrational obstinacy that commonly prompts people to insist that a given method of assessment that they favour will so frequently produce the same outcome as one based on an entirely different principle that the cases in which it will fail to do so can be ignored. To counter it, one would need some estimate of the probability of such cases; but it is in making such an estimate that the difficulty lies.

Most collective decisions lie somewhere between two extreme

---

[1] C. L. Dodgson, *A Method of Taking Votes on more than two Issues*, §3: also reprinted in D. Black, *The Theory of Committees and Elections*, p. 230.

poles. At one pole, the decision affects only those participating in it and is a matter of taste, not judgement: the family going to the theatre was a pure example of this. At the other pole, all differences reflect divergent judgements. The members of an appointments committee may share agreed criteria for the ideal occupant of a post: they differ over which candidate is most likely to prove to satisfy those criteria. Whenever the decision to be taken will affect others than those engaged in making it, judgement plays an important part, as it also does whenever the choice depends upon estimating the future effects of the course of action taken; and most collective decisions have at least one of these features, even when they are not governed by judgements based on criteria agreed by all. When a decision is purely a matter of taste, preferences will be randomly distributed. We could therefore calculate the probability of any given type of distribution on the assumption that every particular distribution was as likely as every other; this would usually be enough to demonstrate that a given procedure would often fail to produce the fairest outcome even when all voted sincerely. Such calculations would be practically worthless, however, because very few collective decisions are pure matters of taste. To the extent that a voting process is a means of reconciling conflicting *judgements*, its purpose is to arrive at that judgement most likely to be correct, given the judgements of the individual voters. When judgement is involved, preferences will not be randomly distributed: the table of voters' preferences is likely to exhibit a good deal of regularity or pattern. It is true that, for this reason, those distributions in which one outcome is glaringly the fairest, and would probably succeed under almost any procedure, will be more frequent than if preferences were distributed quite randomly. It is also true, however, that distributions which will produce different outcomes under different procedures will be more frequent than if there were a random distribution. It is obvious, for example, that, if preferences are randomly distributed, that outcome which is ranked highest by the greatest number of voters is likely to have the highest preference score: there will be plenty of cases in which it does not, but there will be more in which it does. When judgement is involved, however, there can be no such presumption: it will quite frequently happen that an outcome supported by one body of opinion will be strongly opposed by a larger body, or that an outcome regarded as ideal by very few is nevertheless acceptable to almost all.

THE ALTERNATIVE VOTE AND OTHER PROCEDURES 171

For this reason, we can have no ground whatever to judge which types of distribution are likely and which unlikely. If we want to use a procedure that will usually produce an outcome satisfying some favoured criterion for being the fairest, we must adopt a method of assessment that accords with that criterion; it is futile to adopt some other method in the belief that cases in which it will produce the wrong outcome will be of negligible frequency, since there can be no rational basis for such a belief.

We need waste no time considering the simulated relative majority procedure, however modified to handle ties; it requires no demonstration that a procedure treating as decisive the fact that a larger number of voters rank a given outcome highest than so rank any other may often grossly violate principle (4) or principle (13). No body of people engaged in making decisions, and free to choose by what means they shall arrive at those decisions, has ever chosen to employ the relative majority procedure. That is reserved for elections in Britain, the United States, and some other countries, because the electors are not free to choose the method of election they are forced to employ, the choice being left to those who are elected by this method, and who may be afraid that they would not be elected by some other.

When all voters vote sincerely, the outcome under a simulated binary procedure will coincide with that under the actual binary procedure when all vote naïvely; we have already reviewed this in Chapter 5. If all preference scales are strong, and all vote sincerely, then, under simulation of the knock-out procedure with three possible outcomes and a taken first, a will be successful only when a majority of the voters rank it highest. This condition may obviously fail to hold even though a is top and has the highest preference score. For instance, of thirteen voters, six might rank a highest and the other seven second, giving it a preference score of 19 points, the remaining 20 points being divided between b and c, one of which would win. If b won, it might be that ten voters preferred a to it and nine preferred a to c: it could even be that all but one preferred a to b. Under the simulated amendment procedure, things are not quite so bad: if all preference scales are strong, and all vote sincerely, any outcome will be successful if it is top; but the residual outcome a will be successful whenever preferences are cyclic. With $2m + 1$ voters, this could happen when only one had the preference scale abc, while m had the scale bca and m the scale cab: a would then have a preference score of $m + 2$ points, b of $2m + 1$, and c of $3m$. For example, with thirteen voters, a would in such a case have a preference score of 8 points, b of 13, and c of 18.

The relative majority procedure can produce an outcome which is bottom in the sense that, for every other possible outcome y, $yP_{maj}x$. This cannot happen under the alternative vote procedure, which guarantees that the successful outcome will top the set of possible outcomes remaining live before the last stage of the assessment process, which occurs whenever some outcome is credited with an absolute majority of the votes. It may be, however, that there is only one other possible outcome remaining live after the last stage but one of the assessment. No more can be claimed for the procedure in this respect, therefore, than that it will never produce an outcome with the majority number 0.

The procedure is usually advocated for use when the numbers of voters and of possible outcomes are large: we may therefore reasonably consider such an example as the following.

1	2	3	4	5	6	7	8	9	10	11	12	13	14	15	16	17
a	a	a	b	b	b	b	c	c	c	c	d	d	d	e	e	f
g	b	c	f	g	d	a	d	e	g	g	f	g	g	g	f	g
f	e	b	g	f	c	c	g	g	f	f	g	e	f	f	g	a
e	d	f	e	e	a	d	f	f	e	e	e	f	e	b	a	e
d	g	g	d	c	e	e	d	d	d	c	b	a	d	d	d	d
c	f	e	c	d	f	g	a	b	a	b	a	c	c	c	c	c
b	c	d	a	a	g	f	b	a	b	a	b	a	b	a	b	b

Example 1

The majority numbers and preference scores are:

a	b	c	d	e	f	g
1	0	2	3	4	5	6
38	40	48	51	56	59	65

If all vote sincerely, the stages of the assessment under the alternative vote procedure will be as follows:

a	b	c	d	e	f	g	votes redistributed to:
3	4	4	3	2	1	0	a (17)
4	4	4	3	2	—	—	a (16); b (15)
5	5	4	3	—	—	—	a (14); b (13); c (12)
6	6	5	—	—	—	—	a (8, 10, 12); b (9, 11)
9	8	—	—	—	—	—	

The final outcome is therefore a, the worst outcome but one by the standards of principle (6), and the worst of all by those of principle (13). At the first stage, both f and g were eliminated, since it is a waste of time to eliminate only an outcome to which no votes at all have been awarded; though g was in this position, it was top and had the highest preference score. With the exception of a, the outcomes were eliminated in precisely the order in which they are ranked by P_{maj}, which is transitive; the higher an outcome's majority number, the sooner it was eliminated. Since the alternative vote procedure is a majority procedure, the outcome here produced by sincere voting was highly unstable. If all twelve voters who preferred g to a had put g at the head of their lists, they would have given g an absolute majority outright; even those who rated a lowest or lowest but one were numerous enough to do this. Indeed, if just the four voters who ranked a lowest and g second had put g at the head of their lists, this would have been enough to keep g live through all the stages, and so give it eventual victory.

The alternative vote procedure indeed takes into account other preferences than the voters' first choices. It does so, however, in a haphazard fashion: for some voters, it takes account of their second, third, and fourth choices, for others only their first. Moreover, in contrast to preference scores, it assigns exactly the same weight to those second or third choices of which it does take account as to first choices. In the above example, a's eventual majority is composed of three first choices, one third choice, one fourth choice, one fifth choice, and three sixth choices: the 8 votes that b musters against it at the final stage are composed of four first choices, one fourth, one fifth, and two sixth choices. The fact that g is the second choice of eight voters and the third choice of five, on the other hand, counts for nothing, since it is immediately eliminated; the same applies to the fact that f is the second choice of three and the third choice of six. The second and later choices of voters whose first choice is the eventually successful outcome will never be taken into account. Advocates of the alternative vote procedure are disposed to comment that this is only fair, since those voters will be rewarded by the victory of the outcome of their first choice. The argument is quite fallacious: our concern is not to be fair to the *voters*, but to the *outcomes*. It is no excuse for having ignored the later choices of the supporters of the eventually successful outcome that those supporters can have no complaint: it may be

174   THE ALTERNATIVE VOTE AND OTHER PROCEDURES

precisely their second and third choices that show some other outcome to have a better claim to have been selected. The second and later choices of a voter who has the misfortune to rank first an outcome that remains live up to the final stage of the assessment, but is then defeated, are likewise neglected; and in this case there is not even a fallacious argument to be offered in justification.

Let us consider an example with as many as fifty-five voters: the figures standing at the head of each column here indicate how many voters share the cited preference scale.

4	3	2	4	4	4	4	4	4	4	2	1	1	1	3	2
a	a	a	b	b	b	b	b	b	c	c	c	d	e	e	f
c	c	b	a	a	a	d	e	a	a	d	e	e	f	f	a
b	b	d	d	e	f	f	a	a	d	b	a	f	a	c	d
d	f	e	e	d	e	d	e	d	f	d	a	c	a	c	d
e	e	f	f	f	d	e	c	f	e	e	b	c	b	b	b
f	d	c	c	c	c	c	f	b	f	b	f	b	d	d	e

Example 2

The majority numbers and preference scores are:

a	b	c	d	e	f
5	3	1	3	2	1
208	173	122	125	103	94

Given sincere voting, the stages of the assessment under the alternative vote procedure would run as follows:

a	b	c	d	e	f
9	24	14	1	2	5
9	24	14	—	3	5
9	24	14	—	—	8
14	24	17	—	—	—
—	26	29	—	—	—

Of the twenty-seven voters who rank a second, only three contribute to the 14 votes it is allotted at the fourth stage: the high ranking given it by supporters of b and c is ignored, because both outcomes survive until the final stage; the support for a, which is top, is largely masked by the erratic method of assessment.

The alternative vote procedure tends to favour an outcome that has both strong support and strong opposition, especially if the opposition comes mainly from those who favour some one other outcome. It will be unfavourable to an outcome which is ranked high, but not highest of all, by a great many voters: the extreme case would be that of an outcome that was ranked second by every voter, which would then be eliminated immediately, although, if there were four or five other possible outcomes, opinion about which was strongly divided, it would almost certainly have been the best outcome. This is only a general tendency, however. If it were a constant feature, it could be defended on the (surely mistaken) ground that being the first choice of any voter ought to count much more strongly in favour of an outcome than being his second choice. The degree to which this effect of the procedure is felt will depend, however, upon accidents of preference distribution. An outcome which is the second or third choice of many, but the first choice of comparatively few, may do quite well under the procedure if it is not among the first to be eliminated, but ranks second or third to those that are; it will do very badly if those who rank it second or third happen to favour outcomes that remain live until the end. As a method of arriving at decisions, therefore, it cannot be rationally defended, even on the basis of some false general principle.

It would be possible to employ a negative alternative vote procedure, under which outcomes were successively eliminated according to the number of voters ranking each outcome lowest, among those remaining live at any stage. This would be the simulation of the symmetrical elimination procedure with negative voting, and its defects are the mirror image of those of the alternative vote procedure, which therefore need not be spelled out in detail. It will deal harshly with controversial outcomes that attract both fervent support and fervent opposition; it will tend to favour outcomes to which few are strongly opposed, even when few are enthusiastically in their favour. Again, the extent to which this tendency is displayed will depend upon accidents of distribution.

Much better use can be made of the complete list mechanism than is made by the alternative vote procedure or its negative counterpart, and we have now to consider how. Advocates of the alternative vote for electoral purposes may retort to the argument of this chapter on the ground that the object of an election is not to choose the *best* candidate, but the most representative, and that therefore, in this case, we should be more concerned to be fair to the voters than to the candidates. We have some distance to go before we are ready to consider electoral procedures; so we must postpone an evaluation of this retort.

10
The Preference Score and Majority Number Procedures

Those who believe that the fairest outcome is that which gives the greatest overall satisfaction will accept preference scores as furnishing the leading criterion for a fair outcome. For them, there is one obvious method of assessment to suggest: to allot each possible outcome a score, calculated from the ballot papers on which the voters list the outcomes in order in the same manner that its preference score is calculated from the table of preference scales. Under the alternative vote procedure, positive or negative, it is highly inconvenient to allow voters to bracket outcomes; under that here envisaged, there is no such inconvenience, and we shall assume that it is allowed. Thus, for each ballot paper, the outcome standing lowest is awarded 0 points, that lowest but one 1 point, that lowest but two 2 points, and so on; each of a set of bracketed outcomes is awarded the average of the numbers of points that would be awarded to them if they were not bracketed. That obtaining the highest score will be declared successful; if x and y tie for first place, x will be declared successful if more voters rank it higher than y than rank y higher than it. We may call this the *preference score procedure*. A supporter of principle (13) is not bound to regard it as ideal, if it should prove to give exceptional incentives to voters to misrepresent their preference scales, a question here left for later examination; if it does not, he must see it as the best possible procedure.

Originally recommended by Jean-Charles de Borda for use in elections to the French Royal Academy of Sciences, the preference score procedure is in actual, though not widespread, use. As a method of choosing candidates for a post, it is sometimes accused of favouring mediocrity; but the accusation is false. A mediocre candidate is one on whom very few voters are keen, but to whom very few are strongly opposed; a controversial one is a candidate on whom many are keen but to whom many are opposed. The procedure favours neither. An utterly mediocre candidate would be one who was ranked in middle place by every voter, for instance fourth out of seven: he would then receive an average score, namely $\frac{1}{2}n(r-1)$ points, when there are n voters and r candidates, and could not win unless by some extraordinary chance every other candidate received exactly the same score. An utterly controversial candidate would be one who was ranked highest by just half the voters and lowest by the other half: he, too, would receive the average score, $\frac{1}{2}n(r-1)$ points. The procedure gives no advantage to the mediocre candidate, nor any to the controversial one: it measures how far the support for a candidate outweighs the opposition to him. In the extreme case, a candidate whose support marginally outweighs the opposition to him can win, if the support for and opposition to every other candidate but one are equally balanced: but it makes no difference whether the winning candidate in such a case is highly mediocre or highly controversial. Those who criticize the preference score procedure for giving an advantage to a mediocre candidate really mean to charge it with failing to give an advantage to a controversial one. To achieve this, it would be necessary to weight the contributions to a candidate's score from ballot papers on which he was ranked high, so that one ranked highest by half the voters and lowest by the other half would receive a better than average score. This is old ground: we have no reason to think that the fact that one voter regards a candidate as the worst should count against him less than the fact that another regards him as the best counts in his favour.

The preference score procedure, alone among those we have considered, is not in general a majority procedure. Suppose that there are five voters and five possible outcomes. Suppose that three of the voters wish to adopt strategies that will ensure the success of the outcome a. The best they can do is all to put a at the head of their lists, bracketing the other four equal, thus: $a(bcde)$. This is not sufficient to guarantee that a will win: if the other two voters list the outcomes in the order $b(cde)a$, the scores will be:

a	b	c	d	e
12	$12\frac{1}{2}$	$8\frac{1}{2}$	$8\frac{1}{2}$	$8\frac{1}{2}$

and b will win. If the majority had known what the minority intended to do, they could have foiled them by placing b lowest;

under a majority procedure, however, a majority must be able to enforce its collective will *whatever* the minority may choose to do. When there are only three voters, and when there are five voters and only three possible outcomes, the preference score procedure is a majority procedure; in all other cases, it is not.

If, among the members of a committee or other decision-making body, there are people who, imbued with the mystique of the majority, insist on majority preference as an overriding criterion of fairness, they will be unwilling to employ the preference score procedure, but will demand one that conforms at least to principle (5) whenever all vote sincerely. We have seen, however, that no refinement of that principle is likely to select a unique outcome in virtually all instances: it needs to be supplemented by preference scores as a subordinate criterion. For this reason, any rival to the preference score procedure must involve some composite method of assessment. On the face of it, it is easy to specify such a method. If the voters will be satisfied with a method conforming to principle (6), for example, then they may adopt what we may call the *majority number procedure*. The tellers will compute, from the voters' lists, the majority numbers of all the outcomes (taking the lists to represent the true preference scales). Having announced these, they will declare successful an outcome having a higher majority number than any other. If two or more outcomes tie as having the highest majority number, they will then compute and announce the preference scores of those outcomes, that one with the highest preference score being declared successful.

The difficulty of such a procedure lies in inducing the voters to work it exactly as described. It is not only essential that they agree in advance which is to be the overriding criterion: it is also essential that they permit the tellers to divulge no more than is necessary to determine the successful outcome. There is a strong tradition that the voters are entitled to be told, not merely the outcome of the voting process, but how well each possible outcome did. Now suppose that there are four possible outcomes, and the tellers announce that a and b each have majority number 2, while c and d each have majority number 1. There will then be strong pressure on them to disclose the actual P_{maj} relations. If it then emerges that $aP_{maj}b$, many voters will take this as implying that a is a fairer outcome than b: but it may prove that b has a higher preference score than a, and is hence declared successful under the agreed procedure. This will leave a large number of voters, perhaps a majority, aggrieved, thinking that the procedure to which they consented has worked unfairly. There will also be pressure on the tellers to announce the preference scores of c and d as well as those of a and b. If they yield to this pressure, and it proves that c had a higher preference score than any other possible outcome, the supporters of c will also feel aggrieved.

We come here to the heart of the difficulty of devising a satisfactory voting procedure. On the one hand, there is no single criterion which all are likely to acknowledge as selecting a fair outcome and which will almost always select a unique one. If the voters can be brought to accept the preference score criterion, that will yield a unique fairest outcome in the overwhelming majority of cases, and the difficulty will be obviated. They are, however, very likely to reject it in favour of some form of majority preference criterion. Since no one such criterion will yield a unique outcome in almost every case, a composite method is needed. The voters may be well aware in theory that rival criteria may clash, and for that reason lay down in advance which is to override which; but this theoretical awareness will not guard them from disgruntlement if they come to know that a clash has actually occurred in a specific case. It is even more important that the voters accept the procedure used as fair than that it actually be fair. When a procedure is used that does not allow the preference scales of the voters to be deduced from the course of the voting, no announcement of the results, however detailed, will reveal that the successful outcome was not in fact the fairest, by whichever criterion the fairest is to be judged. Even when the complete list mechanism is used, an announcement of the preference scores will not suffice to determine the R_{maj} diagram, and so no clash of criteria will be apparent. But, when a composite method of assessment is employed that appeals both to majority preferences and to preference scores, such a clash is very likely to come to light. No matter with what open eyes the voters have agreed in advance to a method that accords priority to one criterion over another, they will be unable to resist a feeling of chagrin when they discover that the outcome they favoured has been defeated, but would have won if the order of priority between criteria had been reversed. It is a gross defect in any voting procedure that it be liable to prompt such a feeling.

This can be avoided, under the majority number procedure, if the

180 PREFERENCE SCORE AND MAJORITY NUMBER PROCEDURES

tellers are allowed to announce no more than is necessary to determine the successful outcome: if they announce only the majority numbers, not the particular R_{maj} relations obtaining, and announce the preference scores only of the outcomes tying for having the highest majority number, but not of any others. Since this runs counter to the accepted practice of announcing the results in full detail, it is difficult to observe. The difficulty can be mitigated if the majority number procedure be replaced by what may be called the *persistent majority number procedure*, designed to conform, when all vote sincerely, to principle (7). Under this procedure, the tellers may announce all the R_{maj} relations, together with the majority numbers calculated from them. As before, if one outcome has a majority number higher than the rest, it is declared successful. If several tie as having the highest majority number, the rest are eliminated; second-stage majority numbers are now recalculated over just those outcomes that remain. This process is reiterated, if necessary, until either only one outcome remains and is declared successful, or no more can be eliminated: if more than one remains, the preference scores of those remaining are computed and announced, the outcome with the highest preference score being declared successful. In this way, an outcome can be successful only if it persistently has the highest majority number. This procedure will be greatly simplified if voters are *not* permitted to bracket outcomes equal on their lists, and we shall assume that this rule is adopted.

A clash of criteria will not be revealed under this procedure unless it becomes necessary to invoke preference scores, and the voters demand to be told the preference scores of all the outcomes, rather than only of those surviving the earlier stages of the assessment process. Such a clash will only rarely come to light. Suppose that there are r possible outcomes, of which r' tie as having the highest majority number. The second-stage majority numbers will sum to $\frac{1}{2}r'(r' - 1)$; they can therefore all be the same only when r' is odd. We may neglect the case in which $r' = r$, as when each of three possible outcomes has the majority number 1, or each of five has the majority number 2; preference scores will have to be invoked, but there can be no clash of criteria, since not a single outcome was eliminated. We can also neglect the case when $r' = r - 1$. In such a case, each of the r' outcomes must have the majority number $\frac{1}{2}r$, and the remaining one the majority number 0, as when, out of four outcomes, three have the majority number 2 and the fourth 0, or, out of six, five have the majority number 3 and the sixth 0. The second-stage majority numbers will all be $\frac{1}{2}r - 1$, so that preference scores will be invoked; but there is no danger that a clash will be revealed, even if the voters demand to hear the preference scores of all r outcomes, since an outcome with majority number 0 cannot have a preference score higher than any other. When $r' = 2$, preference scores will not be invoked; one of the two outcomes will have a second-stage majority number 1, and the other 0, which is just to say that one will stand in the relation P_{maj} to the other. A clash may therefore be revealed only when r' is greater than 2 and less than $r - 1$. This may happen when there are five outcomes, of which three have the majority number 3, one 1, and one 0: the first three must necessarily each have the second-stage majority number 1, so that preference scores will be invoked. It could then be found that the outcome with the original majority number 1 had the highest preference score, given more than five voters. The same applies when there are six outcomes, of which three have the majority number 4 and the other three the majority number 1, or of which three have the majority number 3 and the other three the majority number 2, and the second-stage majority numbers are all 1, as they may, but need not, be. It is thus possible for a clash between the preference score criterion and the majority preference criterion to come to light even under this procedure, although this will happen far more rarely than under the simple majority number procedure.

The majority number procedure is therefore to be avoided except by voters who are highly self-disciplined and appreciate the importance of knowing no more about how the voting has gone than they need to know; even the persistent majority number procedure will lead to resentment on the part of a section if such self-restraint is not exercised. It is easier to accept a decision that you deplore when you believe it to be an expression of the general will. In devising a voting procedure, one must bear in mind the existence of preference distributions that allow no determinate answer to the question what is the general will; having taken part in a decision arrived at by voting, on the other hand, one does better to remain unaware that the actual distribution is of this kind.

Plainly, only voters who are fairly sophisticated, that is, who are aware of the fundamental facts concerning the theory of voting, are going to contemplate the adoption of a composite procedure, appealing to the distinct criteria of majority numbers and preference scores. They might have been led to do so by a prior grasp of those fundamental facts, together with a disposition to give an overriding weight to the criterion of majority preference. Alternatively, they might have come to discover those fundamental facts for themselves. This could happen if, at some earlier stage, they had been persuaded to adopt the preference score procedure, but, on reflection, had come to realize that it did not always select an outcome which was top even when there was one; or if they had started by using a majority number procedure (or the simple criterion of being the unique top), with no provision for the case when two or more outcomes tied in having the highest majority number, and had then encountered just such a case. However it came about, by the time that a set of voters have seen the point of using a composite procedure, they will have come to grasp far more of the principles of voting theory than most people are aware of. It would be impossible to introduce such a composite procedure without explaining those principles: that is, without explaining both that there may be no top, so that some supplementary criterion such as preference scores may need to be invoked, and that, when there is a top, it may not have the highest preference score, so that one could not rely on preference scores alone if one thought majority preference of greater importance.

Could not voters who had achieved such a level of sophistication be trusted to accept the outcome selected by the procedure on which, with eyes open, they had agreed, even if all the facts known to the tellers were communicated to them? Perhaps they could: but they would have to be an exceptional body of people. It is one thing to be aware in theory of a disagreeable possibility: it is another to be able to resign oneself equably to it when an instance of it occurs in practice, and the result is contrary to one's own hopes and wishes. The likelihood is that, if the voters are of a normal temperament, then, however sophisticated they may be, awareness that, in a specific case, there has been a clash of criteria for the fairest outcome will arouse, on the part of those who are disappointed in the outcome of the voting procedure agreed on, resentment and a loss of faith in that procedure.

The difficulty is of course one that does not arise under most of the voting procedures in ordinary use: the method of assessment embodied in them is such that, from the 'results' as announced, it is impossible for anyone to determine either the majority numbers or the preference scores of the various possible outcomes. The voters must accept the procedure they use as fair if they are to continue to use it; and, if they accept it as fair, then even those disappointed by the outcome of a particular vote under that procedure will be reconciled to it by the belief that it was fairly arrived at and so is an expression of the general will. But they cannot know, in any particular case, that the outcome was in fact fair according to any one of the criteria for a fair outcome that were formulated in Chapters 6 and 7; for the data they are given will not allow them to apply those criteria.

The best and simplest solution of the problem for those who have decided to use the majority number procedure has already been explained: to impose a self-denying ordinance on the information to be divulged by the tellers to the voters, or even to be extracted by the tellers from the ballot papers, so that no one ever comes to know that an outcome having a majority number lower than some other obtained the highest preference score, or, at least, so that only the tellers do. If this rule is strictly followed, then it will never be known, in any specific case, that the criteria of preference scores and of majority preferences yielded distinct outcomes as the fairest; and the difficulty will be obviated with the least possible trouble.

As already remarked, however, this solution runs counter to the tradition that the tellers disclose the 'results', not just the outcome, where the 'results' are understood to include every fact of the kind on which the method of assessment depends; the voters need to be highly sophisticated to see the advantage of flouting this tradition in favour of the rule that only what was needed in order to decide the outcome should be disclosed. Moreover, even if they see the advantage of this in principle, not many people have sufficient self-discipline to refrain from seeking information because they see it to be information that it is better that they should not have. There is, nevertheless, an alternative solution to the difficulty; the rest of this chapter will be devoted to explaining it. The solution is complicated to explain. The complexity does not lie in what has to be conveyed to the voters, either about how they are to vote or even about the method of calculating the form in which the results will be announced. It lies, rather, in demonstrating why the method achieves what is intended, namely to secure exactly the same outcome as under the majority number procedure without giving the voters the means to determine exactly how it was arrived at, that is to say, the majority numbers and preference scores of the individual outcomes.

It needs to be emphasized that this method has a point only for a quite particular type of voting body: one composed of people sophisticated enough not only to perceive the advantage of the majority number procedure, but to acknowledge the importance of their remaining unaware, in any particular case, of a clash of criteria, who nevertheless lack confidence that they will be able to refrain from discovering that such a clash has occurred unless the 'results' of the voting are presented in such a way as to make such a discovery difficult or impossible. If the method were to gain any popularity, it might be adopted, simply as being well thought of, by bodies of voters who were less sophisticated, or more self-confident, than that; it will never be tried at all unless it is tried, in the first instance, by those having the particular combination of qualities here stated.

The method may be called the *composite score procedure*. The principle is to announce the results of the voting in the form of a single numerical score allotted to each possible outcome, that outcome attaining the highest score being declared successful. The manner of computing these composite scores must have two features:

(1) The successful outcome will always be the same as under the majority number procedure, namely one having as high a majority number as any other, and, of those satisfying this condition, having the highest preference score; and the voters will know that this is so.

(2) It will not, in general, be possible to deduce the majority number or preference score of an outcome from its composite score.

It is indeed possible to devise a method of calculating composite scores that satisfies both (1) and (2); but it is not altogether simple, and is best explained in stages. As a first step, let us ask for a method that satisfies (1), but not necessarily (2). It will then be simpler and more convenient not to allow the voters to bracket outcomes equal. To satisfy (1), the composite score u of any outcome x must have two components: a contribution due to x's majority number k, and another due to its preference score p. Clearly, u must be calculated as $f \cdot k + p$, where f is some fixed factor depending only on the number n of voters and the number r of possible outcomes; we have to determine the value of f so as to guarantee that, if y has a preference score p' and a majority number k' less than k, then its composite

PREFERENCE SCORE AND MAJORITY NUMBER PROCEDURES 185

score u' will be less than u, i.e. $fk' + p' < fk + p$. Assume, first, that the number n of voters is odd, say $n = 2m + 1$. Suppose, then, that x's preference score p is the smallest that it can have, consistently with its having the majority number k, and that y's preference score p' is the largest it can have, consistently with its having the majority number k'. By the formulae of Chapter 7, it follows that $p = (m + 1)k$, while $p' = (m + 1)k' + m(r - 1)$. We wish to ensure that

$$fk + (m + 1)k > fk' + (m + 1)k' + m(r - 1)$$

or, equivalently,

$$(f + m + 1)(k - k') > m(r - 1).$$

Since k is greater than k', $k - k' \geq 1$, so that we need only ensure that

$$f + m + 1 > m(r - 1),$$

i.e. that

$$f > m(r - 2) - 1.$$

This will obviously be achieved by setting $f = m(r - 2)$.

By similar reasoning, we find that, when the number of voters is even, so that $n = 2m$, f must be taken as $m(r - 2) + 1$ (so long as we continue to interpret the term 'majority' as comprising a set of half the voters including the chairman). We thus arrive at the following table of values for f:

	3	4	5	6	7	number r of outcomes
3	1	2	3	4	5	
4	3	5	7	9	11	
5	2	4	6	8	10	
6	4	7	10	13	16	
7	3	6	9	12	15	
8	5	9	13	17	21	
9	4	8	12	16	20	
number n of voters						

For illustration, we may take example 4 or 5 of Chapter 7, each of which yielded the same majority numbers and preference scores. With eleven voters and five outcomes, $f = 15$; the composite scores will then be calculated as follows:

186 PREFERENCE SCORE AND MAJORITY NUMBER PROCEDURES

	a	b	c	d	e
majority number (k)	4	3	2	1	0
preference score (p)	24	23	32	21	10
fk	60	45	30	15	0
composite score ($fk + p$)	84	68	62	36	10

This method of computing composite scores satisfies requirement (1) above, but flagrantly fails to satisfy requirement (2). We saw in Chapter 7 that, for an outcome with a given majority score, there is a range of variation within which its preference score can fall, and that there is a considerable overlap between the ranges of variation corresponding to different majority scores. For this reason, one usually cannot determine an outcome's majority score uniquely from its preference score. Since we are presently assuming that voters are not allowed to bracket outcomes equal, there is no distinction between an outcome's majority score and its majority number, as calculated from the voters' lists; but, precisely in order to satisfy requirement (1), we have made the ranges of variation in the composite scores of outcomes with different majority numbers exclusive. Thus the lowest possible composite score of an outcome with majority number 3 will be greater than the highest possible composite score of one with majority number 2; for just this very reason, it will be possible to recover an outcome's majority number, and hence its preference score, from its composite score. We may illustrate this for the case when there are nine voters and five possible outcomes, so that $f = 12$.

majority number k	4	3	2	1	0
fk	48	36	24	12	0
maximum preference score	36	31	26	21	16
minimum preference score	20	15	10	5	0
maximum composite score	84	67	50	33	16
minimum composite score	68	51	34	17	0

Given that an outcome has a preference score of 18, it may have a majority number of 1, 2, or 3; but if we know that its composite score is 42, we know that its majority number must be 2, and hence that its preference score is 18. In fact, since the minimum composite score of an outcome with majority number k is $(f + m + 1)k$ when there are $2m + 1$ voters, we can most easily find the majority number of an outcome with composite score u by dividing u by $f + m + 1$ and ignoring the remainder: in the above example $f + m + 1 = 17$. Since

$f = m(r-2), f+m+1$ can also be expressed as $m(r-1)+1$, which is also the number by which one must divide when there are $2m$ voters, since then the minimum composite score of an outcome with majority number k is mk, and $f = m(r-2)+1$.

It may seem at first sight impossible to modify the procedure so as to satisfy requirement (2) without violating requirement (1); but this is not so. The first step is to allow the voters to bracket outcomes equal. This will immediately force us to revise our estimate for the value, depending upon r and n, of the factor by which we have to multiply the majority number k of an outcome to determine its contribution to the composite score. The formulae for the minimum and maximum preference score of an outcome with majority *score* q remain exactly as before; but q, instead of always coinciding with k, may now vary between k and $\frac{1}{2}k$. The range of possible variation in the preference score of an outcome with given majority *number* is therefore now much greater. Where our new factor is g, this will have the effect that g will in general be greater than our previous factor f. At the same time, to satisfy requirement (2) as fully as possible, it is important to assume as low a value for g as is consistent with requirement (1). To achieve this, rather intricate calculations are necessary, and have been relegated to the appendix to this chapter. It turns out that there is no single formula for the value of g, either when the number of voters is odd or when it is even: we have to give separate formulae, according as $n \leqslant 4$ or $n > 4$, and according as $r < 6$ or $r \geqslant 6$. Since bracketing is allowed, a preference score need no longer be an integer, but may be a fraction with denominator 2; since k is always an integer, it therefore does no harm to allow g to be a fraction with denominator 2. When there are $2m+1$ voters, the formulae for g, whose justification will be found in the appendix, are as follows:

	$m = 1$	$m > 1$
$r < 6$	$r - 2\frac{1}{2}$	$1\frac{1}{2}m(r-2) - r + 2$
$r \geqslant 6$	$2r - 8\frac{1}{2}$	$1\frac{1}{2}m(r-2) + \frac{1}{2}r - 5\frac{1}{2}$

When there are $2m$ voters, g is to be found as follows:

	$m = 2$	$m > 2$
$r < 6$	$2r - 3\frac{1}{2}$	$1\frac{1}{2}(m-1)(r-2) + 1$
$r \geqslant 6$	$3r - 9\frac{1}{2}$	$1\frac{1}{2}m(r-2) - 3\frac{1}{2}$

These formulae yield the following table for g, which may be compared with the preceding table for f.

	3	4	5	6	7	number r of outcomes
3	$\frac{1}{2}$	$1\frac{1}{2}$	$2\frac{1}{2}$	$3\frac{1}{2}$	$5\frac{1}{2}$	
4	$2\frac{1}{2}$	$4\frac{1}{2}$	$6\frac{1}{2}$	$8\frac{1}{2}$	$11\frac{1}{2}$	
5	2	4	6	$9\frac{1}{2}$	13	
6	4	7	10	$14\frac{1}{2}$	19	
7	$3\frac{1}{2}$	7	$10\frac{1}{2}$	$15\frac{1}{2}$	$20\frac{1}{2}$	
8	$5\frac{1}{2}$	10	$14\frac{1}{2}$	$20\frac{1}{2}$	$26\frac{1}{2}$	
9	5	10	15	$21\frac{1}{2}$	28	
number n of voters						

If an outcome has majority number k, its highest possible majority score is k itself, so that its maximum possible preference score remains the same. When bracketing is allowed, the majority score q of an outcome with majority number k may be as little as $\frac{1}{2}k$: the minimum possible preference score of such an outcome is accordingly lowered. This gives us the following table for the ranges of variation in preference score and in composite score for an outcome with a given majority number when bracketing is allowed and, as in the previous table, there are nine voters and five possible outcomes, the value of g then being 15:

majority number (k)	4	3	2	1	0
gk	60	45	30	15	0
maximum preference score	36	31	26	21	16
minimum preference score	10	$7\frac{1}{2}$	5	$2\frac{1}{2}$	0
maximum composite score	96	76	56	36	16
minimum composite score	70	$52\frac{1}{2}$	35	$17\frac{1}{2}$	0

It will be seen that there is now a slight overlap between the ranges of variation in composite score for outcomes with different majority numbers. This does not show an error in the formulae for g: it remains the case that in no one instance can one outcome attain a higher composite score than another while having a lower majority number than it.

In order to comply with requirement (2) and prevent the voters from inferring the original majority numbers and preference scores of the outcomes, a further step must be taken. What the tellers will announce is not the raw composite score u of each outcome, as given by the formula $u = gk + p$, but its *adjusted* composite score v. This is

PREFERENCE SCORE AND MAJORITY NUMBER PROCEDURES 189

to be arrived at as follows. The sum of the majority numbers of the outcomes may vary between $\frac{1}{2}r(r-1)$ and $r(r-1)$. The sum of their raw composite scores may therefore vary between $\frac{1}{2}(g+n)r(r-1)$ and $\frac{1}{2}(2g+n)r(r-1)$. For instance, when there are nine voters and five possible outcomes, $g = 15$, so that $\frac{1}{2}(g+n)r(r-1) = 240$, which is therefore the lowest possible figure to which the raw composite scores can add up, which will happen when the majority number of every outcome is equal to its majority score. If the sum of the majority numbers is just one greater than the sum of the majority scores, which will always be 10, the sum of the raw composite scores will be increased by 15, the value of g: this sum can therefore assume any of the values 240, 255, 270, 285, and so on up to a maximum of 390, which it will attain when every outcome has the majority number 4. The adjusted composite scores will be arrived at by scaling up the raw scores to bring their sum to the maximum possible, in this case 390, in general $\frac{1}{2}(2g+n)r(r-1)$, which we may call T. Thus, where t is the actual sum of the raw scores, each raw score u must be multiplied by T/t; the result must then be rounded to the nearest whole number or fraction with denominator 2, and, if necessary, the minimum adjustment made to ensure that the adjusted scores in fact sum to T. The final result gives the adjusted score of each outcome.

We may again illustrate with $n = 9$ and $r = 5$. In our example, the sum of the raw composite scores is 270, while $T = 390$: in scaling up, we therefore have to multiply by 390/270, or 13/9.

	a	b	c	d	e
majority number (k)	4	4	2	2	0
gk	60	60	30	30	0
preference score (p)	30	20	$19\frac{1}{2}$	$10\frac{1}{2}$	10
raw composite score ($gk + p = u$)	90	80	$49\frac{1}{2}$	$40\frac{1}{2}$	10
raw score scaled up ($u \times 13/9$)	130	$115\frac{5}{9}$	$71\frac{1}{2}$	$58\frac{1}{2}$	$14\frac{4}{9}$
adjusted score (v)	130	$115\frac{1}{2}$	$71\frac{1}{2}$	$58\frac{1}{2}$	$14\frac{1}{2}$

The figures in the last row will be those announced by the tellers. Since, in arriving at the last row from the last but one, they rounded up one figure and rounded down one other, no further adjustment was needed to make the sum of the adjusted scores 390.

Presented with such adjusted composite scores, would it be possible to deduce the original majority numbers and preference scores? It would sometimes be possible, after a great deal of

190 PREFERENCE SCORE AND MAJORITY NUMBER PROCEDURES

laborious calculation; but it would certainly not always be possible. There will be finitely many scaling-up factors that may have been used, in fact $\frac{1}{2}r(r-1) + 1$ of them: thus, when $n = 9$ and $r = 5$, there will be eleven such factors, namely 26/16, 26/17, ..., 26/25, 1. By applying the inverses of these to the adjusted scores, one will arrive, in our case, at eleven possible assignments of raw scores to the outcomes, and, in general, of $\frac{1}{2}r(r-1) + 1$ such. For each of these, it can then be calculated whether it is possible to assign majority numbers and preference scores to the outcomes in such a way as to yield the given raw scores: in carrying out this calculation, it will often be necessary to reconstruct the majority scores, the R_{maj} diagram, and sometimes even the preference scales themselves. In the process, it will be possible to exclude most of the solutions as inconsistent. When only one is left, the majority numbers and preference scores will be known; but it may happen that, when all the work has been done, two distinct solutions remain, between which there is no way of deciding. It is extremely unlikely that anyone should undertake such extensive labour with no guarantee of success. This may be illustrated from the example given above. Suppose that the adjusted scores, as given in the last line of the foregoing table, are announced, and that voter 2, who listed the outcomes in the order *adebc*, wants to discover whether the successful outcome *a* obtained the highest preference score, or won only by having a higher majority number than *b*. He will find that there are two possible solutions. A set of preference scales which might obtain if solution A were correct is:

1	2	3	4	5	6	7	8	9
a	a	a	c	b				
					a b	a b	a b	
c	d	c	e					a b d
				a c				
e	e	e	a		c	c	c	
	b			d	e	d	d	c
b d		b d	b d					
	c			e	d	e	e	e

The R_{maj} diagram will be as shown in diagram 10.1, and the relevant figures for the various outcomes are as given below it.

PREFERENCE SCORE AND MAJORITY NUMBER PROCEDURES 191

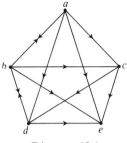

Diagram 10.1

	a	b	c	d	e
majority number	4	4	2	2	0
majority score	$3\frac{1}{2}$	3	2	$1\frac{1}{2}$	0
preference score	30	20	$19\frac{1}{2}$	$10\frac{1}{2}$	10
raw composite score	90	80	$49\frac{1}{2}$	$40\frac{1}{2}$	10

This, then, tallies with the example. Under solution B, however, the preference scales may be:

1	2	3	4	5	6	7	8	9
a	a	a	a	a	b	d	b	b
b	d	d	b	d	c	b	c	c
c	e	b	c	b	d	e	d	d
d	b	e	d	e	e	c	e	e
e	c	c	e	c	a	a	a	a

The R_{maj} diagram is now as in diagram 10.2.

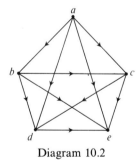

Diagram 10.2

The sum of the raw composite scores will be 240, so that the scaling-up factor is 13/8. The figures are thus:

192 PREFERENCE SCORE AND MAJORITY NUMBER PROCEDURES

	a	b	c	d	e
majority number	4	3	2	1	0
majority score	4	3	2	1	0
preference score	20	26	14	21	9
raw composite score	80	71	44	36	9
scaled-up composite score	130	$115\frac{3}{8}$	$71\frac{1}{2}$	$58\frac{1}{2}$	$14\frac{5}{8}$
adjusted composite score	130	$115\frac{1}{2}$	$71\frac{1}{2}$	$58\frac{1}{2}$	$14\frac{1}{2}$

The last line shows that the adjusted scores tally with those given as data. Under solution A, a and b have the same majority number, and a wins as having the highest preference score. Under solution B, on the other hand, a has a lower preference score than b, but wins in virtue of having a higher majority number. After all the work necessary to arrive at these two solutions and eliminate all other possibilities, voter 2 still does not know the answer to the question in which he was interested.

It is the use of these adjusted composite scores that we shall take as constituting the composite score procedure, since, even when bracketing is allowed, use of the raw scores has scarcely any advantage over the unmodified majority number procedure. Under the composite score procedure, the tellers might complain that they have been given a great deal of work to do; but no one who accepted the majority number procedure as fair could have any objection to the composite score procedure as unfair. Nor is it complicated for the voters to understand or operate. They have only to list the outcomes in order of preference; it is not necessary for them to know more about how the procedure works, in drawing up their lists, than that it will produce the same outcome as the majority number procedure. They will naturally want to be told more than this; but the required explanation is easily given. The complexity of the matter lies in determining the general formulae, but the voters do not need to know these, still less the reasoning required to justify them; they need to know only the general principles, the purpose of those principles, and the actual numerical values on any particular occasion when the procedure is used.

The easiest way to explain the procedure to the voters is as follows. Each voter must list the outcomes on his ballot paper in descending order of preference, bracketing any two or more equal if he likes; any outcomes he omits will be treated as bracketed equal below those he does list. Each outcome will start with a base score;

PREFERENCE SCORE AND MAJORITY NUMBER PROCEDURES 193

this is in order to avoid negative scores, since points will be subtracted as well as added. The base score will in fact be taken to be $g(r-1)$ points; as soon as n and r are known, its numerical value can be announced, for instance as 60 when $n = 9$ and $r = 5$. Points will be added to the base score in accordance with the voters' listings: for each ballot paper, an outcome will be allotted 1 point for each outcome standing lower than it, and $\frac{1}{2}$ point for each outcome bracketed equal with it. Points will be subtracted from an outcome's score in virtue of majority preferences, as revealed by the ballot papers. An outcome will incur a fixed penalty for each outcome which a majority of the voters positively prefer to it; the penalty is fixed so that an outcome cannot obtain the highest score if it has incurred a greater number of such penalties than some other outcome. When n and r are known, the penalty will be taken to be g points and its numerical value announced, for instance 15 when $n = 9$ and $r = 5$. When all additions to and subtractions from the basic scores have been made, the resultant scores will be scaled up, if necessary, so as to bring their sum to a fixed maximum: this is to make it difficult, and often impossible, to work out whether the outcome obtaining the highest score did so by having more additions or by incurring fewer penalties than its nearest rival. The fixed maximum will of course be T, for instance 390 when $n = 9$ and $r = 5$. While voters should in no way be discouraged from bracketing, it should in fairness be pointed out that, by bracketing x and y rather than listing x above y, a voter will be increasing y's chances of success by considerably more than he will be diminishing x's. He will be diminishing x's chance of beating y by exactly the same amount that he is increasing y's chance of beating x; but he will be significantly increasing y's chance of beating an outcome other than x, and diminishing only marginally x's chance of beating one other than y.

The procedure, so explained, is perfectly easy to understand. The easiest method for the tellers is to keep a tally divided into $\frac{1}{2}r(r-1)$ sections (10 when $r = 5$), one for each pair of outcomes. Any one section, for a pair x and y, will be subdivided into three: one for voters listing x above y, one for those bracketing them equal, and one for those listing y above x. From the numbers in each subdivision, it will then be easy to calculate both the majority numbers and the preference scores. When there is an even number of voters, a special mark must be made in each subdivision to which the chairman's ballot paper contributes. Having arrived at the raw scores by this means, the tellers must add them together to find their total t: they then have to scale up by the factor T/t, rounding to the nearest $\frac{1}{2}$ point and making the minimum adjustment to ensure that the sum of the adjusted scores is T. The adjusted scores are then announced, and the outcome with the highest score declared successful.

For voters with sufficient self-restraint not to demand extraneous information from the tellers, and to impose on them an inviolable duty not to disclose it, the composite score procedure has no advantage over the majority number procedure, and may seem less fair than the persistent majority number procedure. Such self-restraint is rare, however. It is common to suppose that there will usually be one outcome which, if the voters' real preferences were known, would be revealed as unequivocally the fairest, and that, when there is not, this can only be because two outcomes have equally good claims of the same kind. It requires some sophistication—that is, some understanding of the elements of the theory of voting—to grasp that there may be two outcomes both of which have, on *different* grounds, strong claims to be the fairest. Only voters who have grasped this can see the point of the majority number procedure: but the tradition that the voters have the right to know the specific 'results' of the voting is so powerful that they will need a greater degree of sophistication to be conscious of the importance of concealing a clash of criteria for the fairest outcome in any specific case. If they cannot trust themselves to refrain from uncovering such a clash, but continue to believe that the majority preference criterion should override that of the preference scores, they will do best to adopt the composite score procedure.

Appendix to Chapter 10

The purpose of this appendix is to justify the formulae for the factor g cited in the body of the chapter. Simpler formulae, yielding larger values for g, could be arrived at with less work, and it will be evident from the following what they would be; but, to make it as hard as possible to recover the majority numbers and preference scores from the adjusted composite scores, g needs to be kept as small as possible.

We assume, first, that there are $2m + 1$ voters. We need to consider only the maximum difference between the preference scores of two outcomes, b and a, when a has majority number k and b has majority number $k - 1$. We shall therefore assume that the majority score q of a is as low as possible, and the majority score q' of b as high as possible, and that a has as small as possible a preference score and b one as high as possible. Three distinct cases arise, according as $aP_{\text{maj}}b$, $aI_{\text{maj}}b$, or $bP_{\text{maj}}a$.

Case 1: $aP_{\text{maj}}b$. Since $aP_{\text{maj}}b$, $q = \frac{1}{2}(k + 1)$, while $q' = k - 1$. When $r = 5$, case 1 is illustrated by the R_{maj} diagram 10A.1.

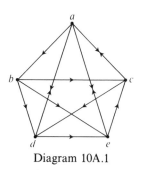

Diagram 10A.1

Here $k = 4$, so that a is top, while $q = 2\frac{1}{2}$. The general formula for the minimum preference score of an outcome with majority score q is $(m + 1)q$, and that for its maximum preference score is $(m + 1)q + m(r - 1)$. These formulae yield, respectively, the following estimates for the preference scores of a and b:

$$
\begin{array}{cc}
a & b \\
\tfrac{1}{2}(m+1)(k+1) & (m+1)(k-1)+m(r-1)
\end{array}
$$

These estimates require correction for certain cyclic triads to which a and b must of necessity belong. For any outcome x such that $bP_{\text{maj}}x$, a will belong to a triad of the form of either diagram 10A.2 or 10A.3.

Diagram 10A.2   Diagram 10A.3

The x of diagram 10A.2 may be taken in diagram 10A.1 as c, d, or e. There will be $k-1$ triads of one or other form; for each of them, a's minimum preference score must be increased by at least $\tfrac{1}{2}$ (by 1 in diagram 10A.3), since there must be at least one voter who definitely prefers a to x. Each such triad will also diminish b's maximum preference score by 1, since at least one voter must prefer x to b. We must therefore add $\tfrac{1}{2}(k-1)$ points to the above estimate of a's preference score, and subtract $k-1$ points from b's, obtaining the revised estimates:

$$
\begin{array}{cc}
a & b \\
\tfrac{1}{2}m(k+1)+k & m(k+r-2)
\end{array}
$$

The difference between the preference scores of b and a will thus be $\tfrac{1}{2}(m-2)k+m(r-2\tfrac{1}{2})$. Provided that $m \geq 2$, this will be at its greatest when k assumes its greatest value $r-1$, so that a is top. The value of the greatest difference d' in case 1, when $m > 1$, is thus given by:

$$d' = 1\tfrac{1}{2}m(r-2) - r + 1.$$

Case 2: $aI_{\text{maj}}b$. The majority score q of a is now $\tfrac{1}{2}k$, while the majority score q' of b is $k - 1\tfrac{1}{2}$, since $aI_{\text{maj}}b$. Case 2 is illustrated by diagram 10A.4.

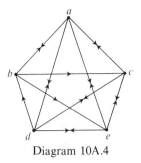
Diagram 10A.4

Here $k = 4$, $q = 2$, and $q' = 2\frac{1}{2}$. The general formulae for the minimum and maximum preference scores yield the following preliminary estimates for the preference scores of a and b:

$$\begin{array}{cc} a & b \\ \frac{1}{2}(m+1)k & (m+1)(k-1\frac{1}{2}) + m(r-1) \end{array}$$

We have again to correct these in view of the cyclic triads to which a and b must belong. For every outcome x for which $bP_{\text{maj}}x$, a belongs to a triad of one of the two forms represented by diagrams 10A.5 and 10A.6.

Diagram 10A.5   Diagram 10A.6

There are $k - 2$ of these; in diagram 10A.4 the x of diagram 10A.5 can be taken as c or e. Each of these triads increases a's minimum preference score by at least $\frac{1}{2}$, since at least one voter must actually prefer a to x. There are also $r - k$ triads of one or other of the forms represented by diagrams 10A.7 and 10A.8.

Diagram 10A.7   Diagram 10A.8

In diagram 10A.4, the y of diagram 10A.7 is d. For each such y, $\frac{1}{2}$ point must be added to a's minimum preference score, since at least one voter must actually prefer a to b. Together, then, the r triads of the forms shown in diagrams 10A.5–8 must increase our estimate of a's preference score by $\frac{1}{2}(r-2)$ points. Triads of forms 10A.5 and 10A.6 must each diminish b's maximum preference score by 1, since at least one voter must prefer x to b; each of those of the form 10A.7 or 10A.8 must diminish it by $\frac{1}{2}$, since at least one voter must prefer a to b. We must thus subtract $\frac{1}{2}(r+k) - 2$ from our estimate of b's preference score, obtaining the revised estimates:

$$\begin{array}{cc} a & b \\ \frac{1}{2}(mk + k + r) - 1 & m(r + k - 2\frac{1}{2}) - \frac{1}{2}(r - k - 1) \end{array}$$

The difference between them will be $m(r + \frac{1}{2}k - 2\frac{1}{2}) - r + 1\frac{1}{2}$, which will necessarily be greatest when $k = r - 1$, so that we must determine d_2, the greatest possible difference in case 2, by:

$$d_2 = 1\frac{1}{2}m(r-2) - r + 1\frac{1}{2}.$$

Case 3: $bP_{\text{maj}}a$. We may take the majority score q of a to be $\frac{1}{2}k$, and the majority score q' of b to be $k - 1$. Case 3 is illustrated by the R_{maj} diagram 10A.9.

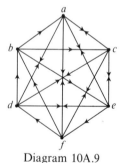
Diagram 10A.9

The preliminary estimates of the preference scores are thus:

$$\begin{array}{cc} a & b \\ \frac{1}{2}(m+1)k & (m+1)(k-1) + m(r-1) \end{array}$$

There are k outcomes x other than a for which $aI_{\text{maj}}x$; since there are only $k - 1$ outcomes to which b stands in the relation R_{maj}, one of which is a, there are at least two such outcomes x for which $xP_{\text{maj}}b$: in diagram 10A.9, these are d and f. There thus exist triads of the form of diagram 10A.10.

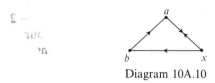

Diagram 10A.10

In such a triad, a's predecessor in the cylic order is b: hence at least one voter must prefer a to b, increasing a's minimum preference score by 1, and decreasing b's maximum score by 1. This yields the revised estimates:

$$a \qquad\qquad b$$
$$\tfrac{1}{2}(m+1)k + 1 \qquad (m+1)(k-1) + m(r-1) - 1$$

The difference between these is $\tfrac{1}{2}k(m+1) + m(r-2) - 3$, which is again at its greatest when k is at its greatest. Since $bP_{\text{maj}}a$, a is not a top, and k can be $r-2$ at most. Putting $k = r-2$ in the foregoing expression for the difference in the preference scores, we obtain $1\tfrac{1}{2}mr - 3m + \tfrac{1}{2}r - 4$.

We may further assume that there is no top, since we are really interested in the excess of b's preference score over a's only when a has a majority number as high as any other outcome. This further assumption, together with the assumption that $k = r-2$, allows us to lower our estimate of the excess still further. Since b has the majority number $r-3$, there must be exactly two outcomes x forming a triad of the form 10A.10. Since x is not a top, there must be an outcome y such that $yP_{\text{maj}}x$: thus, in diagram 10A.9, y is f when x is d, and y is e when x is f. There are therefore cyclic triads of the form of diagram 10A.11.

Diagram 10A.11

Since at least one voter must prefer a to x, each such triad increases a's preference score by $\tfrac{1}{2}$; there being two such triads, we must add 1 to that score. Furthermore, there being only two such outcomes x, there must be one such that, for the corresponding y, $bP_{\text{maj}}y$, producing a further triad of the form shown in diagram 10A.12.

Diagram 10A.12

In diagram 10A.9, x is f and y is e. Since there must be at least one voter preferring y to b, we must subtract 1 more point from b's preference score. This lowers our estimate of the maximum possible difference d_3 between the two scores in case 3 by a further 2 points altogether, so that our final formula is:

$$d_3 = 1\tfrac{1}{2}m(r-2) + \tfrac{1}{2}r - 6.$$

We have thus arrived at different estimates for the greatest possible difference between the preference scores of b and of a, depending upon m and r, in each of our three cases. We can ignore d', because it is always smaller than d_2. When $r > 5$, $d_3 > d_2$, but, when $r \leqslant 5$, $d_2 \geqslant d_3$. We need also to check that our assumption, in the foregoing argument, that we may assume a to have its smallest possible majority score, and b to have its greatest, actually accords to them their smallest and greatest possible preference scores respectively. It might fail to do so if the adjustments rendered necessary by the existence of cyclic triads had a greater effect than the difference in majority scores. It is easily seen that this will in fact happen only when $m = 1$, i.e. when there are only 3 voters. We earlier found that, when there are no cyclic triads, the maximum difference d_1 between the preference scores of b and a is $m(r-2) - 1$. When $m > 1$, d_2 will be greater than d_1, so that we need not bother about this effect. When $m = 1$, however, d_1 is greater than d_2 when $r > 3$, and equal to it when $r = 3$, though less than d_3 when $r > 6$, and equal to it when $r = 6$. It will be recalled that, in case 1, d' was not the correct estimate when $m = 1$; it will readily be verified that, for $m = 1$ and $r < 6$, cyclic triads will contrive to make the difference less when a's majority score is smaller than k than when its majority score equals its majority number: for this reason, d_1 is the relevant estimate in this case.

For given values of m and r, we have to take d as the greatest of d_1, d_2, and d_3, and set $g = d + \tfrac{1}{2}$. The upshot of the foregoing discussion is that we must take d as d_3 when $r \geqslant 6$, as d_2 when $m = 1$ and $r < 6$, and as d_1 when $m = 1$ and $r < 6$. This will be found to accord with the formulae given in the body of the chapter for when $n = 2m + 1$.

Little more work is needed to extend these results to the case when the number n of voters is $2m$, since we have only to modify the preliminary estimates for the preference scores of a and b in each case; the effects of cyclic triads remain the same. The general formulae for the minimum and maximum preference scores of an outcome with majority score q are now mq and $m(q + r - 1)$ points respectively. When P_{maj} is transitive and a is top, the greatest difference between the preference score of b and that of a is $m(r - 2)$ points. Assume, for all our three cases, that k is as large as possible. The preference scores and differences will now be:

	a	b	
case 1	$\frac{1}{2}mr + \frac{1}{2}(r - 2)$	$m(2r - 3) - r + 2$	$d' = 1\frac{1}{2}(m - 1)(r - 2)$
case 2	$\frac{1}{2}m(r - 1) + \frac{1}{2}(r - 2)$	$m(2r - 3\frac{1}{2}) - r + 2\frac{1}{2}$	$d_2 = 1\frac{1}{2}(m - 1)(r - 2) + \frac{1}{2}$
case 3	$\frac{1}{2}m(r - 2) + 2$	$m(2r - 4) - 2$	$d_3 = 1\frac{1}{2}m(r - 2) - 4$

As before, d' may be ignored, as always being less than d_2. When $m > 2$, d_1 is never greater than d_2. When $m = 2$ and $r < 6$, d must be taken as d_1; when $m = 2$ and $r \geqslant 6$, it must be taken as d_3. When $m > 2$, d must be taken as d_2 if $r < 6$, and as d_3 otherwise. This completes the justification of the formulae given in the body of the chapter.

11
There is no Straight-forward Procedure

Suppose that there were a voting procedure that offered a straightforward strategy to every voter, whatever his preference scale: we may say that the procedure itself would be straightforward. A straightforward procedure would have immense advantages. No voter would ever need to hesitate how to cast his vote: the outcome of the voting would never depend upon the voters' erratic predictions how others are going to vote. We might well be willing to tolerate considerable deviation from the fairest outcome for the sake of such advantages. Unfortunately, there is no such procedure.[1]

No two non-equivalent voting strategies can be straightforward for the same strong preference scale. Hence, when all preference scales are strong, a straightforward procedure must be fully determinate: each voter can choose only between equivalent strategies if he is to vote admissibly, and so each admissible situation will produce the same outcome. We proved earlier that, whenever a binary procedure determined an outcome outright, that outcome must be a top. It follows that no binary procedure can be straightforward, since there may be no top. The same would hold for any class of voting procedures of which we could prove the same, namely that a procedure in that class could determine an outcome outright only if it was a top. It is possible that a proof could be given

---

[1] This result was conjectured by Farquharson and myself in our article 'Stability in Voting' of 1961, and first proved by Gibbard in 1973, and subsequently by Satterthwaite, Gardenfors, Jain, Pattanaik and Schmeidler and Sonnenschein. The proof here given was devised by me before I was aware that the theorem had already been proved; in its original form, it used a stronger assumption, namely that the procedure is symmetrical with respect to the voters. Having learned of the content of Gibbard's theorem, but not its proof, I strengthened my version to yield a similar result. It remains slightly weaker, since Gibbard assumes only that there is no voter who, for *each* outcome, has a strategy that will ensure its success, whereas I have assumed that there is no voter who has such a strategy for *any* outcome.

THERE IS NO STRAIGHTFORWARD PROCEDURE

that all procedures symmetrical with respect to the outcomes have this property.

Symmetry can be explained by appeal to the notion of a permutation of a set. A permutation p of a set A is simply a way of associating, with every member x of A, a member $p(x)$ of A, where $p(x)$ may or may not be different from x, but $p(x)$ must be different from $p(y)$ for any two distinct members x and y of A. If A were infinite, we should have to add that every member x of A was the image $p(y)$, under the permutation, of some member y of A; when, as in our case, we are concerned only with finite sets, this is automatically guaranteed. A procedure may then be said to be *symmetrical with respect to the outcomes* if the effect of any permutation p of the outcomes can be nullified in the following sense. Suppose that the procedure is altered by leaving the voting mechanism as before, but changing the method of assessment so that, whenever a situation s produced an outcome x under the original procedure, it will now produce $p(x)$. Suppose further that, for each voter i, there is a permutation q_i of the strategies open to i such that, if s produced x under the original procedure, s' will produce x under the new procedure if, for each i, s'_i is $q_i(s_i)$. We may then say that the permutations q_i *nullify* the effect of p. This means that a procedure is symmetrical with respect to the outcomes if, when the procedure is changed by a permutation of the outcomes, strategies under the new procedure can be made to correspond with strategies under the old one so as to exhibit the new procedure as equivalent to the old.

No binary procedure is symmetrical with respect to the outcomes, if there are more than two of them. For instance, the amendment procedure treats the outcome a, representing the defeat of the motion, amended or unamended, in a different way from the other two outcomes b and c. The permutation p under which $p(a) = c$, $p(b) = b$, and $p(c) = a$ transforms the procedure represented by the diagram 11.1 into that represented by diagram 11.2.

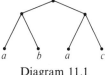
Diagram 11.1

Diagram 11.2

The two procedures are not equivalent. Under both, each voter has a choice of eight strategies: but there is no way of making strategies under the new procedure correspond to those under the old so that the outcome produced under the old one when the voters make any choice of strategies will always be produced under the new one when they choose corresponding strategies. Any procedure requiring a special majority, say of two-thirds, for one or more of the outcomes is evidently asymmetrical. Nevertheless, most non-binary procedures are symmetrical with respect to the outcomes; any property shown to be possessed by all binary procedures and all symmetrical ones is therefore shared by most procedures in actual use.

We shall not proceed in this way, however, since greater generality is readily obtainable. In passing, we may note that the property of being symmetrical with respect to the voters is definable in a similar way. So far, we have assumed only that each voter has a choice between finitely many strategies open to him: we have made no general assumption that each voter has the same choice, or that it even makes sense to speak of one voter's adopting the same strategy as another. Under a procedure symmetrical with respect to the voters, each voter has to choose from among the same finite set of strategies, and all that will matter for the outcome is how many select each strategy. More exactly, if the situation s produces the outcome x, then, for any permutation p of the voters, s' will also produce x if, for each i, $s'_{p(i)}$ is s_i. The procedures we have actually considered have all been symmetrical with respect to the voters when the number n of voters is odd; when it is even, they are not quite symmetrical, because of the chairman's casting vote.

What we have to do is to derive a contradiction from the supposition that there is a procedure that affords every voter a straightforward strategy, whatever his preference scale, given that there are more than two possible outcomes. We shall show that there can be no such procedure for any fixed number of outcomes greater than two. Suppose, first, that there are just three possible outcomes, a, b, and c, and that there is a voting procedure affording a straightforward strategy to a voter with any preference scale. If a voter with a strong preference scale has more than one straightforward strategy, they will be equivalent, and we may pick out one of them at random as representative. We may thus denote the representative strategy straightforward for a given voter with the preference scale xyz by '$|xyz|$'. It is evident that the strategies straightforward for distinct preference scales cannot be equivalent, but we do not need to assume, or to prove, this fact. We shall assume that each of the three outcomes is genuinely possible, i.e. that there is at least one situation that produces it. We shall further assume that any one voter can be overridden by the rest: that is, for each voter i and outcome x, there can be no strategy σ such that s will produce x whenever s_i is σ.

In the technical literature on voting, what we have been calling 'situations' are often called 'points'. It is useful in the present context to think of them as points in a space divided into regions corresponding to the outcomes. In our case, there will be three regions, one comprising all situations producing the outcome a, and the other two those producing the outcomes b and c respectively. For convenience, we may delete all points or situations save those in which each voter adopts a representative strategy straightforward for a strong preference scale: this is in effect to consider only situations in which each voter votes straightforwardly and has a strong scale. With this simplification, there is a natural way to conceive of contiguity between points: two points will be *contiguous* if there is a minimal difference between them, namely when either can be obtained from the other by altering the strategy $|xyz|$ of some one voter to $|yxz|$ or to $|xzy|$, leaving the strategies of the other voters unchanged. If two contiguous points lie in different regions, we may say that there is a *boundary* between the regions that passes between the two points. A *path* is a sequence of points in which each point, save the last, is contiguous to the next one in the sequence. It is plain that there is a path between any two points.

The voting mechanism may be any that allows a sufficient choice of strategies; but, since each of the strategies we are considering corresponds to a strong preference scale, we may, whenever it allows a simpler form of expression, pretend that the complete list mechanism, without bracketing, is being used. We may thus describe a voter's adopting the strategy $|abc|$ as his listing the outcomes in the order *abc*, and his replacing that strategy by $|bac|$ as his interchanging a and b on his list. Let us label the three regions $R(a)$, $R(b)$, and $R(c)$, according to the outcome produced by the points in them. Now suppose that s lies in $R(a)$ and that t is contiguous to s and lies in $R(b)$. Then, for some voter i, t_i differs from s_i by the interchange of two adjacent outcomes, while, for every j other than i, $s_j = t_j$. Now s_i cannot be $|bca|$. For, if it were, then, if i's preference scale were *bca*, the strategy $|bca|$ would not be straightforward for him, since in this contingency he would have obtained the outcome b, which he preferred to a, by adopting the strategy t_i; and this is contrary to the specification of $|bca|$ as a strategy straightforward for i when his preference scale is bca. By the same argument, s_i cannot be $|bac|$ or $|cba|$ either, in sum any strategy straightforward for i when he prefers b to a. Likewise, t_i cannot be $|acb|$, $|abc|$, or $|cab|$. If, for example, it were $|acb|$, then, if i's preference scale were acb, the strategy $|acb|$ would not be straightforward for him, for in this contingency he would obtain an outcome that he preferred by adopting the strategy s_i. This leaves only two possibilities: that s_i is $|abc|$ and t_i is $|bac|$, or that s_i is $|cab|$ and t_i is $|cba|$.

We have shown that a path can cross the boundary from $R(x)$ to $R(y)$ only between a point at which a voter listed x just above y and one at which the same voter interchanged x and y on his list. It follows that there must be a boundary between any two regions $R(x)$ and $R(y)$. Since there are no empty regions, any point at which every voter lists x highest must lie in $R(x)$, for otherwise some voter's strategy at that point would not be straightforward for him if his preference scale corresponded to his listing. If u is such a point, we can construct a path from u each step in which consists in moving y upwards in some voter's list at the expense of either x or z, and terminating at a point v at which every voter lists y highest, and which therefore lies in $R(y)$. No step along this path can cross the boundary between $R(x)$ and $R(z)$; the path must therefore somewhere cross the boundary between $R(x)$ and $R(y)$, which accordingly exists.

A similar argument shows that there is a path entirely inside $R(x)$ from any point s in $R(x)$ to any other point s' in $R(x)$. There will be a path from s terminating at a point u at which every voter lists x highest, each step of which consists in moving x upwards in some voter's list at the expense of either y or z: such a path cannot lead outside $R(x)$. There will be a similar path from s' to a point u' at which every voter lists x highest. Finally, there will be a path from u to u' at each point of which every voter lists x highest. The three paths together make a path from s to s' entirely inside $R(x)$: hence no region can consist of two disconnected subregions, like Pakistan before the independence of Bangladesh. It follows from this and the previous result that there is always a path from any point in $R(x)$ to any point in $R(y)$ that never crosses $R(z)$.

Consider again a point s lying in $R(a)$ just inside the boundary with $R(b)$. Let A be the set of voters who, at s, list a higher than b. There is some point t contiguous to s and lying in $R(b)$: hence there is a voter i in A on whose list a stands just above b and who, by interchanging a and b, would cause a shift from $R(a)$ to $R(b)$. Conversely, let s' be any point at which all the voters in A list a higher than b. To construct a path from s to s', it will never be necessary to move b upwards at the expense of a. The path will therefore not lead directly from $R(a)$ to $R(b)$. It may lead to $R(c)$, however, since there may be steps that consist of moving c upwards at the expense of a. Since there may also be steps that involve moving b upwards at the expense of c, we have to verify that these can all be taken before the path leaves $R(a)$, since otherwise it might lead from $R(c)$ into $R(b)$. That this cannot happen follows from our earlier result, that, if s' lies in $R(b)$, there will be a path from s to s' that does not cross $R(c)$. In detail, we may construct the path as follows. We first take a sequence of steps that consist either of interchanging b and c in some voter's list in which they are adjacent, or in moving a upwards at the expense of b or of c. No such step can lead from $R(a)$ to $R(b)$ or $R(c)$. Finally, to arrive at s', we may have to take some steps that consist of moving c upwards at the expense of a, possibly followed by moving c upwards at the expense of b. By means of such steps, the path may cross into $R(c)$, but cannot lead either from $R(a)$ or from $R(c)$ into $R(b)$. We have thus shown that s' cannot be in $R(b)$.

We may call a set U of voters *decisive for x against y* if no point at which every voter in U lists x higher than y lies in $R(y)$. Plainly, if s lies in $R(x)$, the set of all voters who list x higher than y at s is decisive for x against y. If U is decisive for x against y, and there is a point in $R(y)$ at which a voter i in U lists y just above x and every other member of U lists x higher than y, we may call i a *critical member* of U and say that U is *critically decisive* for x against y. In the case considered, A was critically decisive for a against b. If U is decisive for x against y, and i is a critical member of U, then the set U' consisting of i together with all voters not in U is decisive for y against x, and i is a critical member of U'. Not every member of a critically decisive set need itself be critical. However, among the sets decisive for x against y will be those having no subsets decisive for x against y except themselves; these may be called *minimally decisive* sets. If U is minimally decisive for x against y, every member i of U is a critical member: for the point t at which every voter lists both x and y higher than every other outcome, i lists y higher than x, as does every voter not in U, and all the other voters in U list x higher than y, must lie in $R(y)$, since the set of all voters is necessarily decisive for y against z, for any z.

Now suppose that A is minimally decisive for a against b, and B minimally decisive for b against c. If, for any set X, $\bar{X}$ is the set of all voters not in X, and, for any sets X and Y, XY is the set of all voters both in X and in Y, we may partition the voters into four sets, according as they belong or do not belong to each of A and B. Consider the point s at which the voters in these four sets adopt strategies corresponding to the following lists:

$A\bar{B}$	AB	$\bar{A}B$	$\bar{A}\bar{B}$
c	a	b	c
a	b	c	b
b	c	a	a

s cannot lie in $R(b)$, since every member of A lists a higher than b; nor can it lie in $R(c)$, since every member of B lists b higher than c. It must therefore lie in $R(a)$, from which it follows that AB is decisive for a against c, and hence cannot be empty.

Let i be any member of A and j any member of B. Since every member of A is a critical member, the set A' consisting of i together with all members of $\bar{A}$ is decisive for b against a; similarly the set B' consisting of j together with all members of $\bar{B}$ is decisive for c against b. Consider any point t at which every member of A' lists b higher than a, every member of B' lists c higher than b, and every member of AB lists a higher than c. It is plain that no such point can exist: for it could not lie in $R(a)$, $R(b)$, or $R(c)$. It follows that no conditions that would allow it to exist can obtain.

At any such point t, every member of $\bar{A}\bar{B}$ must adopt the strategy $|cba|$; voter i must list b higher than a, and voter j must list c higher than b. If i is in B, he is in AB, and hence must list a higher than c: he must therefore adopt the strategy $|bac|$. If i is not in B, he must list c higher than b, and hence must adopt the strategy $|cba|$. Similarly, if j is in A, he must adopt the strategy $|acb|$, and, if he is not in A, he must adopt the strategy $|cba|$. These demands are all compatible with one another provided that i and j are distinct: since we know that the demands cannot be simultaneously satisfied, it follows that i and j are identical. But i was taken to be any member of A, and j any member of B: it follows that A and B must themselves be identical, each consisting solely of the same single voter i. Thus the set consisting solely of i is decisive for a against b and also for b against c, and, as constituting AB, for a against c. Hence, if i places a highest on his list, a is bound to be successful. This, however, is contrary to one of our initial assumptions, namely that, for each voter i and outcome x, i has no strategy that will guarantee the success of x. We have thus shown that there can be no straightforward procedure satisfying both that assumption and the assumption that, of three possible outcomes, each is genuinely possible.

We have now to generalize the result to any case in which there are more than two possible outcomes; this presents no difficulty. It will remain the case that the passage from a point in $R(x)$ to a contiguous point in $R(y)$ can be effected only by interchanging x and y in some voter's list in which x stands immediately above y. For instance, if there are four possible outcomes, the replacement by one voter of the strategy |*cadb*| by |*cabd*| could not cause a shift across the boundary from $R(a)$ into $R(b)$, since otherwise the strategy |*cabd*| would not be straightforward for that voter if he had the preference scale *cabd*. The entire argument now goes through as before: in characterizing the points s and t, in terms of the sets A and B, in the last stage of the proof, we must specify that at both points every voter lists a, b, and c higher than any other outcome.

We have tacitly assumed that every voting procedure is definite in the sense that every situation produces a unique outcome: the method of assessment yields a rule correlating a single outcome with every possible course of the voting. The principle that no procedure can afford a straightforward strategy to every voter, whatever his preference scale, applies only to definite procedures; if we were prepared to tolerate the incorporation of some random process into our procedure, the matter would stand differently. Imagine that the complete list mechanism were employed, and the preference score of each outcome calculated. For each outcome, $2p$ slips of paper bearing its name were then placed in a box, where p was its preference score. The box would be shaken and a slip drawn at random, the outcome whose name it bore being declared successful. Under such a procedure, there would be no incentive for any voter to record anything but his true order of preference: but it is clear that all but those most securely confident of the protection of Providence would prefer the most arbitrary definite procedure to one involving the random intervention of mechanical rather than psychological forces.

12
Strategic Voting: The Alternative Vote

When Arrow's theorem was first discussed in Chapter 2, it was denied to entail that there can be no reasonable social welfare function, on the ground that the principle of independence of irrelevant alternatives lacks intuitive justification; and this position has been maintained throughout this book. The principle lacks such justification for the reason which has been repeatedly insisted on, that the number of outcomes intervening on a voter's preference scale between x and y is a rough guide to the strength of his preference for x over y. The true significance of the theorem lies elsewhere. To see what that significance is, we must ask what would follow from its falsity. All of Arrow's principles can be construed as characteristics of a method of assessment for a voting procedure using the complete list mechanism. In particular, such a method of assessment might be said to satisfy the principle of independence of irrelevant alternatives if the following were true. Suppose that, for a given set of ballot papers returned under the complete list mechanism, an outcome x were successful; and suppose it then discovered that some other particular outcome y had been eliminated before the vote was taken (y might be the election of some candidate who had withdrawn or died). Suppose that at that stage the vote were taken again, with y eliminated from the list of possible outcomes, and suppose that every voter then listed the remaining outcomes in the same order as before: his new ballot paper was exactly like his earlier one save for the deletion of y. If the method of assessment satisfied the principle of independence of irrelevant alternatives, then, in such a case, x would necessarily still be the successful outcome.

Now suppose that there were a voting procedure with the following characteristics:

(i) it used the complete list mechanism;

(ii) for a voter to list x higher than y always increased x's chances of success as against those of y;

(iii) the method of assessment satisfied the principle of independence of irrelevant alternatives.

Then the procedure would be straightforward: every voter would have a straightforward strategy, namely to list the outcomes according to his actual order of preference. Since we know that there can be no straightforward procedure, it follows that no procedure can satisfy the principle of independence of irrelevant alternatives unless it violates condition (ii).

The significance of Arrow's theorem thus does not lie in showing that there can be no intuitively reasonable criterion for a fair outcome, given the actual preference scales. We have seen that there is no single such criterion capable of commanding universal assent; but we have canvassed a number of criteria each of which is fairly reasonable by intuitive standards. The significance of the theorem lies, rather, in its close connection with the result proved in the last chapter, that there can be no straightforward procedure, and hence no procedure that will with certainty elicit from the voters their true preference scales. It is for this reason that it deserves to be considered the fundamental theorem of voting theory.

Since no voting procedure is straightforward, it is not to be held against any particular procedure that it offers to certain voters a choice of admissible strategies. The concept of a 'sincere' strategy is certainly to be shunned in discussing voting procedures generally, both because of its inappropriate moral connotations and because it often has no clear application. Under a procedure in which the complete list mechanism is used, however, the application is evident, and we may employ the notion so long as we strip it of moral content. If we say that a voter votes *strategically* whenever he departs from his sincere voting strategy, we may regard it as a defect in a voting procedure that it offers a substantial incentive for strategic voting. This chapter is devoted to enquiring how far the alternative vote procedure offers such an incentive.

When the number of voters is large, there is a certain artificiality, which is nevertheless harmless, in studying such a question in the framework we have been using. The circumstances in which there is a set of voters who, under a given majority procedure, have an incentive to enter an alliance to vote strategically, and perhaps inadmissibly, are clear: they are those in which the sincere situation—that in which every voter votes sincerely—produces an outcome which is not a top. We have been principally concerned with the case in which a voter who has not entered any alliance has to choose his voting strategy: and we have represented him as estimating the probability of each possible contingency, and working out the effect, in each such contingency, of his adopting this or that admissible strategy. Since a contingency consists in a choice of strategy by each of the other voters, this in effect involves his taking the way every other voter votes as given, that is, as beyond his control. When the voters are members of a small committee, this is a reasonable representation of the way any individual voter is likely to think; but it is psychologically unrealistic when the number of voters is large, as in a parliamentary or municipal election. In such cases, no voter will be disposed to regard it as in the least likely that the outcome would be affected by a change in any one voter's vote. It might be retorted that it is only the possibility of such a contingency that gives him any incentive to vote at all, so that he must base his decision how to vote upon the supposition that some one such contingency obtains, improbable as that may be: but this is not an accurate representation of how voters think.

Hardly anyone would ever participate in a parliamentary election if he believed that it was pointless to do so unless there was a significant chance that his vote would affect the outcome. People do so because they are swayed by the thought, not merely that it would have a bad effect if everybody refrained from voting, but that it would be especially disastrous if just those who share their political opinions refrained. It is an intricate problem to say just when the argument, 'Think what would happen if everybody did that', is legitimately suasive, and when it is rightly answered by, 'They won't'; this is closely allied to the question when 'If I don't do it, someone else will' is a legitimate defence, and when not. The more the issue belongs to ethics than to prudential calculation, the more force 'What if everyone did that?' will have: but the line is not simply to be drawn along the divide between the moral and the prudential. The question has to do with responsibility for the effects of action. If an individual action is unlikely to have any great effects in itself, but is such that some great good could be obtained or evil averted if many were to perform similar actions, one may reasonably regard oneself as incurring a responsibility for the loss of that good or the occurrence of that evil if one does not take the action, however little hope one may have had of success. This applies especially when it is a moral responsibility; but, even when it is not, one may reasonably be guided by the thought, 'I shall have no right to complain if I do not do what I can.'

This explains, not only why people vote at all in parliamentary or local elections, but why they vote as they do. A voter who, in a British or American election, votes for the candidate of his second choice because he believes that the one he likes best is unlikely to get in cannot be presumed to think it at all likely that the candidate he votes for will win by one vote. If he thought of the votes of the other voters as something unalterably given, the only rational motive for his voting as he did would be the possibility that he might just tip the scale: but he does not so think of them. He votes, rather, as he hopes that others who share his opinions and preferences will decide to vote: he acts as if his decision were a sign of what the decisions of all who have the same preferences as he will turn out to have been. Is this a rational way to think? It is, provided that it is how most people think, for then those with the same preferences are quite likely to arrive at the same decision. If most people did not think in this way, it would not be rational for anyone to do so; but it is in fact how most people think when deciding how to vote, and, if it were not, it is doubtful that parliamentary democracy would work at all.

None of this invalidates an investigation of the incentive for strategic voting by considering a single voter who regards the choice of strategies by the other voters as fixed independently of his own. This is because it would always be easy to modify any example in which an individual voter could gain an advantage by departing from his sincere strategy so as to yield one in which a whole group of like-minded voters could gain such an advantage by all deviating in the same way from their sincere strategies. To discuss the matter in terms of the advantage to be gained by a single voter on the assumption that no other voter will vary his strategy is thus no more than a convenience: it will still pick out just those strategies which a voter with a given preference scale might consider adopting even when he was assuming that other voters with the same preference scale were likely to arrive at the same decision as he. The disadvantage of discussing the question in this framework is that the contingencies in which it will be advantageous for a single voter to depart from his sincere strategy will be comparatively rare, whereas it will happen far more frequently that it will profit a whole group of like-minded voters to do so. For this reason, it is as wrong to dismiss such contingencies as hardly likely to arise as to criticize someone who votes for B in an election because he thinks that his favourite candidate C has no genuine chance on the ground that it is hardly likely that B will win by a single vote.

Advocates of the alternative vote procedure invariably make great play with the concept of a wasted vote, claiming it as the great merit of the procedure that it reduces the number of voters who waste their votes. Unfortunately, they hardly ever attempt to specify what it means to say that someone has wasted his vote. The primary application of the concept is to the relative majority procedure; but it needs to be explained in general terms if we are to judge that some other procedure will involve fewer wasted votes. Suppose that, in an election for a city councillor under the relative majority procedure, the following votes are cast for each of three candidates:

A	B	C
4,500	4,000	1,500

A voter who voted for C and whose preference scale is CBA will be tempted to think that he has wasted his vote, on the ground that, if all who voted for C had voted instead for B, B would have been elected: but this ignores the question whether they would have had any motive to do so. We cannot say which voters, if any, have wasted their votes until we know what the preference scales are. Suppose that they were as follows:

voted for	A	A	A	B	B	C	C
preference scale	A	A	A	B	C	C	C
	BC	C	B	C	B	A	B
		B	C	A	A	B	A
number	4,300	150	50	3,000	1,000	1,300	200

Here 1,000 voters, impelled by the thought that they would be wasting their vote by voting for C, the candidate they liked best, gave their votes to B. Provided that every voter voted admissibly, however, B had no chance of winning. The voters with the preference scale $A(BC)$ could vote admissibly only for A, who is therefore guaranteed at least 4,300 votes. A voter cannot vote admissibly for the candidate he ranks lowest: hence at most 4,250 votes could go to B. On the other hand, if all those who ranked C highest had voted for C, together with at least 2,001 of those who ranked B highest, C would have been elected. In this case, therefore, if we use the notion of a wasted vote at all, we must say that those who voted for B wasted their votes, not those who voted for C.

When the relative majority procedure is used, therefore, we may say that a voter wastes his vote if he votes for a candidate who had no chance of winning, given the preference scales of the voters, provided that they voted admissibly. The only way of generalizing this is to say that, under any procedure, someone wastes his vote if he adopts a 2-inadmissible strategy. The 'wasted vote' terminology of course implies that it is a bad thing for a voter to waste his vote: and we may agree that it is a pity when voters adopt 2-inadmissible strategies, for then they are voting as they would not have done if they had known the preferences of the other voters. It is not always an unmitigated pity, however: under a procedure that produces the fairest outcome whenever all voters vote sincerely, it is more of a pity when some vote strategically; if, under such a procedure, a sincere strategy happens to be 2-inadmissible for a certain voter, it is more for the general good that he should adopt it than that he should depart from it. If, then, a procedure has a good claim frequently to produce a fair outcome under sincere voting, a further claim to discourage 2-inadmissible voting will not be an unalloyed merit: we have to see whether this is achieved by encouraging 2-admissible departures from a sincere strategy. The relative majority procedure has, of course, no claim to produce the fairest outcome; in the above example, a departure by the 3,000 voters who sincerely voted for B from their sincere but 2-inadmissible strategy would have been in no way regrettable, since C was the only top and had the highest preference score.

We may therefore begin our examination of the alternative vote procedure from a simpler standpoint than that of the ambiguous concept of the wasted vote. There are three properties whose possession by a procedure employing the complete list mechanism would simplify a voter's choice of strategy:

(i) listing a highest always maximizes a's chances of success;

(ii) listing a highest never increases c's chances of success at the expense of b's (c being different from a);

(iii) listing a first and b second never gives a a poorer chance of success than listing a first and c second.

A modified relative majority procedure is one using the complete list mechanism but disregarding all but the highest outcome on each voter's list except when two or more outcomes tie for having the greatest number of first choices. A modified relative majority procedure obviously has property (i); so do the preference score and majority number procedures. Notoriously, the relative majority procedure lacks property (ii): it is just this lack that gives rise to all the talk about wasted votes. The property is also lacked by the preference score procedure. Suppose that there are five possible outcomes, and that bracketing is allowed. A voter i has to decide how to list the outcomes. The other voters' lists give c $3\frac{1}{2}$ points more than b, and put both well ahead of the rest. If i lists b highest and c lowest, b will finish with the highest preference score, $\frac{1}{2}$ point ahead of c; but if he lists a highest, b second, and c lowest, c will be $\frac{1}{2}$ point ahead of b. The same is true of the majority number procedure: for listing a above b may just prevent b from having as high a majority number as c. The preference score procedure likewise lacks property (iii). Suppose that the voters other than i have put a and b well ahead of the rest, and a $1\frac{1}{2}$ points behind b. Then, if i lists a highest and b second, b will finish $\frac{1}{2}$ point ahead of a, whereas, if he lists a highest and b lower than second, b will finish at least $\frac{1}{2}$ point behind a. Similar considerations evidently apply to the majority number procedure. As for the modified relative majority procedure, the question turns entirely on the nature of the modification: if a and b tie as having the greatest number of voters listing them highest, the fact that b stands second in some voter's list might be decisive in its favour.

All three of these procedures thus possess property (i) and lack properties (ii) and (iii), although the modified relative majority procedure comes close to having property (iii) by dint of taking so little notice of second and third choices at all. Advocates of the alternative vote procedure make much of the fact that it possesses property (iii), and for a similar reason: the assessment process will pay no attention to the second and third choices of a voter who has listed a highest until the stage, if any, at which a is eliminated. Hoag and Hallett, in their book *Proportional Representation*, even propose that, in elections conducted by means of this procedure, the words, 'You cannot hurt the chances of any candidate you prefer by making lower choices for others', be printed on the ballot papers.[1] How,

---

[1] Op. cit., p. 83.

then, does it stand with the alternative vote procedure in respect of properties (i) and (ii)?

In practice, the tellers will at stage 1 of the assessment process eliminate all outcomes receiving no votes at that stage, i.e. standing highest on no voter's list, together with one other outcome. Furthermore, they will apply the rule that an outcome which at any stage receives an absolute majority of the votes is thereupon to be declared successful, the assessment process being broken off. For simplicity of exposition, however, it is convenient to assume that only one outcome is eliminated at each stage, so that, with r possible outcomes, the assessment process always goes through $r - 1$ stages: when two or more outcomes tie at any stage as having the smallest number of votes (which may be 0), that one of them ranked lowest by the chairman will be eliminated. To proceed in this way would in practice sometimes waste a great deal of the tellers' time, but could not affect the final outcome.

The analysis of the alternative vote procedure resembles closely that of the symmetrical elimination procedure with positive voting. At any stage, at most two of the outcomes remaining live at that stage will be at risk from any one voter i other than the chairman, when the lists submitted by the other voters are taken as given. If x is not at risk from i, we may say that it is *secure from* i; if x is the only outcome at risk from i, we may say that it is *doomed* at the stage in question. For each live outcome x, let x receive k_x votes from the voters other than i: that is to say, just k_x of those voters list x higher than any other live outcome. Let k be the smallest value assumed by k_x for any x; and let K be the set of those outcomes x for which $k_x = k$. If K has more than one member, every outcome not in K is secure from i. If K has two members b and c, both of them are at risk from i: if c stands lower than b on the chairman's list, it is at acute risk from i, and will be eliminated unless i has placed it higher on his list than any other live outcome; if he has, b will be eliminated. If K has more than two members, let c be that which stands lowest of them on the chairman's list, and b that which stands lower than any but c: then c is at acute risk, and b at risk, from i, and the other members of K are secure. If K has only one member c, it is doomed if there is no outcome receiving only $k + 1$ votes from the voters other than i. If there is one or more such outcome, let b be that standing lowest on the chairman's list: then c is at acute risk from i, and b at risk.

218   STRATEGIC VOTING

Now suppose that there are only three possible outcomes, and that the preference scale of a voter i, who is not the chairman, is abc. Can he, by listing the outcomes abc, increase c's chances at the expense of b's? If so, the procedure lacks property (ii). The contingency is specified when we know which outcomes are at risk from i at stage 1, together with what we may call the $\overline{R_{maj}}$ diagram. We may define '$xR_{maj}\,y$' to mean 'If i lists x higher than y, a majority of voters will have done so' (where 'majority' is interpreted in our usual way). Then '$x\overline{P_{maj}}y$' will mean 'However i votes, a majority of voters will have listed x higher than y.' We may further write 'i: (x)' to mean 'x is doomed at stage 1', 'i: (x, y)' to mean 'x is at acute risk from i at stage 1 and y at risk', and 'i: $(x|y)$' to mean 'i: (x, y) or i: (y, x)', i.e. 'x and y are both at risk from i at stage 1'. We have, then, to ask whether there is a contingency in which, if i lists the outcomes in the order abc, c will be successful, whereas, if he votes in some other way, b will be.

The answer is clearly that there is. One such type of contingency is that in which i: (b, c), $c\overline{P_{maj}}a$, and $b\overline{R_{maj}}a$. Unless i puts b at the head of his list, it will be eliminated at stage 1 and c will be the final outcome: if he lists the outcomes in the order bac, c will be eliminated at stage 1 and b will be the final outcome. An example is as follows:

1–7	8–10	11–16	17	18, 19	20–5
a	a	b	b	c	c
b	c	c	a	a	b
c	b	a	c	b	a

Example 1

If every voter save voter 2 votes sincerely, the two stages of the assessment process will go as follows, according as voter 2 votes sincerely or strategically:

2 votes sincerely:			2 votes bac:		
a	b	c	a	b	c
10	7	8	9	8	8
11	—	14	11	14	—

The second type of contingency in which c will be the final outcome if i votes sincerely, but b will be successful if he lists it highest, is that in which i: $(a|b)$, $c\overline{P_{maj}}a$, and $b\overline{R_{maj}}c$. An example is:

1–5	6	7–9	10, 11	12–14	15–19
a	a	b	b	c	c
b	c	c	a	a	b
c	b	a	c	b	a

Example 2

Given sincere voting by all save perhaps voter 2, the two possible courses of the assessment process are:

2 votes sincerely:			2 votes *bac*:		
a	b	c	a	b	c
6	5	8	5	6	8
8	—	11	—	10	9

The alternative vote procedure thus lacks property (ii). This forms no basis for any criticism of it, since the defect is shared with almost all other procedures. The simulated amendment procedure (diagram 12.1)

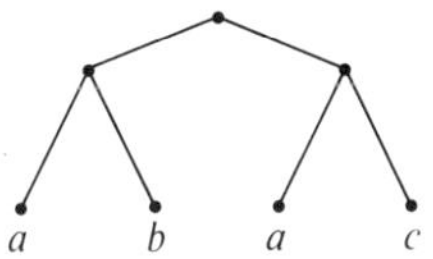

Diagram 12.1

indeed has property (ii) as stated above: listing *a* highest cannot increase *c*'s chances of success. The procedure is asymmetrical with respect to the outcomes, however; listing *b* highest *can* increase *a*'s chances of success at the expense of *c*'s. To say that no voter can bring about the success of *z* rather than *y* by listing *x* above *y* is to say that the only feature of his list relevant to which, of *y* and *z*, is successful is the relative position on it of *y* and *z*. This cannot hold, under any voting procedure, for every voter and every pair of outcomes *y* and *z*, except of course when they are the only possible outcomes: and so it cannot hold, for *any* pair of outcomes and every voter, under any procedure symmetrical with respect to the outcomes.[2]

[2] Under a method of assessment for which listing *x* higher than *y* always increased *x*'s chances of success as compared to *y*'s, property (ii) would thus be a consequence of Arrow's principle of independence of irrelevant alternatives, considered as a feature of that method of assessment. The same is true of property (iii); for it will follow from that principle that *a*'s chances of winning, when a voter has listed it first, cannot be affected by his relative placing of any other two outcomes. The impossibility of devising a voting procedure having property (ii), for every voter and every trio of possible outcomes, thus reflects the impossibility of a straightforward procedure, and illustrates the close connection between the latter result and Arrow's theorem remarked on at the opening of the chapter.

The lack of property (ii) by the alternative vote procedure is nevertheless important, because so much of the propaganda in its favour suggests that it is superior to the relative majority procedure precisely in virtue of possessing property (ii). The celebrated phenomenon of the wasted vote occurs under the relative majority procedure when *a* has no chance of winning, and a group of voters with the preference scale *abc* allow *c* to win by voting for *a* although, by voting for *b*, they could have caused *b* to win. Advocates of the alternative vote procedure point out, quite correctly, that, when *a* is doomed to be eliminated at stage 1, no voter with the preference scale *abc* stands to lose by listing *a* highest; they omit to point out that this is not the only case in which *a* has no chance of final success. If a majority of the voters have listed *b* higher than *a*, and a majority have listed *c* higher than *a*, *a* will be defeated at stage 2 even if not eliminated at stage 1; and a group of voters who list *a* highest may then well bring about the elimination of *b* at stage 1. Or, again, if a majority of voters have listed *c* above *a*, and *c* is secure from a group of voters at stage 1, *a* has no chance of winning, whatever those voters do; and it may be that their only chance of preventing *b* from being eliminated at stage 1 is to list it higher than *a*. It is unfair both to those who have to decide what procedure to adopt and to those who have to operate the procedure adopted to advertise the alternative vote procedure as having merits it does not possess.

A genuinely grave defect in that procedure is its lack of property (i). Consideration of the first type of contingency discussed above easily shows that it does not have it. If *a* is secure from *i* at stage 1, he has no need to list it highest in order to prevent its elimination; but the eventual success of *a* may depend upon the elimination of the outcome not at acute risk. If *i*: (*b*, *c*) and $c\overline{P_{\text{maj}}}a$, but $a\overline{P_{\text{maj}}}b$, the only way *i* has to prevent *c* from winning is to cause it to be eliminated at stage 1, which he can do only by listing *b* highest; if he does this, *a* will be the final outcome. An example is:

1–4	5–8	9–13	14–17	18, 19
a	*a*	*b*	*c*	*c*
b	*c*	*c*	*a*	*b*
c	*b*	*a*	*b*	*a*

Example 3

If all but voter 2 sincerely, the possible courses of the assessment process are:

	2 votes sincerely:			2 votes *bac*:	
a	*b*	*c*	*a*	*b*	*c*
8	5	6	7	6	6
8	—	11	11	8	—

Conversely, if i: (c, b), $b\overline{P_{\text{maj}}}a$, and $a\overline{P_{\text{maj}}}c$, i will bring about the victory of a if he lists the outcomes in the order *cab*; if he votes sincerely, b will be the final outcome. An example is:

1–5	6, 7	8	9–13	14	15–19
a	*a*	*b*	*b*	*c*	*c*
b	*c*	*c*	*a*	*a*	*b*
c	*b*	*a*	*c*	*b*	*a*

Example 4

Given sincere voting by all but voter 2, the possible courses of the assessment process run:

	2 votes sincerely:			2 votes *cab*:	
a	*b*	*c*	*a*	*b*	*c*
7	6	6	6	6	7
8	11	—	11	—	8

The lack of property (i) by the alternative vote procedure, like its lack of property (ii), gravely weakens the strength of the case usually made for it; but it is also a severe defect in itself. It bears in the first instance upon an individual voter's confidence that he is voting in a manner most likely to be favourable to his hopes. A voter with the preference scale *abc* who is very strongly committed to the success of *a*, but whose preference for *b* over *c* is only slight, will doubtless be comforted by the knowledge that the procedure has property (iii): if he lists *a* highest, he will not do any harm to its chances by listing *b* second. But he will be greatly perturbed to know that the procedure lacks property (i): he may not assume that, by listing *a* highest, he is not harming its chances. If a voter with this preference scale is at least as committed to the defeat of *c* as to the success of *a*, property (iii) will not seem very important to him: he would be prepared to diminish *a*'s chances somewhat if he thereby reduced those of *c*. The possibility that, by listing *a* highest, he might thereby be increasing *c*'s chances at the expense of *a*'s, on the other hand, is something no voter who likes *a* best and *c* least can view with equanimity: under most procedures, this possibility does not arise, but under the alternative vote procedure it does. The sentence, 'You cannot hurt the chances of any candidate you prefer by making lower choices for others', which Hoag and Hallett wanted to see printed on the ballot papers in elections under the alternative vote procedure, might well lead someone to believe that he could not hurt a's chances by listing a first and b second, and, if so, he would have been deceived. The only honest instruction to the voter would involve adding, 'but you can in some cases hurt the chances of the candidate you prefer by listing him first'.

It may be retorted that cases of this kind—namely those in which the sincere situation (that in which each voter votes sincerely) is vulnerable to any one voter who ranks a highest—are very rare. So they are, but that is beside the point. First, in accordance with what was said at the beginning of this chapter, the relevant question is how often the sincere situation will be vulnerable to some *group* of voters all of whom rank a highest; such cases will be far less rare. Secondly, if the alternative vote procedure lacked only one of the properties (i) to (iii), the failure of that property would provide the principal incentive for strategic voting, just as it is the failure of property (ii) that provides the incentive for strategic voting under the relative majority procedure. Property (ii) fails also under the alternative vote procedure, however; its failure is not so drastic, but this fact is counterbalanced by the failure of property (i). If a voter with the preference scale *abc* believes that, by voting *bac*, he will prevent c from winning and will bring about the victory of either a or b, he has a motive so to vote. He does not need to know that he will bring about the victory of a; if he believes that to be his only chance of bringing about the defeat of c, that will be motive enough, a motive that is reinforced by, but does not rest on, the hope of causing a to be the final outcome.

Suppose that some voters with the preference scale *abc* know that well over a third, but well under a half, of the voters support a. They will therefore not fear that a will be eliminated at stage 1, but not hope that it will gain an absolute majority outright. If they know further that most supporters of b prefer c to a, they will think it of great importance to prevent the elimination of b, since otherwise c will win. They will therefore have a motive for listing b highest, even if they do not know whether the effect will be that a or b will win, something that will in large part depend on the second choices of c's supporters. Conversely, if they know that a large body of c's supporters prefer a to b, they will again have a motive for listing b first, in order to bring about a victory for a, even if they are in the dark about the preferences of b's supporters as between a and c. The preference scales might in fact be as follows, there the figure at the head of each column indicates the number of voters with the preference scale shown:

5	35	22	6	21	11
a	a	b	b	c	c
b	c	c	a	a	b
c	b	a	c	b	a

Example 5

If all vote sincerely, b will be eliminated at stage 1 and c will win at stage 2 by 54 votes to 46; if the five voters with the preference scale abc vote bac, c will be eliminated at stage 1 and a will win at stage 2 by 56 votes to 44. These five voters do not need to know or guess both of these facts to perceive the advantage of a strategic vote: it will be apparent to them if they guess either one.

The strongest incentive for strategic voting under the alternative vote procedure, as under the relative majority procedure, lies in its lack of property (ii). Suppose that b and c are rather similar proposals, between which the opponents of a are split; it is then likely, and may well become clear from discussion, that most supporters of either b or c prefer the other to a. If it is also clear that a does not command an absolute majority, any supporter of a who feels strongly about the choice between b and c is probably wise to abandon hope of a's success, and to place highest on his list that one of b and c which he prefers to the other. His motive is the same as that of voters under the relative majority procedure who vote for their second choice instead of their first. Again, if a voter with the preference scale abc knows that b's supporters overwhelmingly prefer c to a, and that the supporters of c number over a third but under a half of the voters, he has a clear motive to list the outcomes bac, especially if he cares more that c should be defeated than that a should win. His principal object is to defeat c; his motive is strengthened by the possibility that he may be helping to bring about a victory for a. When a is eliminated at stage 1, a voter with the preference scale abc will admittedly have done himself no harm by listing a highest, but he will also have done himself no good thereby; but when a is defeated at stage 2 by c, it may be that he could have averted that disaster by listing the outcomes bac.

When there are only three possible outcomes, a voter with the preference scale *abc* may admissibly list the outcomes in any of the three orders *abc*, *bac*, and *cab*: it is obvious that these are his only admissible strategies. The peculiar characteristics of the alternative vote procedure come out in their full strength only when there are more than three possible outcomes, however; for then, if two outcomes are at risk from a voter at stage 1, it may depend upon which of them is eliminated which outcomes are at risk from him at stage 2. What strategies are admissible to a voter *i* with a strong preference scale when there are four possible outcomes?

In any given contingency in which, under any voting procedure, the voter *i* may be, we may call *y* a *possible winner* if *i* has a strategy that will result in *y*'s being the final outcome; and we may call *x* the *best attainable outcome* for *i* if it is that possible winner which he prefers to any other. A strategy is then *optimal* for *i* in that contingency if it results in the best attainable outcome. A strategy σ is admissible for *i* if there exists a contingency in which σ is optimal and if it rivals every other strategy τ optimal in that contingency; in particular, σ will rival τ if there is some other contingency in which σ is optimal but τ is not. If there is some contingency in which σ is the unique optimal strategy, we may thus conclude immediately that σ is admissible. Under the alternative vote procedure with four possible outcomes, there is no contingency in which a voter *i* has a unique optimal strategy. A strategy is in fact admissible for him if it involves listing the outcomes in an order *xyzw* such that zP_iw. Let us call the strategy of listing the outcomes in the order *xyzw regular* if yP_izP_iw, and *smooth* if xP_iy and zP_iw. Thus, if *i*'s preference scale is *abcd*, his only strategy that is both regular and smooth is the sincere strategy of listing the outcomes *abcd*: his other regular strategies consist of listing them in one of the orders *bacd*, *cabd*, and *dabc*; and his other smooth strategies consist of listing them in one of the orders *acbd*, *adbc*, *bcad*, *bdac*, and *cdab*. In every contingency, *i* will have a regular optimal strategy: he may reasonably confine his choice of strategy to those that are either regular or smooth. The strategy *cbad*, for example, is admissible, though neither regular nor smooth. There will be contingencies in which both it and the regular strategy *cabd* are optimal, but the smooth strategy *bcad* is not; and others in which both it and the smooth strategy are optimal, but the regular one is not; and yet others in which *cabd* is optimal, but neither *cbad* nor *bcad* is, or in which *bcad* is optimal, but neither *cbad* nor *cabd* is.

It is in a high degree unlikely that i would be in a position to judge the contingency to be of either of the first two kinds, without being able to judge of which of the two it was specifically. For this reason, he would have little motive to adopt the strategy *cbad* or either of the other two admissible strategies neither regular nor smooth, *dbac* and *dcab*.

Any specific contingency may impose certain constraints on a strategy for it to be optimal for the voter i. Since i must have an optimal strategy, the constraints must be compatible with one another; any strategy that satisfies all the constraints will be optimal. The constraints can be classified according as they arise out of stage 1, stage 2, or stage 3 of the assessment process. There will be a stage-1 constraint only if two outcomes y and z are at risk from i at stage 1, and i has no optimal strategy that results in the elimination of y at that stage. If y is at acute risk, the constraint will be that i list y highest; if z is at acute risk, it will be that i should not list z highest. A stage-2 constraint, if there is one, must arise in the same way. Suppose that i has an optimal strategy that results in the elimination of an outcome z at stage 1. If, then, two outcomes v and w will be at risk from i at stage 2 if z is eliminated at stage 1, and i has no optimal strategy that results in the survival of w to stage 3, there will be a stage-2 constraint. If v is at acute risk, the constraint will be that i list v higher than any other outcome save z; if w is at acute risk, it will be that i list w lower than some outcome other than z. If i followed an optimal strategy, he can have placed the outcome z eliminated at stage 1 highest on his list only if z was doomed at stage 1. In that case, such a stage-2 constraint can be as well satisfied by his placing z highest and v second as by his placing v highest. When no outcome is doomed at stage 1, a stage-2 constraint can only limit i's choice of the outcome to be listed highest, in addition to the limitation imposed by any stage-1 constraint that holds. Finally, a stage-3 constraint must take the form of requiring i to list x higher than some outcome u, perhaps conditionally upon his choice of outcomes to be listed first and second, where x is the best attainable outcome. From all this the statements made in the preceding paragraph may be deduced.

A complete analysis of the opportunities for strategic voting under the alternative vote procedure when there are four possible outcomes is extremely complex, because of the large number of distinct types of contingency that may obtain. We may rest content with one

226   STRATEGIC VOTING

example to show the failure of property (i) and one to show that of property (ii). We may write 'y is at acute risk from i, and z at risk, at stage 1' as '$i: (y, z)_1$', and 'if z is eliminated at stage 1, v is at acute risk from i, and w at risk, at stage 2' as '$i: \not z \to (v, w)_2$'; '$i: (z)_1$' is to mean that z is doomed at stage 1, and similarly for stage 2.

In both examples, we assume that voter 2 has the preference scale $abcd$ and that every other voter votes sincerely. The preference scales are:

1	2	3	4	5	6	7	8	9	10	11	12	13	14	15	16	17	18	19	20
c	a	a	a	a	a	a	b	b	b	b	c	c	c	d	d	d	d	d	d
a	b	c	d	d	d	b	c	c	c	d	a	a	d						
d	c					d	a	a	a										
b	d					c	d	d	d										

Example 6

It makes no difference to the example how the blank spaces in the above table are filled in: as usual under this procedure, determinate assumptions about how the assessment process will go under sincere voting by every voter but one still leave room for wide variation in the R_{maj} relations and preference scores. This fact illustrates how little correlation there is between the outcome under the alternative vote procedure, even with sincere voting, and the fairest outcome by either criterion. Thus, in example 6, we know from the data in the table only that a has a majority number of at least 1, b and c one of at most 2, and d one of exactly 2; and that a has a preference score of from 27 to 41, b one of from 16 to 35, c one of from 21 to 37, and d one of from 30 to 33, so that any one of them could conceivably have the highest preference score and as high a majority number as any.

Relatively to voter 2, the contingency has the following features:

$$2: (b, c)_1$$
$$2: \not b \to (a)_2 \qquad 2: \not c \to (b)_2$$
$$\overline{dP_{maj}c} \qquad \overline{aP_{maj}d}$$

The marked preference of the chairman (voter 1) for c over b puts b at acute risk from voter 2 at stage 1. The fact that a, though a possible winner, is doomed at stage 2 if b is eliminated at stage 1 imposes the stage-1 constraint on voter 2's optimal strategy that he list b highest. The following are the stages of the assessment process according as voter 2 votes sincerely or adopts the regular strategy of listing the outcomes $bacd$:

2 votes sincerely:				2 votes *bacd*:			
a	*b*	*c*	*d*	*a*	*b*	*c*	*d*
6	4	4	6	5	5	4	6
6	—	7	7	8	5	—	7
—	—	9	11	12	—	—	8

Thus *d* is the final outcome if voter 2 votes sincerely, but *a* is if he adopts his optimal strategy.

In the next example, *b* is the best attainable outcome for voter 2.

1	2	3	4	5	6	7	8	9	10	11	12	13	14	15	16	17
a	*a*	*a*	*a*	*b*	*b*	*b*	*c*	*c*	*c*	*c*	*c*	*d*	*d*	*d*	*d*	*d*
c	*b*	*b*	*b*	*d*	*d*	*d*						*b*	*b*	*b*	*a*	*a*
d	*c*	*d*	*d*												*b*	*c*
b	*d*	*c*	*c*												*c*	*b*

Example 7

The decisive features of the contingency are:

$$2\colon (b, a)_1$$
$$2\colon \not{b} \to (a)_2 \qquad 2\colon \not{d} \to (b, d)_2$$
$$d\overline{P_{\text{maj}}}c \qquad\qquad b\overline{P_{\text{maj}}}c$$

It is thus again a stage-1 constraint that voter 2 list *b* highest: the course of the assessment process, according as he votes sincerely or adopts the strategy *bacd*, is:

2 votes sincerely:				2 votes *bacd*:			
a	*b*	*c*	*d*	*a*	*b*	*c*	*d*
4	3	5	5	3	4	5	5
4	—	5	8	—	6	6	5
—	—	7	10	—	10	7	—

If voter 2 votes sincerely, *d* will be the final outcome; if he votes *bacd*, it will be *b*.

It is difficult to estimate how much strategic voting will occur under the alternative vote procedure when there are more than three possible outcomes. Regarded in one way, it matters little. The claim of the preference score and majority number procedures is to produce the fairest outcome whenever voting is sincere; the existence of a strong incentive to depart from a sincere strategy would then lessen the value of the claim. A procedure, like the alternative vote, that frequently fails to produce the fairest outcome when voting is sincere will probably not fail more frequently when strategic voting occurs; from this standpoint, therefore, the strength of the incentive to vote strategically is unimportant. It is, indeed, a disadvantage to a voter that he lacks a straightforward strategy, or even one that will be optimal in almost all contingencies. The chief reason for investigating strategic voting under the alternative vote procedure is to dispel the suggestion only just below the surface of the propaganda of its advocates that it achieves the impossible feat of providing a straightforward strategy for every voter. There will be little or no strategic voting by those who know or surmise little about other voters' intentions: as under every procedure, a sincere strategy will be optimal in more contingencies than any other. Equally, voters unfamiliar with the procedure are likely to vote sincerely under it. But a voter who has understood the working of the procedure, and who has some information about the probable intentions of the others, will have nearly as much incentive to vote strategically as under the relative majority procedure. Advocates of the alternative vote harp on the fact that a voter who ranks a highest derives no incentive for not listing it highest from the probability of its elimination at stage 1. This is counterbalanced by the fact that in such a case he has little incentive for listing it highest; and by the further fact, not stressed by partisans of the procedure, that such a voter has little incentive for listing a highest if he is confident that it will *not* be eliminated at stage 1: in either case, he may have a strong incentive for listing some other outcome highest. The voter likewise has little incentive for listing a highest if he is convinced that it will either be eliminated at a later stage or defeated at the final stage. Advocates of the procedure tend to write as though the only ground for believing an outcome to have no chance is the knowledge that it has few committed supporters, making it likely to be eliminated at stage 1. This is obviously untrue: one may know of an outcome that, although it has significantly many supporters, there is also strong opposition to it, dooming it to defeat at a later stage.

When there is a very large number of voters, as in an election, it is highly improbable that any single voter can affect the outcome; but a group of like-minded voters may do so. Voters whose first choice is a, but who despair of a's success, may bring about a victory for their second choice b by all listing b highest. It is very much more tricky for supporters of a to achieve a victory for a by voting strategically. Unless they engage in some carefully planned collusion, they are likely to do so only as a by-product of a plan whose principal purpose is to prevent a victory by some outcome they particularly dislike, as in example 5. In that example, the strategy of the voters with the preference scale *abc* was based on their confidence that *a* was secure from elimination at stage 1; if there had been as many as nine of them, the result of their voting *bac* would have been that *a*, not *c*, was eliminated. With detailed and reasonably accurate information about the intentions of the voters, such as can be obtained from well-conducted opinion polls, and with a thorough canvass to identify its own supporters, an organized group such as a political party can evade this danger if its supporters are well disciplined: it can instruct sufficiently many supporters to list *a* highest to ensure that *a* is not eliminated at stage 1, and instruct the rest to list *b* highest, in order to bring about the elimination of *a*'s principal rival *c*. It is not far-fetched to imagine a political organization's acting in this way: an instance of instructions of just this kind, under a different voting procedure, issued by the Birmingham Liberal Association in the Parliamentary election of 1880 is cited by Bogdanor in his book *The People and the Party System*.[3]

There remains the question of 'wasted votes'. We earlier proposed to identify a wasted vote with the adoption of a 2-inadmissible strategy, i.e. a vote cast in a manner that could not be advantageous, given the preference scales of the other voters. On this definition, there would never be any wasted votes under the alternative vote procedure. This is because each voter has so many admissible strategies that a knowledge of the voters' preference scales, combined with the presumption that they will all vote admissibly, will never even restrict the possible course of the assessment process: hence every admissible strategy is also 2-admissible. This can hardly be held to capture what is meant when 'wasted votes' are discussed: our definition was too restrictive. Let us say, rather, that i's vote is wasted if the actual situation was vulnerable to a set A of voters containing i, but not vulnerable to the set formed from A by dropping i from it. This is to say that i wastes his vote if he, together with certain other voters, could have obtained an outcome they all preferred by voting differently, this time on the assumption, not merely that all the rest voted admissibly, but that they voted as in fact they did; the second clause of the definition is required in order to guarantee that, to obtain the preferable outcome, i would actually

[3] Op. cit., pp. 103–4.

have had to vote differently, given that no one outside the set *A* did so. On this definition, then, there will be voters who have wasted their votes whenever the situation is unstable. When a majority procedure is being used, there will have been wasted votes whenever the outcome is not a top; in particular, there will be wasted votes, whatever the outcome, when there is no top. This of course depends solely on the preference scales, and not upon the details of the procedure, provided only that it is a majority procedure. In this respect, therefore, no majority procedure has an advantage over any other. Votes will be wasted, according to this definition, even when there is a top, if the actual outcome is not a top; they will also be wasted when the situation is not stable, even though it produces a stable outcome. Under the alternative vote procedure, as indeed under any procedure, symmetrical with respect to the outcomes, that takes a significant account of second or later choices, the situation in which all vote sincerely will more frequently be stable than under the relative majority procedure; that is only to say that it is an improvement upon the very worst of all procedures. As we have seen, however, the 'sincere situation' can quite easily be unstable under the alternative vote. It is entirely possible that the proposed definition of a wasted vote does not accord with the intentions of those who employ the concept; there is no way of eliminating that possibility, since they never trouble to explain what they do mean. The reader may like to see if he can devise any more plausible definition.

13
Strategic Voting: Preference Score and Majority Number Procedures

What are the admissible strategies under the preference score procedure? Suppose that there are six possible outcomes and fourteen voters, with preference scales as follows:

1	2	3	4	5	6	7	8	9	10	11	12	13	14
e	a	a	b	c	d	e	f	d	c	b	f	a	b
d	b	b	c	d	e	f	a	c	b	f	a	e	c
c	c	c	d	e	f	a	b	b	f	a	e	d	d
b	d	d	e	f	a	b	c	f	a	e	d	c	e
f	e	e	f	a	b	c	d	a	e	d	c	b	a
a	f	f	a	b	c	d	e	e	d	c	b	f	f

Example 1

Suppose that all the voters other than voter 2 vote sincerely: they will then collectively make the following contributions to the preference scores of the various outcomes:

a	b	c	d	e	f
31	35	34	33	32	30

In what order must voter 2 list the outcomes if his first choice a is to win? Clearly he will give a the best chance if he puts it at the head of his list, in which case it will obtain a total preference score of 36. Voter 2 must therefore ensure that b has a total preference score of less than 36: if it ties for top score with a, the chairman (voter 1) will give his casting vote for it against a. The total preference score of b will be less than 36 only if voter 2 puts it last on his list; he could put it equal last with one other if bracketing is allowed, but let us suppose for simplicity that it is not. Similarly, c will get a preference score of less than 36 only if voter 2 puts it no higher than fifth: since b must occupy the sixth place, he must place c fifth. Likewise he must place d fourth and e third: f must therefore be second. Hence the only winning strategy for voter 2 is to list the outcomes in the order *afedcb*, in which case the total preference scores will be:

a	b	c	d	e	f
36	35	35	35	35	34

and *a* will win. Listing the outcomes in this order is thus an admissible strategy for a voter with the preference scale *abcdef*. It is obvious that we could vary this example by applying any arbitrary permutation to the outcomes other than *a*. It therefore follows that any listing of the outcomes in which *a* occupies the highest place represents an admissible strategy for a voter who ranks *a* highest.

Suppose, now, that the voters other than voter 2 together contribute the following numbers of points to the various preference scores:

a	b	c	d	e	f
25	32	36	35	34	33

It will then be impossible for *a* to win, however voter 2 votes. His optimal strategy is therefore one that results in a victory for *b*: and the only listing that will achieve this is *bafedc*, which will yield the following total preference scores:

a	b	c	d	e	f
29	37	36	36	36	36

When voter 2's optimal strategy requires him to put *b* at the head of his list, he can in no case gain any advantage by not putting *a* in second place. On the other hand, the example could be varied by applying any arbitrary permutation to the outcomes *c*, *d*, *e*, and *f*. Thus for voter 2 any listing with *b* in first place and *a* in second represents an admissible strategy.

By similar reasoning, if voter 2 has no strategy that will result in a victory for either *a* or *b*, his optimal strategy may consist in putting *c* at the head of his list, followed by *a* and *b* in that order, and then the remaining outcomes *d*, *e*, and *f* in any one specific order. As before, his optimal strategy may require that *a* and *b* occupy the second and third places between them, and can never require that they do not.

Generalizing this, we may pick out certain conditions on the list returned by a voter i, of whom we assume only that he is not indifferent between all the outcomes. Let us say that an outcome z is *worst* for i if yR_iz for every outcome y (there may thus be more than one worst outcome); and let x be the outcome listed highest by i. Then the relevant conditions are: (1) x is not a worst outcome for i; (2) if yR_ix and z is worst for i, y stands higher on i's list than z; (3) if wP_iyR_ix, then w stands higher on i's list than y; and (4) if yR_ixP_iu, then y stands higher on i's list than u. We may call a strategy *regular* if it consists in listing the outcomes in an order that satisfies all the conditions (1) to (4). If i adopts a regular strategy, he will list highest some outcome x that is not worst for him; x will then be immediately followed on his list by those outcomes he regards as at least as good as x, in their true order of preference (save for arbitrary choices of precedence between those of them between which he is indifferent). In every contingency, some regular strategy will be optimal for i. To be admissible, a strategy need not satisfy condition (4). For example, in a contingency in which d and f are the only possible winners, the listing *deabcf* will be optimal for the voter 2 discussed above, as will the regular listing *dabcef*; but *deabcf* will also be optimal in certain contingencies in which e and f are the only possible winners. Thus, if we call a strategy *semi-regular* if it consists in listing the outcomes in an order satisfying conditions (1) to (3), but not necessarily (4), there will be no single regular strategy that dominates one that is semi-regular but not regular. In fact, if voter 2 despaired of victory for a, b, or c, but was anxious above all to prevent f's being the final outcome, the listing *deabcf* might appear quite attractive to him. Nor does condition (3) govern all admissible strategies. For instance, if voter 2 is mistaken in believing c to have no chance of success, it may be that, by listing the outcomes in the regular order *dabcef*, he will bring about a victory for d, or even for f, whereas, if he had listed them in the order *dcabef*, c would have been the final outcome: again, there is no single semi-regular (or regular) strategy that dominates that of listing the outcomes in the second of these two orders. Thus a listing is admissible for a voter i provided only that it satisfies conditions (1) and (2), namely that any outcome that is worst for him is listed lower than any he ranks at least as high as the outcome x he lists highest.

Thus, if there are four possible outcomes, a voter who has a strong preference scale will have 11 admissible strategies, out of the 24 available to him, of which 9 will be regular (one will violate condition (3) and one condition (4)); of the 9 regular strategies, 6 will involve listing a highest, where a is the outcome he prefers to all others. This compares with 12 admissible strategies under the alternative vote procedure, of which 9 are either regular or smooth, only 3 of which involve listing *a* highest. With six possible outcomes, such a voter has 274 admissible strategies, out of 720 available to him, of which 153 are regular, 120 of them requiring *a* to be listed highest, as against 360 admissible strategies under the alternative vote procedure, of which 60 involve listing *a* highest.

Under the preference score procedure, a well-informed voter has considerable incentive to vote strategically, and in particular to adopt a regular strategy. He will then put at the head of his list that outcome x which, of those he believes to have some chance of success, he most prefers. After x he will place, in order of preference, those outcomes he prefers to it, which, by hypothesis, he believes to have no chance of winning. Below these, he will place those outcomes to which he prefers x, in inverse order of their estimated chances of success. Thus, if his preference scale is *abcdef*, and he believes that *a*, *b*, and *e* have no genuine chance of success, and that, of the other three, *d* is the most likely to win and *f* the least, he will list the outcomes in the order *cabefd*. In voting in this way, he runs comparatively little risk. If his estimates were right, *d* is *c*'s chief rival: he has increased *c*'s preference score by five points as against *d*'s, instead of by the one point that would have resulted from his voting sincerely. If his estimates were mistaken, he has probably done little harm. As against his sincere strategy, he has diminished the preference scores of *a* and *b* by only one point each, and increased those of *e* and *f* by only one point each. He may, indeed, have had the very worst effect, and caused *f* to win instead of *a*: but, for that to happen, his calculations must have gone very far astray.

A preliminary conclusion, then, is that the preference score procedure gives an exceptionally strong incentive for strategic voting to one who believes himself to have a sound knowledge of the intentions of other voters. This is so because, under this procedure, a strategic vote is far less dangerous than under others. For just this reason, however, it appears that strategic voting is unlikely gravely to distort the final outcome: it will, at the most, replace a popular outcome by one almost equally popular.

This conclusion—that, under the preference score procedure, strategic voting will have only a minor effect—will hold good, however, only so long as no more than a few voters indulge in it. If all of them do, the effect may be large. Suppose that the preference scales of the voters are as follows:

1	2	3	4	5	6	7	8	9	10	11	12	13	14	15	16	17
a	b	b	a	c	d	c	e	d	d	d	f	f	e	c	d	f
b	a	d	f	a	c	d	d	c	f	c	d	e	a	f	c	c
c	e	f	d	b	f	f	c	b	c	e	c	a	b	e	e	a
d	f	e	e	e	b	b	f	f	a	f	e	d	f	b	f	d
e	d	c	c	f	e	a	b	a	e	a	b	c	c	d	b	b
f	c	a	b	d	a	e	a	e	b	b	a	b	d	a	a	e

Example 2(a)

If all vote sincerely, the preference scores will be:

a	b	c	d	e	f
33	33	51	52	37	49

Suppose, on the other hand, that every voter correctly estimates that the chances of a, b, and e are negligible, that of e being slightly better than those of the other two, and that, of the remaining three, d stands the best chance and c the second best; and suppose that, on this basis, each voter adopts the strategic policy indicated above. They will then record their votes as follows:

1	2	3	4	5	6	7	8	9	10	11	12	13	14	15	16	17
c	f	d	f	c	d	c	d	d	d	d	f	f	f	f	d	f
a	b	b	a	a	b	b	e	b	a	a	b	a	a	b	b	a
b	a	a	b	b	a	a	b	a	b	b	a	b	b	a	a	b
e	e	e	e	e	e	e	a	e	e	e	e	e	e	e	e	e
f	c	f	c	f	c	f	f	f	f	f	c	c	c	c	f	c
d	d	c	d	d	f	d	c	c	c	c	d	d	d	d	c	d

Example 2(b)

As a result, the preference scores will be:

a	b	c	d	e	f
58	59	23	35	38	44

and b will win instead of d in spite of not having been listed highest by a single voter. Since, under the table 2(a) of the voters' true preference scales, the majority numbers of the outcomes were:

a	b	c	d	e	f
0	1	4	5	2	3

this is a most inequitable, as well as a quite unintended, result.

We have here a particular example of an oscillatory process, quite different from that of narrowing down the admissible strategies to the ultimately admissible ones. A voter who has an idea what other voters' preferences are may work out his own best strategy on the assumption that they will all vote sincerely. If, now, he assumes that they are equally well informed about the preferences of other voters, and that they will reason as he does, this may greatly affect what he takes to be the most probable contingency: he may therefore completely revise his estimate of the merits of the strategies open to him. He may then reflect that other voters may likewise carry their reasoning to this second stage; on this basis, he will need to revise his estimate once more. There is no reason why reiteration of this process should lead his estimates to converge: on the contrary, they may swing back and forth, according to how far he carries his analysis. To succeed in a strategic vote, he needs to be a jump ahead of the other voters, as in a bluffing game: one jump, no less, but also no more. He has no way of knowing when he is one jump ahead; so, having once begun this non-convergent process, his safest course is to abandon it altogether, and revert to his sincere strategy. A voting procedure may offer a strong incentive for strategic voting to a voter who believes others to be ill-informed, and himself to be well informed, about the distribution of preferences; but the stronger the incentive it offers to such a voter, the weaker the incentive it offers to one who believes others to be as well informed as himself. More exactly, this will be so whenever each voter has so wide a choice of admissible strategies that they all remain 2-admissible: it is just then that there will be no convergence.

This is clearly illustrated by the above example 2. The chances of a, b, and e were rightly reckoned negligible by each voter, but only on the assumption that the other voters would vote sincerely: a and b were therefore placed high by virtually all the voters, precisely because they did not expect either of them to win. Each voter was attempting to give the maximum chance to that one of c, d, and f which he favoured, by reducing the chances of the other two and using a, b, and e as filling-in material: but the effect of this was to overturn the originally well-founded assumption that a and b had no serious chance of success.

Under the preference score procedure, therefore, a voter who expects most of the other voters to vote strategically must rate as highly likely to win those outcomes which he thinks the other voters will believe to have poor chances. If he expects the other voters to base their strategies on the assumption that most others will vote sincerely, he will probably do best to vote sincerely himself. If an outcome is generally expected to do badly, its likely use as filling-in material will probably counterbalance the effect of its unpopularity, supposing this to have been correctly estimated; if an outcome is expected to do well, its popularity, when correctly estimated, will probably be counterbalanced by its being marked down by voters anxious to promote the chances of its rivals. The overall effect may well be to make the preference scores much more uniform: even if this does not happen, the effects will be too unpredictable to warrant a strategic vote. The given voter may, indeed, suspect that others will reason in the same way, and so decide to vote sincerely themselves; but, as we have seen, this path of reasoning has no natural termination, and cannot rationally lead to a decision to vote strategically. A departure from sincere voting thus ought to recommend itself only to a voter who believes himself to be uniquely, or all but uniquely, well informed, in which case the other voters would vote sincerely *faute de mieux*. For such a voter, but only for him, the incentive remains strong; but it is still true that, if only one or two vote strategically, their doing so will have only a slight effect under the preference score procedure.

Under the majority number procedure, the problems facing a voter who contemplates a strategic vote are very different. His chief concern must be with how he may change the majority numbers to his advantage; but also with how to avoid doing so inadvertently and to his disadvantage. Suppose that there are seven voters and four possible outcomes, and that the preference scales are as follows:

1	2	3	4	5	6	7
c	a	c	b	b	c	a
b	b	d	a	d	a	b
a	c	a	d	c	b	d
d	d	b	c	a	d	c

Example 3

If all vote sincerely, the majority numbers and preference scores will be:

a	b	c	d
2	2	2	0
12	13	11	6

so that b will win. Since a, b, and c all have the same majority number, it might seem that voter 2 can make a the winner by listing the outcomes in the order *adcb*, yielding the preference scores:

a	b	c	d
12	11	11	8

This is not so, however. By listing *c* above *b*, voter 2 will give *c* a majority over *b*, so that *c* will now be top, the new majority numbers being:

a	b	c	d
2	1	3	0

Such a strategic vote will thus work to voter 2's disadvantage, replacing the outcome *b* by *c* rather than by *a*.

There are contingencies in which a voter can tamper with the majority numbers to his advantage. Suppose that there are four possible outcomes and nine voters, with preference scales as follows:

1	2	3	4	5	6	7	8	9
a	a	c	b	a	a	c	c	d
b	b	a	c	b	d	d	a	c
d	c	b	a	d	c	a	d	a
c	d	d	d	c	b	b	b	b

Example 4

Under sincere voting, the majority numbers and preference scores will be:

a	b	c	d
2	1	3	0
19	10	15	10

and *c* will win. If, however, voter 2 lists the outcomes in the order *abdc*, the rest still voting sincerely, he will deprive *c* of its majority over *d*, thus altering the majority numbers and preference scores to:

a	b	c	d
2	1	2	1
19	10	14	11

As a result, *a*, now having the same majority number as *c* and a higher preference score, will become the winner.

A small change in a voter's list can thus have a big effect under this procedure, because, if one outcome has a bare majority over another, a reversal of their order by a single voter can overturn that majority and so alter two of the majority numbers. A voter with the preference scale *abcd* may confidently list *d* higher than *c* in the hope of lowering *c*'s majority number if he is sure that *d*'s majority number is low. If he is unsure of that, such a strategy is dangerous. Fairly minor changes in the preference scales of voters 3, 4, and 8 in example 4 would yield a very different R_{maj} diagram: thus, if the preference scales were:

1	2	3	4	5	6	7	8	9
a	*a*	*c*	*b*	*a*	*a*	*c*	*c*	*d*
b	*b*	*d*	*c*	*b*	*d*	*d*	*d*	*c*
d	*c*	*a*	*d*	*d*	*c*	*a*	*a*	*a*
c	*d*	*b*	*a*	*c*	*b*	*b*	*b*	*b*

Example 5

the majority numbers and preference scores would be:

a	*b*	*c*	*d*
1	0	3	2
16	9	15	14

If, in this case, voter 2 were to list the outcomes in the order *abdc*, the rest continuing to vote sincerely, the figures would change to:

a	*b*	*c*	*d*
1	0	2	3
16	9	14	15

and the effect of his strategy would be that *d* would win instead of *c*. A strategic vote, under this procedure, can be particularly dangerous; to have an incentive to risk it, a voter needs a very precise knowledge indeed of the voting intentions of the other voters.

A detailed analysis of voting strategies under the majority number procedure would be very complicated; but it is hardly needed in order to establish that the procedure is relatively immune to strategic voting. Unlike the preference score procedure, it is not true of the majority number procedure that the departure of only one voter from a sincere strategy will have at most a minor effect: on the contrary, its effect may be dramatic. The incentive for strategic voting is, however, minimal, because of the difficulty of being sure what its effect will be. In order to risk a strategic vote under the preference score procedure, a voter needs simply to have a good general idea of the relative popularity of the various outcomes. Under the alternative vote procedure, he needs to know the distribution of first preferences, and of some, but not all, of the second preferences; although a few third preferences may be relevant, he need not know for certain about these in order to think it worth while trying to prevent the elimination of a particular outcome at stage 1. To have a basis for a strategic vote under the majority number procedure, on the other hand, a voter must be rightly informed about all the R_{maj} relations; and this he will seldom be, or think himself to be.

Thus the majority number procedure offers as little incentive for strategic voting as may be hoped for from any voting procedure; the preference score procedure, though it offers considerably more, is unlikely to be gravely affected by only a few voters' departing from their sincere strategies. If a great many voters do so, on the false assumption that most of the other voters will vote sincerely, the outcome of the preference score procedure may be grossly distorted. The same is true of the majority number procedure, though the danger is less acute under it, since the risks of strategic voting are so much higher. The danger must be acknowledged; but it must also be accepted, if the voting procedure employed is to come near to satisfying any reasonable criterion for being fair. A procedure whose outcome will seldom be greatly affected by strategic voting by a large number of voters, provided that they are well informed, is not difficult to devise: the relative majority procedure is one such, in that, although the outcome may be affected by strategic voting, it will usually be affected in favour of an outcome that would have come close to success under sincere voting. Any such procedure will, however, necessarily be insensitive to all but coarse features of the preference scales, and hence will have a feeble claim to be fair. A method of assessment employing a globally sensitive leading criterion will inevitably be more responsive to changes of voting strategy, and therefore more severely affected by widespread strategic voting: it must accordingly rely upon the riskiness of departing from a sincere strategy to deter voters from doing so. The preference score procedure, being comparatively inflexible when only a small number of voters vote strategically, may safely be used when most are likely to refrain from so voting because of the risks involved or because of their poor knowledge of the preferences of others. The majority number procedure is much more flexible under strategic voting by a few: but the risks of such voting are so much higher under this procedure that there is a good chance that all will vote sincerely.

The preference score and majority number procedures have by far the strongest claim to produce a fair outcome under sincere voting, for the obvious reason that they alone employ methods of assessment expressly designed to reflect one or other of the only possible criteria for a fair outcome. The preference score procedure lends itself easily to adaptation when the voters desire to skew the scores in one direction or the reverse, which they are particularly likely to do—misguidedly, in my opinion—when electing a candidate to a post. If they agree in preferring a candidate with strong support, though strong opposition, to one generally ranked as rather better than middling, they can give extra weight to a candidate's having a high place on a voter's list; for example, when there are seven candidates, by assigning scores of 9, 6, 4, 3, 2, 1, and 0 points to the candidates on a voter's list. If, conversely, they agree in preferring a generally acceptable candidate to one who rouses strong opposition, they can skew the scores in the reverse direction, say by assigning the scores 9, 8, 7, 5, 2, 1, and 0. The more the preference scores are skewed, the greater will be the temptation to strategic voting, but those who wish to skew them may accept this as the lesser evil; anyone who understands that there can be no ideal voting procedure is prepared to choose between evils. The possibility of a skewed preference score procedure has been mentioned only to forestall the objection to the unmodified procedure that it 'favours mediocrity' or, conversely, that it 'gives insufficient weight to strong opposition'. Both objections are unsound; but, if either is strongly felt, it can be accommodated without abandoning the general principle of this method of assessment.

If a voting procedure falls very far short of producing a fair outcome whenever voting is sincere, as the relative majority procedure does, strategic voting, provided that it is guided by correct information, will tend to make the outcome fairer: this is why it is misguided to object to opinion polls during an election conducted under such a procedure. A voting procedure, such as the alternative vote, that lies, in this respect, about half-way between the relative majority procedure and the preference score procedure, is likely, on average, to produce as fair an outcome under strategic as under sincere voting, although, of course, it will often produce different outcomes in the two cases. The effect of strategic voting on a procedure, like the preference score or the majority number procedure, which always or almost always produces the fairest outcome under sincere voting must necessarily be to make it less fair. The conclusion of this chapter is that the opportunities for strategic voting under either of these procedures are not so great as to vitiate their claims to be fairer than other voting procedures. Whenever the complete list mechanism is practicable and the aim is to arrive at that outcome which, on the basis of the voters' preferences, is to be judged most probably the best, one or other of these procedures will be superior to any other that could be devised or is in general use.

14
Voting with Many Possible Outcomes

The preference score procedure is unsuitable when there is a very large number of possible outcomes, and the majority number procedure still more so. If there are, say, twenty possible outcomes, the task of deciding the precise order of preference in which he ranks them may induce a kind of psychological paralysis in the voter; and, for the tellers, the labour of reckoning the preference scores becomes very tedious. We have, therefore, to devise new or modified procedures for use in this case.

The most usual example in which many distinct outcomes are possible occurs when the object of the voting is to select one or more candidates for a position; it will be assumed in this chapter that the vote is for this purpose. Let us suppose, first, that a single appointment is to be made from among a large number of candidates. When there is a small appointing body or selection committee, the differences between whose members are differences of judgement according to shared criteria, it is usually unnecessary to resort to voting until a late stage, when the candidates have been whittled down to a short list. When what is being undertaken is more naturally described as an election than as an appointment, for instance when the master of a college or the chairman of a political organization is to be chosen, the criteria will not be shared: different electors may value different qualities or favour different policies. In such a case, it may be necessary to employ a voting procedure from the outset. If the number of candidates is large, and the process of selection can be extended over a period, it will be advisable to proceed in stages, first arriving at a short list, and then holding the final election between the members of the short list, with some form of interview of the short-listed candidates intervening between the two stages, when this is suitable. If there was initially a very large number of candidates, it may be necessary to split the process into three stages: first the drawing up of a 'long short list'; then its curtailment to a shorter list; and finally the actual election. Even when the selection process cannot be extended over weeks, but must take place in a single day, it will usually be advantageous to split it into stages.

This case presents few difficulties. The final election will be between the three or four candidates on the final short list, and may be conducted by means of the preference score procedure or the majority number procedure, according to the inclination of the electors. To draw up the short list, and, if there is one, the long short list before it, a modified form of the preference score procedure is much the best suited to ascertaining the overall preferences of the electors in a manner that does not place an undue strain on either voters or tellers. Suppose that there are fifty candidates. A reasonable decision would be first to draw up a long short list of about seven, and subsequently to cut this down to a final short list of three or four. In the first vote, then, to determine the long short list, the electors may be asked to list, on their ballot papers, in order of preference, the eleven candidates of whom they most approve, bracketing any between whom they are indifferent. On the basis of these ballot papers, the candidates' preference scores are computed and announced. It will then be open to the chairman to propose that the long short list shall consist of the six, seven, or eight, according to his judgement, who have obtained the highest scores: such a proposal would be then voted on by a simple for-or-against vote. It would, of course, be possible to agree in advance on the size of the long short list: if it were fixed at seven, then the seven obtaining the highest scores would be automatically placed on the long short list, unless there happened to be two or more candidates tying for seventh place, in which case all of these would be placed on it. This is not advisable, however. When the preference scores are computed on less than the full preference scales of the voters, a difference of one or two points is not significant. It is therefore better for the chairman to look to see at what point, near to the seventh place, a large gap occurs between the preference score of a candidate and that of his nearest rival, and propose that a break between those who go through to the next stage and those who are eliminated should be made at this point.

The only detail that might cause uncertainty is how to compute the preference scores. When the voters have been asked to list eleven candidates, it would be quite misleading to allot 11 points to a candidate for appearing at the head of a voter's list, 10 points for appearing second, and so on down to 1 point for appearing in last place: to do so would be to give far too small an award to a candidate for being listed at all. Under such a method of assessment, a candidate could get on to the short list or long short list by having enthusiastic support from a quite small proportion of the electors; and this will be a waste of time, since he is certain to be eliminated at the next stage. The proper way to think of the matter is as follows. Imagine that the voters had been asked to list all fifty candidates in order of preference, with bracketing allowed: candidates not appearing on a voter's list would be treated as if he had bracketed them equal below all those he actually listed. Then, on the standard way of computing preference scores, the candidate appearing eleventh on a voter's list would receive 39 points, and the one appearing at the head of the list 49. Now if a voter listed only eleven candidates, the remaining thirty-nine would be treated as bracketed equal below them, and hence would each be allotted the mean score of 19 points. Hence, when each voter has been asked to list only eleven, the preference scores should be computed in essentially the same way. It will, of course, be a waste of time to accord 19 points to each candidate for failing to appear on a given voter's list: we may therefore subtract 19 points from the scores awarded to each candidate appearing on a list. The candidate appearing at the head of a given list will therefore be awarded 30 points, the one appearing second 29 points, and so on down to the one at the bottom of the list, who will receive 20 points. Generalizing, we may lay down that if there are r candidates, of whom each voter is asked to list k in order of preference, the candidate at the head of any list should be awarded $\frac{1}{2}(r + k - 1)$ points, with 1 point difference between successive candidates, down to $\frac{1}{2}(r - k + 1)$ points to the kth candidate on the list. When r is even, it is best to choose k to be odd, and conversely, so as to avoid scores that are not integers.

Computing the scores in this way guarantees that just those candidates are short-listed who have the best chance of winning if they reach the final stage. It also makes possible a substantial improvement of the procedure, in that it is no longer necessary to require each voter to list a fixed number of candidates. Instead, they may be given a maximum number, or not even that: it might merely be suggested to them about how many they are expected to list. The scores can then be computed according to the same formula as before, where now k is taken to be the number of candidates a given voter has actually listed; if, out of fifty, he lists only seven, they will be allotted from 28 down to 22 points, according to their positions on his list. A voter who knows little about most of the candidates will now have no reason to fill up the lower places on his list with names picked almost at random; as a means of drawing up a short list, the procedure will thus become more accurate. No voter ought to be allowed to gain the impression that, to do the best by the candidate of his first choice, he ought to list as many candidates as possible. By listing eleven candidates instead of seven, a voter will increase the advantage of each of the first seven candidates on his list over those he does not list by 2 points; but, when r is 50, he is also reducing, by from 18 to 21 points, the advantage they had over those he lists in the eighth to eleventh places.

Voters, while feeling lukewarm towards many candidates, may be strongly opposed to some while enthusiastic about others. It might therefore seem better to allow them to express negative feelings, by listing some candidates 'below the line', thereby indicating that they preferred all other candidates to them: candidates listed below the line would then receive suitable negative scores. There is no difficulty in reckoning what these scores should be: if, out of r candidates, a voter listed k above the line and j below, the one he listed highest above the line should receive $+\frac{1}{2}(r + k - j - 1)$ points, and the one he listed lowest below the line $-\frac{1}{2}(r - k + j - 1)$ points, the scores of successive candidates differing as before by 1 point. The idea is a bad one, however, because it offers the strongest temptation to strategic voting. A voter who feels strong hostility to a particular candidate should be made to wait until a later stage of the selection process to take specific steps to prevent his election.

When a long short list of about seven has been drawn up by this means, the next step will be to reduce it to the final short list of three or four. The voters might be asked to list all candidates on the long short list in order of preference; or it might be found more convenient to ask them to list no more than, say, four. In the latter case, the same formula as before should be used to allot points to each candidate: if the voters are to list four candidates out of seven on the long short list, we put $r = 7$ and $k = 4$, so that a candidate will receive 5 points for being at the head of a voter's list, and 4, 3, and 2 points respectively for being placed from second to fourth by a voter. As before, when the scores have been announced, it should be left to the chairman to propose the top three or four candidates for the final short list, according to where the signficiant gap occurs.

A different type of case is that in which there may be comparatively few candidates, of whom more than one must, or may, be elected. Suppose that there are only five candidates, but two places to be filled. There will then be ten possible overall outcomes, there being ten ways of selecting two out of five. Now, as we have seen, when the possible outcomes of a decision-making process can be regarded as composite, much more information is given by a participant's scale of preferences between the outcomes than by his scales of preferences between the components. In the present case, therefore, the electors' scales of preference between the overall outcomes tell us much more than their scales of preference between the individual candidates. This is partly because an elector may have conditional preferences: he may think, for example, that A and B are individually the best candidates, but that, for one reason or another, it would be a mistake to elect both of them, because they would not work well together or because they specialize in the same thing. It is only partly for this reason, however. Even when an elector's preferences between the overall outcomes are additive, they cannot be determined simply from his preferences between the candidates. His preferences will be additive if it is possible to assign satisfaction values, positive or negative, to the individual candidates in such a way that he will be found to prefer the election of any one pair of candidates to that of any other pair just in case the sum of the satisfaction values of the first two is greater than that of the second two. If an elector's preferences are additive in this sense, he does not have conditional preferences; but his scale of preferences between the candidates will still not determine his scale of preferences between the outcomes, because there will be many different ways of assigning satisfaction values to the candidates consistently with his preferences between them individually. As we saw earlier, an elector's scale of preferences between the overall outcomes serves to a large extent as a surrogate for numerical weightings by him of the individual candidates.

For these reasons, whenever it is practicable, it is far better to ask the electors to list the *outcomes* in order of preference than to ask them so to list the *candidates*. The borderline of feasibility for the complete list mechanism may be regarded as lying between seven and twelve possible outcomes. With six or fewer, there can be no doubt that it is practicable; with thirteen or more, it is evidently not. In cases of the present type, however, the advantages of having the electors list the outcomes rather than the candidates are so strong that it should be done wherever possible, and in particular when there are no more than five candidates, of whom exactly two or exactly three are to be elected. It is then better to assess the results by calculating the preference scores of the outcomes than by determining their majority numbers, because there is a particularly high probability of cyclic triads.

If there are more than five candidates, and they cannot conveniently be reduced to a short list of five or fewer, or if the electors are for some reason unwilling to list the overall outcomes, the next best method is to use the preference score procedure applied to candidates, electing the two or three who obtain the highest scores. We have, of course, been assuming that there is no distinction between the posts to which the successful candidates will be appointed. If appointments are to be made to two distinct posts from among five candidates, there will be twenty distinct possible overall outcomes, and the voters cannot be asked to list them all. If the posts are distinguished only by grade, not by function, it will then be best to use the preference score procedure applied to candidates, appointing the one with the highest score to the higher post and his closest rival to the other. If the posts differ in function, it will probably be necessary to vote to fill each separately, even though this may create a quandary for some electors about the voting strategy they should adopt; a sympathetic hearing should be given to objections to the proposed order in which the two votes will be taken. There is, however, no excuse for adopting the method of voting separately on the two posts when there is no real distinction between them, although this is quite often done in practice. To do so presupposes the use of some method of assessment other than preference scores, and probably of some voting mechanism other than listing all the candidates: it would be pointless, having elected one candidate by means of preference scores, to recalculate the preference scores omitting that candidate, thereby losing relevant information. Hence, when a merely notional distinction is made between the two posts for the purpose of voting, it is probable that each post will be voted on by some crude method. Either a relative majority will suffice for election, each elector voting for just one candidate, or repeated votes will be taken until a candidate attains an absolute majority. Suppose, now, that there are five candidates and nineteen electors, with preference scales as follows:

1–6	7–9	10–13	14	15–19
C	C	A	A	B
A	B	B	C	A
B	A	D	B	E
D	E	E	E	D
E	D	C	D	C

Example 1

If the preference score procedure, applied to candidates, is used, the scores will be:

A	B	C	D	E
59	55	39	19	18

If two are to be elected, A and B will be successful, as, on the basis of the preference scales, they clearly deserve to be. If, however, the two posts, though only notionally distinguished, are voted on separately, each elector voting for only one candidate, then, on the first ballot, A and B will receive 5 votes each and C 9. If the relative majority procedure is being used, C will be elected outright. If an absolute majority is required, then, on the second ballot, the opponents of C will not know which way to switch their votes. They probably cannot prevent C's election, since elector 14 will probably switch to C on the second ballot, or subsequently. Some of A's supporters may switch to B, and some of B's to A; but, since there will never be any incentive for any of C's supporters to switch, it will be impossible to get either A or B elected to the supposititious 'first place' if there is no opportunity for collusion. Furthermore, the only chance of successful collusion is to persuade all B's supporters to switch to A; in that case, C will be elected to the 'second place', so that no difference will be made to the overall outcome. In addition to gross disadvantages of its own, this thoroughly inequitable procedure has the disadvantages of the STV procedure, to be discussed in Chapter 16. This example illustrates the well-known phenomenon of the 'split vote': nine electors favour C, but the nine with a low opinion of C are divided over which of A and B, whom they all agree in regarding highly, is the best. Without collusion, C's opponents have no way of knowing which of A and B to vote for. Moreover, a procedure that fails to take account from the outset of the second preferences of all the voters cannot reveal that both *A* and *B* have a stronger claim to election than *C*.

Somewhat different problems arise when it is open to the electors to elect fewer than the maximum number of candidates. The simplest case is that in which not more than one is to be elected, but it is open to the electors to make no election. Here there is only one equitable way of proceeding. If necessary, the slate of candidates must first be reduced to a short list; then, at the final stage, the electors must be asked to list the possible *outcomes* in order of preference, and the outcome determined by either the preference score or majority number procedure. This means, in effect, that the electors must treat 'no election' precisely as if it were the name of a candidate. In other words, they will list the candidates in order of preference, drawing a line to separate those they think individually worthy of election from those they do not; in computing the result, the tellers will treat this line as an item on each elector's list, assigning it a preference score and, if required, a majority number. There will then be no election if, and only if, 'no election' qualifies as the winning outcome according to the criterion adopted. Under this procedure, it will probably be felt more equitable to adopt the majority number criterion (supplemented, when necessary, by preference scores). Thus, if it proves that 'no election' is top, that means that there is no candidate whom a majority of the electors think worthy of election (if they have voted sincerely): in such circumstances, it would probably be agreed to be a mistake to make an election, even if one candidate had a preference score higher than 'no election'.

This procedure is greatly to be preferred to taking a separate vote on whether to make an election, either as a preliminary to choosing between the candidates, if it is decided to elect one, or after choosing which candidate is to be elected, if any. If a preliminary vote is taken on whether or not to elect, any elector who thinks some of the candidates worthy of election but others not is in a quandary how to vote; and it can easily happen that the electors commit themselves to making an election even though no single candidate is thought by a majority to be worthy. Conversely, if the vote on whether to make an election is taken after a candidate has been selected, it may have a negative outcome even though there was a candidate whom most would regard as worthy; if so, those who voted for the candidate selected will regret that they did not vote for a candidate they liked less well, the selection of whom might have led to a positive outcome of the final vote on whether to elect at all.

The matter is more complex when it is allowable to elect more than one candidate, but not required to elect up to the maximum. If there are only four candidates, of whom up to two may be elected, there will be eleven possible outcomes: six possible elections of two candidates, four of only one, and the decision not to elect any. In this case, it is still practicable to ask the electors to list all the possible outcomes in order of preference; for familiar reasons, it is far better to do so. In this case, it is better to determine the successful outcome by the majority number procedure than by preference scores alone, despite the likelihood of cyclic majorities. This is because the assumption that the distances between successive outcomes on an elector's preference scale are equal is highly implausible in this case: small differences between preference scores are therefore likely to reflect nothing but the manner of computing them, even when preferences are additive.

When there is a greater number of possible outcomes, it is no longer feasible to ask the electors to list them all. When there are five candidates, of whom up to two are to be elected, there will be sixteen possible outcomes, including the decision to make no election. If there are eight or more candidates, of whom up to two may be elected, it may be possible to handle the process of selection by drawing up a short list of no more than four, and then asking the electors to list the outcomes. If there are only five or six candidates to start with, however, this will probably seem unreasonable, and may not be acceptable when there are more, of whom at least five attract determined support. It will be equally impossible to proceed in this way if it is open to the electors to elect more than two. If, out of four candidates, the electors may elect up to three, there will be fifteen possible outcomes, including 'no election'. What should be done in these cases?

If, as in cases of this kind, it is impossible to ask the electors to list the outcomes, we have to fall back on a procedure under which they are asked to list only the candidates. This has the great disadvantage that they are unable to express conditional preferences, but there is no remedy for this; once the point has been reached at which voting takes place, they will have to be treated as if their preferences were additive. A method having considerable merit, and sometimes employed, requires each elector to list all the candidates in order of preference, but with a line, representing 'no election', separating those he thinks worthy of election from those he thinks unworthy: the voting mechanism is thus exactly the same as the complete list mechanism applied to outcomes in the case when not more than one candidate is to be elected, but no election need be made. The method of assessment is by preference scores: a score is computed for each individual candidate, exactly as under the preference score procedure applied to candidates, save that 'no election' is treated as a separate item on each elector's list. Taking 'O' to denote 'no election', we may use '$ABOCDE$' to represent the list of an elector who puts A and B, in that order, above the line, and C, D, and E, in that order, below the line: in the standard manner, such a list will result in the award of 5 points to A, 4 points to B, 3 points to 'no election', 2 points to C, 1 point to D, and none to E. If 'no election' proves to have the highest overall score, there will then be no election; otherwise, the candidates having the highest scores will be declared elected, up to the maximum allowable number, save that no candidate can be elected unless his score is greater than that of 'no election'. We may call this the 'individual PS procedure'. A variant is what we may call the 'straight individual SV procedure'. Under this, 'no election' is assigned a fixed score of 0: the candidates above the line on an elector's list are awarded positive points, and those below negative points. For instance, the list $ABOCDE$ will result in the award of $+2$ points to A, $+1$ to B, -1 to C, -2 to D, and -3 to E. A candidate may then be elected only if he has a positive total score.

These two procedures are completely equivalent: the score of a candidate under the SV procedure is simply the result of subtracting, from his score under the PS procedure, the score of 'no election'. The SV method suggests, however, that the points awarded to a candidate on the strength of any elector's list represent the satisfaction value to that elector of the election of the candidate; hence the name of the procedure. This in turn suggests a somewhat better method, which we may call the 'graded individual SV procedure'. Under this, each elector awards points, positive or negative, to each candidate, in the following way. When there are five candidates, he distributes the whole numbers from 1 to 5 among them, attaching to each a plus or minus sign as he pleases. If he thinks them all worthy of election, he will allot positive numbers to all of them; if he thinks none worthy of election, he will allot negative numbers to all. In general, he will allot positive numbers to some and negative numbers to others: but, having allotted $+3$ points to one candidate, he may not allot either $+3$ or -3 to any other. The numbers to be distributed among the candidates always run, ignoring sign, from 1 to r, where r is the number of candidates. The rest is as under the straight SV procedure: a candidate may not be elected unless he has a positive total score; the candidates with the highest positive total scores are declared elected, up to the maximum allowable number of them.

This procedure allows each elector to represent his preferences more exactly; at least when his preferences are additive, the points he awards to the candidates will come closer than under the straight SV procedure to an assignment of satisfaction values that would yield his scale of preferences between the overall outcomes. To see how to award points on his ballot paper, an elector should first draw up a list in order of preference, with a line dividing those worthy of election from those unworthy of it. Say that this list has the form $ABOCDE$. He must then first ask himself whether he would prefer the election of both B and C to the election of no one. If he would, he must allot -1 point to C: this will guarantee that the sum of the points he allots to B and to C will be positive. Conversely, if he would rather that no one was elected than that B and C were, he should allot $+1$ point to B. Suppose that he has decided on this basis to give -1 point to C: he must next ask himself whether he would prefer the election of both B and D to the election of no one. Say that his answer is 'No': he must accordingly allot $+2$ points to B. If, now, he would prefer the election of A and D to 'no election', he must give -3 points to D. Finally, he must consider whether he would prefer the election of both A and E to the election of no one: if so, he must give $+5$ points to A and -4 to E. At each stage, he considers the combination of the lowest candidate above the line to whom he has not yet assigned a score with the highest candidate below the line to whom he has not yet assigned a score, and asks whether he would prefer the election of that pair to 'no election': if so, the number least in absolute magnitude, of those yet unassigned, must be given, with a minus sign, to the candidate below the line; if not, that number, with a plus sign, must be given to the one above it. This is not, of course, a rule of the procedure, but merely indicates how an elector may best assign points to represent the relative strengths of his preferences.

It cannot be pretended that the points so awarded will always lead to a faithful reconstruction of an elector's scale of preferences between possible outcomes. In the foregoing example, the elector allotted $+2$, -1, and -3 points to B, C, and D respectively: it cannot be inferred that he would be indifferent between the election of B and D together, on the one hand, and the election of C alone, on the other. Nor, if it is open to the electors to elect as many as three candidates, can we deduce from the fact that he allotted $+5$, -1, and -3 points to A, C, and D respectively that he would prefer the election of all three to the election of no one. It would be possible, but it would be pointless, to devise a system of numerical scores by means of which one could answer correctly, from any elector's ballot paper, whether he preferred any given possible outcome to any other. The principal reason for not employing the complete list mechanism, applied to outcomes, when the possible outcomes are numerous is not to save the tellers trouble but to avoid perplexing the voters, who cannot be expected to decide what their preference scales are if there are too many items to arrange in order. Under any system which allowed the reconstruction of a voter's scale of preferences between the outcomes from his numerical awards to the individual candidates, an elector would have to make all the comparisons necessary to determine his preference scale between the outcomes in order to decide what awards to make; if so, he could more simply have been asked to list the outcomes. The graded individual SV procedure is the best practical compromise: simple to explain, to understand, and to operate, yet yielding substantially more information than the straight SV procedure or its equivalent the individual PS procedure.

15
Electing Representatives

When representatives are to be elected, the criteria for a good voting procedure differ from those which apply when the objective is to select those best qualified for a job or, more generally, to arrive at the best decision. There are conflicting requirements on a good electoral system, and people vary in the weights they attach to each: but all agree that a Parliament should be to some extent representative of public opinion, and this requirement is quite distinct from that of containing wise or able legislators.

We shall not be concerned, in these last two chapters, with electoral systems as a whole, but only with the narrower question what voting procedure should be used in a given constituency. When they are electing representatives, the voters may reasonably demand that the procedure be fair to them—to the voters, rather than to the candidates. When the object of voting is simply to select the best possible outcome, according to the criteria being variously applied by the voters, it is irrelevant to speak of being fair to the *voters*: that is why we characterized a fair procedure as one that produces the fairest *outcome*. The distinction becomes prominent when the alternative vote procedure is discussed. Under that procedure, the second preferences of those whose first choice was eliminated at an early stage will go to determine the final outcome, whereas the second preferences of those who supported the eventually successful outcome are never taken into account. If we are concerned to be fair to the outcomes, that is most unfair; it is beside the point to reply that those whose first choice was selected as the final outcome can have no complaint. If we are concerned with the election of representatives, on the other hand, talk of fairness to the voters is not in the same way out of place. That is not to say that the reply just cited is reasonable: if it happened that, when the second preferences of those who supported the winning candidate were taken into account, some other candidate appeared to have had better claims, the procedure might well be judged to have been very unfair to the supporters of that other candidate. Nevertheless, the notion of being fair to the voters is at least in place when representatives are being elected: there may be groups of voters who are entitled to be represented, even though the candidate they support does not by other criteria merit election.

The use of the majority preference criterion in place of the preference score criterion for judging which outcomes is the fairest is in itself a concession to the principle of being fair to the voters. If we are simply trying to estimate which outcome is probably the best, there is no reason to give a special weight to majority opinion: what matters is the prevalent opinion, as judged by giving equal weight to each voter's preference between any two possible outcomes. To adhere to the majority preference criterion, as a matter of justice and not merely of prudence, is to accord a group of voters a special entitlement to affect the outcome, just by virtue of constituting a majority. Whether, in general, majorities have any such rights is open to dispute; but it cannot be denied that not only majorities, but minorities, too, have special rights when representatives are being selected, unless the sense of the word 'representative' is to be altogether lost.

There are, indeed, intermediate cases: elections which have some of the character of selecting representatives and some of the character of appointing the best qualified to fill certain positions. Our concern in this chapter will be with voting procedures that are used for elections that have at least some of the former character, and that involve the election of two or more candidates. In parliamentary elections, minorities stand a better chance of being represented under almost any system with constituencies returning several members of parliament than under one in which each constituency is represented by a single member. Since what principally distinguishes electoral procedures from other uses of voting procedures, from a theoretical standpoint, is the need to ensure representation for minorities, the method to be used by a single body of voters to elect a fixed number of candidates, greater than one, is central to the topic.

A method not in use for parliamentary elections, but in common use for other purposes, is the multiple vote procedure. Under this, each ballot paper bears a list of all the candidates, and each voter has as many votes at his disposal as there are places to be filled: he need not use them all, but may vote for up to that number of candidates. He is not allowed, however, to cast more than one vote for any one candidate. The votes given by a voter for different candidates are not distinguished in any way; in particular, he does not order the candidates for whom he votes. The total number of votes received by the various candidates are announced by the tellers, and those receiving the highest totals, up to the number to be elected, are declared successful. The procedure is extremely popular for the election of university committees, executive committees of organizations, and the like. It tends to be used in cases of two kinds: when the number of electors is very large; and when the number of places to be filled is very large.

The multiple vote procedure does little to ensure the representation of minorities. The best that a set M of voters can do to secure the election of a candidate to represent their interests is to pick a suitable candidate A and agree each to cast one vote for A. If there are m voters in M, A will then receive at least m votes. If k candidates are to be elected, and n voters altogether, the $n - m$ voters not in M might, at the worst, each cast one vote for each of k other candidates, who would then receive $n - m$ votes each. It follows that M must constitute a majority of the voters in order to be certain of bringing about the election of A. It is, of course, unlikely that the voters not in M will all vote for the same k candidates, even if none of them votes for A; but it is clear that this procedure offers little protection to minorities. The only reason for the use of the multiple vote procedure is the convenience of the tellers: it is much easier to count unweighted votes than to compute preference scores. The procedure is a very blunt instrument: it involves giving as much weight to a voter's kth preference as to his first. When there is a large number of places to be filled, for instance fifteen seats on an executive committee, most of the inaccuracies of the procedure are likely to cancel out, especially when there are fewer than twice as many candidates as places; in such a case, there are likely to be at least four times as many voters as places to be filled, and the convenience of both tellers and voters will be far greater if the multiple vote procedure is used than any involving listing candidates in order. Even so, the procedure will deliver only rough justice: one or two candidates may fail to be elected even though, if the preference score procedure applied to candidates had been used, they would have had higher scores than some of those elected. The same, however, is true of almost any practicable procedure, for instance if voters are asked to list in order the six candidates they think best, and preference scores are computed from these in the manner described in the last chapter for drawing up a short list. As long as it is not a matter of intense importance, to voters or to candidates, just who is elected, the multiple vote procedure is good enough, in a case of this kind, as a rough and ready method that is also quite practicable.

It is otherwise when a small number of candidates are to be elected. The crude basis of the assessment can now produce quite bizarre outcomes. Consider, for instance, the following set of preference scales between seven candidates:

1	2	3	4	5	6	7	8	9	10	11	12	13	14	15	16	17	18	19
A	A	A	A	A	A	A	A	A	B	B	B	B	C	C	C	E	F	F
B	B	C	C	C	C	D	D	G	C	C	C	C	A	A	B	B	B	B
C	C	B	D	D	D	B	B	C	D	D	D	D	D	D	D	D	C	D
D	E	E	B	B	B	C	C	B	A	A	A	A	B	B	A	A	G	A
E	G	F	E	F	F	E	E	E	E	E	F	G	E	G	F	C	A	E
F	F	G	F	E	G	G	G	F	F	G	E	F	G	E	E	F	E	G
G	D	D	G	G	E	F	F	D	G	F	G	E	F	F	G	G	D	C

Example 1

The voters show a marked preference for A, B, and C, and, to a lesser extent, for D. Of these, A is the most popular, being ranked highest by nearly half the voters; he is also top, and has the highest preference score, the majority numbers and preference scores being:

A	B	C	D	E	F	G
6	5	4	3	2	1	0
87	84	82	61	35	29	21

Yet, if there are three candidates to be elected, and all vote sincerely, A will not be successful when the multiple vote procedure is used. When the number k of candidates to be elected is 1, this procedure of course reduces to the relative majority procedure; A would then have a walk-over. The relative size of the vote for each candidate will vary markedly according to the value of k; in the following table, the figures for the successful candidate or candidates are underlined.

	A	B	C	D	E	F	G
$k=1$	<u>9</u>	4	3	0	1	2	0
2	<u>11</u>	10	<u>11</u>	2	1	2	1
3	11	<u>13</u>	<u>15</u>	<u>14</u>	1	2	1
4	<u>18</u>	<u>19</u>	<u>17</u>	<u>15</u>	3	2	2

When only two are to be elected, it is B's turn to be unfairly treated;

he will not be elected, even though eleven of the nineteen voters prefer him to C. The distribution of preferences in this example is in no way improbable, but it illustrates very clearly the haphazard effects of this coarse method of selecting candidates. It is even possible to devise an example in which, when $k = 1$, A is elected, when $k = 2$, F and G are, when $k = 3$, C, D, and E are, and, when $k = 4$, A, B, F, and G are. It is only when k is very large that the crudity of the method becomes unlikely to lead to a grossly inequitable outcome; when it is small, the multiple vote procedure will be hardly fairer than it is when $k = 1$, that is, when the relative majority procedure is used to select a single candidate. When it is a matter of any serious importance who is elected, and there are only a small number of places to be filled, the use of the multiple vote procedure is quite inexcusable; it can be intended only to save trouble for the tellers. The preference score procedure applied to candidates will always lead to fairer outcomes; when the number of candidates is too great to make this practicable, the voters can always be asked to restrict themselves to listing no more than a certain number of candidates, which should not be less than four or less than k.

The multiple vote procedure has two variants, both intended to secure better representation for minorities. Minorities, in this connection, should not be thought of only as those composed of supporters of relatively unpopular political parties; they include all groups who feel their interests to differ from those of the majority, whether they are distinguished by religious allegiance, racial origin, or occupation. Schemes of proportional representation are often designed to secure a more equitable representation of political parties; racial or religious minorities are then unable to benefit from these arrangements unless they form political parties of their own. In this chapter and the next, we are not concerned with electoral systems that give an explicit role to political parties as such, but only with voting procedures that help any group that feels itself to have special interests to obtain representation, whether or not it has a formal organization.

The electoral system at present in use in Britain and the United States is notoriously ineffective at affording minorities a chance to secure the election of those who will represent their interests. This is indeed a scandal and a reproach to the professedly democratic character of those two countries. Imperial Britain, both while acting as a colonial ruler and when supervising arrangements for independence, repeatedly introduced formally separate representation for minorities. In India there were, under the British Raj, separate seats for Muslims and for other minority groups such as the 'scheduled castes'; as late as the constitutional conference on Zimbabwe at Lancaster House, a proportion of seats was reserved for whites out of all proportion to their share of the population. Yet in Britain itself, although Mrs Thatcher declared, in a celebrated statement, that the native population was being swamped by black people, she does not see around her in the House of Commons a sea of black faces: she does not see one, however apprehensively she may peer. The only two members of the racial minorities to be found in Parliament are both peers, which is why, as things are at present, it is undemocratic to propose abolishing the House of Lords. If there were the same proportion from those minorities in the House of Commons as in the population at large, there would be about twenty-five black MPs; yet the prospect of getting even one seems bleak. This may not be surprising in a country in which for many years it has been standard for politicians to remark, without seeing anything odd about it, that it is in 'areas of high immigrant concentration' that people are most concerned to tighten the immigration controls yet further, as if their black constituents were not people. Surprising or not, it is utterly inequitable; it is one of many things that have to be rectified if we are ever to nullify the effects of two decades of encouragement of racialist feelings by the two main political parties. The adequate representation of minorities is one of the criteria by which a democratic system is to be judged.

Suppose that there is, among the electorate, a significant level of prejudice against some minority within the population, say racial prejudice against a racial minority. If every constituency returns only one member, political parties will tend to believe that they would lose more than they would gain by putting up a candidate from that minority. If each constituency returns three or more members, on the other hand, they are likely to suppose that, in constituencies where the minority forms a substantial part of the electorate, they would gain more than they would lose by putting up one candidate who belongs to the minority group. For this reason, an electoral system with multi-member constituencies will of itself be more favourable to minorities, whatever the voting procedure used. The matter goes further than the selection of candidates: under such an electoral system, political parties will feel a greater need to woo the votes of a minority group; the history of British since 1965 is ample proof that, under the electoral system now in force, politicians see their best advantage as lying in an appeal to the prejudices of the majority and in a complete disregard for the minority. A fairer electoral system would have changed more than the identity of British MPs: it would have changed their behaviour.

The first variant of the multiple vote procedure is the limited vote. For some number j less than the number k of candidates to be elected, each voter may cast up to j undifferentiated votes, no two of them for the same candidate: the multiple vote procedure is thus the special case when $j = k$. Giving each voter as many votes, without ranking, as there are seats to be filled has a psychological advantage, in that the voters feel able fully to express their opinions about which candidates they would like to see elected; they are in effect asked to state which overall outcome they would prefer. The limited vote procedure was designed for the express purpose of giving a better chance to minorities. When $j = k - 1$, we may call the procedure the *simply* limited vote, and, when $j = 1$, the *strictly* limited vote. Under the Second Reform Act, the simply limited vote procedure was used in Britain for the thirteen three-member constituencies and one four-member constituency (the City of London) then created.[1] Example 1 illustrates how the simply limited vote can produce a fairer outcome than the multiple vote: when $k = 3$, A, B, and C would be elected under the former, but B, C, and D under the latter.

We can best estimate how good is the protection given by a voting procedure to minorities by asking how large the minority must be to be certain of electing a candidate of its choice, providing that its members vote in the manner best calculated to achieve that end. With k seats to be filled, a minority M of m voters can guarantee a selected candidate A just m votes. If the voters not in M vote as unfavourably for the minority as possible, they will divide their votes equally between k other candidates. If each voter has j votes, and there are n voters altogether, each of these other candidates will receive $j(n - m)/k$ votes. Hence, if A is nevertheless to be elected, m must be greater than $j(n - m)/k$, i.e. m/n must be greater than $j/(j + k)$. We may call $j/(j + k)$ the *critical ratio*: a minority M that forms a proportion of the electorate greater than that can be sure of

---

[1] Vernon Bogdanor, *The People and the Party System*, p. 101.

getting a candidate elected. When m/n falls somewhat below the critical ratio, the members of M still have a good chance of getting a candidate elected if the other voters divide their votes unevenly or between more than k other candidates: but they are certain of being represented only if m/n surpasses the critical ratio. It might be thought that, in that case, they could be sure of getting as many as j candidates elected, since they can all vote for each of that number of candidates. This follows only when the other voters divide their votes equally between k other candidates, however; if they divide them between only $k-1$ others, not more than one of the candidates favoured by M will be elected unless m/n exceeds $j/(j+k-1)$.

If the simply limited vote procedure is being used, $j = k-1$, so that the critical ratio becomes $(k-1)/(2k-1)$. Obviously this is smaller when k is smaller: under the simply limited vote, the critical ratio assumes the values:

$k =$	2	3	4	5	6	7
	1/3	2/5	3/7	4/9	5/11	6/13

Under the strictly limited vote, the critical ratio becomes $1/(k+1)$, which of course decreases as k increases:

$k =$	2	3	4	5	6	7
	1/3	1/4	1/5	1/6	1/7	1/8

In general, we obtain the following table, where the columns represent values of k and the rows values of j:

	2	3	4	5	6	7
1	1/3	1/4	1/5	1/6	1/7	1/8
2	1/2	2/5	1/3	2/7	1/4	2/9
3	—	1/2	3/7	3/8	1/3	3/10
4	—	—	1/2	4/9	2/5	4/11
5	—	—	—	1/2	5/11	5/12
6	—	—	—	—	1/2	6/13

The principal diagonal shows the critical ratios under the simply limited vote. In practice, the strictly limited vote is unlikely to recommend itself, since it calls for voters only to nominate their first choices: constituencies returning either three or four members are the most likely to be created, and j will probably not be set at less than $k-1$. A minority forming less than 40 per cent of the electorate in any one constituency will then be unable to be certain of electing someone to represent it. In practice, if no voter not in M votes for a candidate A acceptable to the members of M, but only 60 per cent of the majority vote for the same k candidates, A will be able to be elected if M forms about 30 per cent of the electorate (more than 28.6 per cent if $k = 3$, more than 31 per cent if $k = 4$). This still does not make the simply limited vote procedure a very effective means of securing representation for the racial minorities in Britain, which are unlikely to form more than 20 per cent of the electorate in any constituency. Their chances will, of course, be increased by the likelihood that some white voters will vote for a black candidate representing the political party they favour: but a lack of solidarity among the minority will have a disastrous contrary effect.

The preference score procedure (applied to candidates) is of very little use for the present purpose: it is designed to select the most generally acceptable candidates. Suppose that the m voters in M favour r candidates $A_1, \ldots, A_r$, and that there are k other candidates $B_1, \ldots, B_k$ and k seats to be filled. Suppose also that the members of M all list $A_1, \ldots, A_r$, in that order, above $B_1, \ldots, B_k$, whom they bracket equal: to achieve this, collusion will be essential. And suppose, finally, that the voters not in M all bracket $B_1, \ldots, B_k$ equal, and, not knowing in which order the members of M have listed $A_1, \ldots, A_r$, have listed them all equal below $B_1, \ldots, B_k$. Then A_1 will receive $(k + r - 1)m + \frac{1}{2}(r - 1)(n - m)$ points, while each of $B_1, \ldots, B_k$ will receive $\frac{1}{2}(k - 1)m + \frac{1}{2}(k + 2r - 1)(n - m)$ points. A_1's score will be found to be greater than any of $B_1, \ldots, B_k$ provided that M forms a proportion of the electorate greater than $(k + r + 1)/(2k + 3r - 1)$. This critical ratio will not fall below $\frac{1}{2}$ unless the number r of candidates acceptable to M is greater than 3: even so, when $r = k = 4$, it is only 9/19, and when $r = k = 5$, still as high as 11/24. The position becomes more unfavourable for M if there are more than k candidates unacceptable to it, but the voters not in M agree in ranking k particular candidates higher than all others. The preference score procedure is thus revealed as useless for the protection of minorities.

The second variant of the multiple vote is the cumulative vote procedure. Under this, with k candidates to be elected, each voter has k undifferentiated votes, which he may distribute between the candidates as he pleases: there is no prohibition on giving more than one vote, or even all k votes, to a single candidate. The system was originally proposed by J. G. Marshall, specifically in order to protect minorities, in 1853; Robert Lowe lost an amendment to the Second Reform Bill proposing its introduction in three-member constituencies, but it was used from 1870 until 1902 for the election of school boards in Britain.[2] Under this procedure, the critical ratio is $1/(k + 1)$, $1/4$ when $k = 3$, and $1/5$ when $k = 4$: m voters could give km votes to one candidate A, while the $n - m$ other voters must give $n - m$ votes to each of k other candidates to prevent A's election.

To guarantee the election of a candidate representative of them, members of a minority must co-operate closely. If they scatter their votes, they may fail to win a seat for any candidate they favour, while, if they concentrate them too intensely, they may get only one elected where they could have got two. The same applies to any group, whether a minority or a majority: they need to plan how to distribute their votes so as to get the maximum number of candidates favourable to them elected. Suppose that 50,000 voters in a constituency electing three representatives are divided into 26,000 favouring one party and 24,000 favouring another, which we may call the Republican and Democratic Parties respectively. If each Republican distributes his three votes equally between three Republican candidates A, B, and C, and each Democrat distributes his between D, E, and F, the three Republicans will be elected. To be certain of winning, a candidate must receive just over a quarter of the total votes cast, namely 37,501 or more. The Democrats' best plan is therefore for 13,501 of them to cast two votes for D and one for E, and the remainder to cast one vote for D and two for E: D will then receive 37,501 votes and E 34,499. If the Republicans then divide their votes equally between A, B, and C, both D and E will be elected. The Republicans must therefore likewise ensure 37,501 votes for two each of their candidates, say A and B: if 11,501 give two votes to A and one to B, another 11,501 give one vote to A and two to B, and the remainder give one vote each to A, B, and C, A and B will receive 37,501 votes each and C will receive 2,998, so that A, B, and D will be elected. Naturally, no political party would in practice risk such narrow margins, nor would their supporters ever be quite so well disciplined: but essentially this was what happened in Britain when the procedure was in use for electing school boards.[3] Under the cumulative vote procedure, any group of voters must organize

---

[2] Ibid., pp. 99–101.
[3] Ibid., p. 103.

very carefully to ensure its maximum representation: it must identify its supporters and instruct them precisely how they are to cast their votes.

Exactly the same is true of the simply limited vote procedure, used in Britain for certain constituencies from 1867 to 1884. In Birmingham, where three members of Parliament were returned, the Liberal Party machine or Caucus went to great trouble to identify probable Liberal voters in advance, and distributed cards to them instructing each voter which two of the three Liberal candidates to vote for. In this way, by equalizing the numbers of cards recommending the three different pairs, they contrived to ensure that all three Liberal candidates were returned and the Conservatives deprived of representation. Thus the results of the 1880 election, cited by Vernon Bogdanor, were as follows:

P. H. Muntz (Lib.)	22,969
John Bright (Lib.)	20,079
Joseph Chamberlain (Lib.)	19,544
F. Burnaby (Cons.)	15,735
A. Calthorpe (Cons.)	14,208

As Bogdanor remarks, without prior planning, the voters, left to themselves, might well have given Chamberlain insufficiently many votes to have gained him a seat, preferring to vote for Muntz and Bright and so allowing Burnaby to obtain the third seat. Under the cumulative vote procedure, the Conservatives, constituting well over a quarter of the electorate, could have ensured the election of one of their candidates; under the simply limited vote procedure actually in force, they could not, since they fell very slightly short of the critical ratio of one-third.

The limited and cumulative vote procedures thus put a high premium on organization, and so give much power to political parties and take it away from less well-organized groups without the money to carry out extensive canvassing. A method is needed that will ensure the representation of sufficiently large minorities without requiring them to be efficiently, and expensively, organized, or even organized at all.

16
STV and a New Alternative to it

The rationale of the alternative vote procedure is that as many votes should count as possible. Suppose there are just three candidates for a single seat. If the alternative vote procedure is used, and C is eliminated at stage 1, the votes of his supporters are redistributed according as A or B is the second choice of each. A will then win just in case $AP_{maj}B$, at least as shown on the ballot papers. In this case, it is claimed, voters who listed the candidates CAB will not have 'wasted their votes': they will have contributed to the victory of A. True, the second preferences of the supporters of A have been ignored, but they have no complaint, since their candidate has been elected. Even those who voted BAC might take comfort in the fact that they helped to get C eliminated. Those who voted BCA or CBA have no consolation: but someone must be unfortunate.

It may be objected that to ignore the second preferences of the supporters of A and of B may have been unfair to C, or, if we are concerned to be fair to the voters rather than to the candidates, to C's supporters. Suppose the preference scales were as follows, the figures at the head of each column representing the number of voters sharing that preference scale:

1,000	6,000	5,000	1,000	2,000
A	A	B	C	C
B	C	C	A	B
C	B	A	B	A

Example 1

The assessment process would then run:

A	B	C
7,000	5,000	3,000
8,000	7,000	—

If B had been eliminated instead of C, the second choices of his supporters would have been taken into account, and C would have won:

A	B	C
7,000	—	8,000

If A had been eliminated, the second choices of *his* supporters would have been taken into account, and C would again have won:

A	B	C
—	6,000	9,000

C was top, being preferred to A by a majority of 1,000 and to B by a majority of 3,000. Not even those who voted CAB should therefore be consoled by the thought that, in the actual case, their votes went to effect A's victory: their first choice C deserved to win. If C had won, only the thousand who voted ABC would have been quite without consolation: with A's victory, the five thousand who voted BCA and the two thousand who voted CBA have none.

How, then, could the alternative vote procedure be modified so that its outcome no longer depended upon which candidate happened to be eliminated at stage 1? The obvious solution is to add up the final votes that each candidate would obtain, were some other candidate to be eliminated; in example 1, this would give us:

A	B	C
8,000	7,000	—
7,000	—	8,000
—	6,000	9,000
15,000	13,000	17,000

C would then be seen as having the best claim. This is not a new method of assessment, however: we have simply reinvented the preference score procedure. A candidate's preference score is simply the sum of the votes he would receive if pitted against each other candidate in turn: the preference score procedure is therefore just the alternative vote procedure, adapted to remove the random effects of the distribution of first choices. We have already seen that the number of votes each candidate has as against each of the other candidates leaves a wide margin of variation for the distribution of the particular preference scales, and hence of first choices. For instance, if the preference scales were as in example 2, the pairwise

1,000	2,000	4,000	1,000	5,000	2,000
A	A	B	B	C	C
B	C	A	C	A	B
C	B	C	A	B	A

Example 2

majorities would have been exactly the same; only the numbers of first choices would differ:

A	B	C
3,000	5,000	7,000
8,000	7,000	—
7,000	—	8,000
—	6,000	9,000

It would be misleading to explain this by saying that the alternative vote procedure attaches more weight to first choices than do preference scores. When votes are redistributed after the elimination of a candidate at stage 1, the redistributed second choices are given exactly the same weight as the first choices to which they are added: what is given special importance is only the fact of having the *smallest* number of first choices.

It is not only in the special case that there are three candidates that the suggested method of modifying the alternative vote procedure yields the preference score procedure, but in all cases. If, for instance, there were four candidates, we should have to consider six possibilities, according as one or another pair of candidates were eliminated before the final stage. For each of these six possibilities, the votes would be divided between the two uneliminated candidates: by adding together the votes received by each candidate in the three possible cases in which he survived until the final stage, we should obtain the preference scores.

The alternative vote has been adapted in quite a different manner for the election of two or more candidates. This adaptation is known as the STV (single transferable vote) procedure, and is by far the most popular with advocates of proportional representation who do not like systems involving lists drawn up by political parties; it is in use in Eire, Northern Ireland, and Malta. Each voter lists as many candidates as he chooses in order of preference, but may leave as many as he likes off his list. The assessment process is carried out in stages, at each of which votes are redistributed from candidates no longer in the running; but they fall out of the running, not only by being eliminated, but also by qualifying for election. The proponents of STV usually justify it by appeal to the principle, whose meaning we have found to be so obscure, that as few votes as possible should be 'wasted'.

Suppose that there are r candidates competing for k seats, and that n ballot papers are returned. The method of assessment requires a quota to be determined: this is the minimum number of votes a candidate needs to be accorded at any stage except the last in order to qualify for election. The quota normally employed is known as the Droop quota (after its inventor): it is the smallest whole number larger than $n/(k + 1)$. Thus, if 20,000 people actually vote, and there are 3 seats to be filled, the quota will be set at 5,001; if there had been 5 seats to be filled, it would have been set at 3,334. The Droop quota is the smallest number for which it is impossible that more than k candidates should attain it: it is not certain that as many as k will eventually do so, since no voter is required to list all the candidates. It is quite possible for a candidate to attain the quota at stage 1, and so immediately qualify for election, even though each of the ultimately unsuccessful candidates is preferred by a majority to him.

At each stage of the assessment process, one or more candidates fall out, either by attaining the quota or by being eliminated. If, at any stage, any one or more candidates are found to have attained the quota, they then qualify for election; if there nevertheless remain further seats to be filled, some of their votes are redistributed, as explained below, but no candidate is eliminated. If, at a given stage, no candidate still remaining in the competition is found to have attained the quota, the candidate who at that stage has the lowest number of votes is eliminated, and his votes are redistributed. In either case, the redistribution carries the process to the next stage.

The redistribution is effected in the following way. A candidate will here be called *live* at any stage if he has neither qualified for election nor been eliminated at a previous stage. Now suppose that, at a given stage, a candidate X is to be eliminated. In this case, each of the votes accorded at that stage to X is redistributed to the next live candidate below X on the voter's list, provided that there is one; if there is none, that vote is not redistributed. Let us assume, for example, that there are 20,000 voters, 7 candidates, and 3 seats to be filled, so that the quota is 5,001. At stage 1, only first preferences are counted: 7,001 voters list A first, so that he qualifies for election at stage 1; but he is the only candidate to do so. After redistribution of some of A's votes, it is found, at stage 2, that the quota has still not been attained by any of the remaining 6 candidates: so G, who has the smallest total of votes at stage 2, namely 700, is eliminated. Suppose that 200 voters listed G first and B second: all these 200 votes will then be redistributed to B at stage 3. If 100 voters listed G first and D second, these 100 votes will be redistributed to D. If a further 200 voters listed G first, A second, and B third, their votes will also be redistributed to B, as being the next live candidate below G on their lists: B will thus obtain altogether 400 extra votes in the redistribution which carries the assessment process from stage 2 to stage 3. 100 voters, say, voted only for G, while a further 100 listed G first and A second, but put no other names on their ballot papers: their votes therefore cannot be redistributed. Thus, in all, when G is eliminated, 400 of his 700 votes go to B, 100 to D and 200 fall away.

When, at a given stage, a candidate attains the quota and so qualifies for election, only a proportion of the votes accorded him are redistributed, namely the difference between his total and the quota. In our example, A received 7,001 first preferences: since the quota was 5,001, the surplus to be redistributed in passing from stage 1 to stage 2 is 2,000 votes. These are redistributed according to the proportions of those listing other candidates second among the 7,001 who listed A first. Suppose, for instance, that, of these, 876 (just over 1 in 8) put no other name on their ballot papers: then, of the possible 2,000 votes to be redistributed, 250 will fall away, without being assigned to any of the other candidates. If, of the remaining voters who listed A first, 1,750 listed B second, 1,750 listed C second, and 2,625 listed D second, then 500 of A's votes will be assigned to B, 500 to C, and 750 to D.

At later stages, the redistribution follows the same general principles, but becomes more complicated. To continue the example, suppose that, at stage 1, B received 4,401 first preferences. 500 of A's votes are redistributed to him, so that, at stage 2, he is accorded 4,901 votes, not yet attaining the quota. G is eliminated at stage 2, 400 of his votes going to B. Hence, at stage 3, B has 5,301 votes, surpassing the quota by 300. He thus qualifies for election, and 300 of his votes are redistributed. They will be redistributed according to the next live preferences of the 5,301 voters; to speak more accurately, of the 4,801 actual voters and the 500 notional voters transferred from A. The matter is more easily illustrated by example than stated in full generality. Assume that the relevant lists began as

STV AND A NEW ALTERNATIVE TO IT 271

follows, the figures at the top of each column indicating the numbers of lists involved:

(250)	(250)							
875	875	517	517	767	1,000	1,000	600	400
A	A	B	B	B	B	B	B	G
B	B	A	A	A	C	D	E	B
C	D	C	D	E				E

The 1,750 voters who listed A first and B second are represented by 500 notional votes redistributed to B from A at stage 2. Exactly half of these 1,750 voters listed C next after B, and the other half listed D after B. Hence 250 of these notional voters count as favouring C higher than other candidates live at stage 4, and 250 as favouring D, as shown by the bracketed figures. 517 voters listed B first, followed by A and then C: their votes will therefore count in favour of C at stage 4, as will those of the 1,000 voters who listed B first and C second. We must thus take $250 + 517 + 1,000 = 1,767$ of B's 5,301 votes as favouring C highest of the 4 candidates remaining live after stage 3. In the same way, we must also take 1,767 as favouring D, since there were likewise 517 voters whose lists began BAD and 1,000 whose lists began BD. The same number again must be taken as favouring E, but arrived at differently: 600 put B first and E second, another 400, redistributed at stage 3 from G, put B second and E third, and 767 put B first, A second, and E third, while none of those who put A first and B second listed E third. Thus, in respect of their next live preferences, B's total of 5,301 votes (4,801 actual, 500 notional) must be reckoned as divided equally between C, D, and E. The surplus of 300 votes to be redistributed from B must therefore also be divided equally: 100 will go to C, 100 to D, 100 to E, and none to F. C's acquisition of 100 votes represents the second preferences of 1,000 voters, and the third preferences of 1,392, and likewise for D; E's represents the second preferences of 600 voters and the third preferences of 1,167.

Whenever k candidates have attained the quota, the assessment process is terminated. It is also terminated at any stage at which there are only as many candidates remaining as seats as yet unfilled, or at which no further redistribution of votes can affect the outcome. This will happen if just one seat remains to be filled, and at a certain stage one candidate has an absolute majority of the votes; he then immediately qualifies for election, even if he has not attained the quota. Suppose, again, that two seats remain to be filled, the quota being 4,000. If, at some stage, X has 3,108 votes, Y 3,350, Z 1,900, and W 1,190, X and Y now qualify for election, since each of them has more votes than the sum of those of Z and W: even if all of W's votes were redistributed to Z, Z would still be eliminated at the subsequent stage. The required number of seats will always be filled; attainment of the quota is thus not necessary for election.

The simplest way to envisage the entire assessment process under STV is as follows. At the outset the ballot papers are distributed in piles representing the various candidates, according to the candidate listed first by each voter, and the piles are counted. If, at any stage, a candidate is to be eliminated, his name is deleted from every ballot paper on which it occurs; a ballot paper no longer containing any undeleted names is set aside. When a candidate has been eliminated, the ballot papers in his pile are redistributed according to the highest undeleted name occurring on each. A candidate found at any stage to have a total surpassing the quota qualifies for election; if seats remain to be filled, his name, too, is then deleted from every ballot paper on which it occurs. The ballot papers in the successful candidate's pile are then marked with a fraction, and henceforward count as no more than that fraction of a vote. The fraction is arrived at by dividing the candidate's surplus by the total number of votes accorded to him at the given stage. Any ballot paper with more than one fraction marked on it counts only for that fraction of a vote found by multiplying them together. Having been marked with the appropriate fraction, the ballot papers in the pile of a candidate attaining the quota are then redistributed as before. This description is picturesque, and obviously does not represent the actual procedure of the tellers, but it is equivalent in effect to the calculations they will make, save that they will round to the nearest integer. Instead of dealing in notional votes, each representing a certain number—not necessarily a whole number—of actual votes, the foregoing description deals in actual ballot papers, some of which are reduced in value to a fraction of a vote. It thus allows a completely accurate statement of the method of assessment, something which is not in fact achieved by those who essay popular accounts of STV, assuring their readers that it is not really complicated. It *is* complicated. Sliding over the complications that occur when a vote is redistributed more than once will somewhat disguise the complexity, at the cost of accuracy, but still cannot give the appearance of simplicity. The voter, indeed, does not have to do anything complicated: he has only to list as many candidates as he chooses in order of preference. He is, however, entitled to understand the method of assessment, and it is unfair to inform him that it is perfectly simple, because it is not: it is very much harder to explain and to grasp than the preference score procedure or even the composite score procedure. It is very doubtful whether many of those who vote under this system in the countries where it is in use could explain its working or give clear instructions to the tellers.

Let us examine an actual example, cited by David McKie in an article on STV in the *Guardian* for 10 December 1981. This is the election in West Belfast in April 1925: out of a total electorate of 65,550, there were 49,484 votes cast, and four seats to be filled, yielding a quota of 9,897. There were seven candidates: these, with their parties and the abbreviations we shall use, were:

De	J. Devlin	Nationalist
Wo	P. J. Woods	Independent Unionist
Bu	T. H. Burn	Labour Unionist
Ly	Sir R. Lynn	Unionist
Di	R. Dickson	Unionist
MC	J. McConville	Republican
MM	W. McMullan	Labour

The assessment process went through six stages. In the table below, an underlined figure indicates one that surpasses the quota, the candidate in question therefore gaining one of the seats; a bracketed figure indicates a candidate eliminated at the stage in question. In

	De	Wo	Bu	Ly	Di	MC	MM
Stage 1	<u>17,558</u>	9,599	4,808	8,371	3,133	3,146	2,869
Stage 2	—	1,472	70	136	305	1,310	4,368
	—	<u>11,071</u>	4,878	8,507	3,438	4,456	7,237
Stage 3	—	—	43	92	185	55	558
	—	—	4,921	8,599	(3,623)	4,511	7,795
Stage 4	—	—	1,068	1,838	—	34	207
	—	—	5,989	<u>10,437</u>	—	4,545	8,002
Stage 5	—	—	520	—	—	7	13
	—	—	6,509	—	—	(4,552)	8,015
Stage 6	—	—	6	—	—	—	2,330
	—	—	6,515	—	—	—	<u>10,345</u>

Example 3

the stages after the first, the upper figure indicates the number of votes gained by a candidate by redistribution of the surplus of a successful candidate or of the total vote of an eliminated candidate, and the lower figure gives the total number of votes accorded to the given candidate at that stage.

The final outcome was therefore that Devlin, Woods, Lynn, and McMullan were elected. The first three of these had, in that order, the three highest totals of first preferences, but McMullan had the lowest number of first preferences, gaining greatly in the redistributions at the second, third, and sixth stages.

To estimate the significance of such an example, we really need to know the preference scales of all the voters; although the numbers of votes redistributed at each stage tell us something of the voters' second and third preferences, they obviously do not allow us to reconstruct them exactly. It is nevertheless worth making a rough attempt. If we were to stick to the actual figures, and allow for all the possible preference scales that voters might plausibly be thought to have, the example would become far too complex to survey; we have therefore to simplify it, while retaining an essential plausibility. For this purpose, we may begin by dividing the above figures by 100, rounding up or down. As a result, we obtain the following simplified table, in which altogether 494 votes are cast, with a quota of 99:

	De	Wo	Bu	Ly	Di	MC	MM
Stage 1	175	96	48	84	31	31	29
Stage 2	—	15	1	1	3	13	43
	—	111	49	85	34	44	72
Stage 3	—	—	0	1	2	1	6
	—	—	49	86	(36)	45	78
Stage 4	—	—	11	18	—	0	2
	—	—	60	104	—	45	80
Stage 5	—	—	5	—	—	0	0
	—	—	65	—	—	(45)	80
Stage 6	—	—	0	—	—	—	23
	—	—	65	—	—	—	103

Example 4(a)

It will be noted that, although at stage 2 Wo achieved a surplus of 12, only 10 of these are redistributed at stage 3: this must be due to some of the voters' having listed only Wo, and perhaps also De, on their ballot papers. Similarly, at stage 4, only 31 of Di's 36 votes are redistributed, and, at stage 6, only 23 of MC's 45. Even with this simplified example, to give a wholly plausible reconstruction of the preference scales of the voters would be intolerably complex: with seven candidates there are altogether 5,040 possible preference scales. With only 494 voters, not all of these could be represented: but it would be perfectly possible for there to be between 300 and 400 different preference scales distributed among the voters. In guessing at the preference scales that might produce the foregoing result, it is still necessary to simplify beyond what perfect realism would demand. Given this need, however, example 4(b) on p. 276, in which 22 distinct preference scales are represented, is reasonably plausible: it is consistent with the result, and accords quite well with the political affiliations of the actual candidates, as listed above. In each preference scale a line occurs at one level or another. This line separates the preferences of which, in the assessment process, account was taken at some stage from those of which no such account was taken. It would therefore be consistent with the facts, though not very plausible, to take it as also representing the distinction between those candidates actually listed by the voters and those not listed by them. Since, as observed, at most, though not all, the stages, fewer votes were redistributed than might in principle have been, it is, for certain of the voters, necessary to suppose that they did not list any of the candidates below the line: in these cases, the line is doubled. The figures standing at the head of each preference scale indicate the number of voters with that scale.

Of the 494 voters, the 77 who rank either Bu or MM highest never have their second preferences taken into account, since both these two candidates survive until the last stage. Of the remaining 417, 107 have their third preferences taken into account, and the other 310 only their first and second preferences.

A different reconstruction would, of course, be possible; this one has been devised with the sole aim of being as plausible as the demand of relative simplicity allows, not with an eye to any specific consequences. The majority numbers and preference scores obtained by each candidate, according to example 4(b), are:

De	Wo	Bu	MM	Di	MC	Ly
5	5	4	3	2	2	0
1,792	1,702	1,866	1,335	1,377	1,275	1,123

34	2	30	7	100	21	9	9	3	54	1	13	11	2	84	9	14	8	48	29
De	De	De	De	De	Wo	Wo	Wo	Wo	Wo	Di	Di	Di	Di	Ly	MC	MC	MC	Bu	MM
Wo	Ly	MC	Di	MM	Ly	MC	Di	Di	MM	Ly	Ly	Bu	MM	Bu	MM	De	Wo	–	–
Di	Bu	MM	Ly	=	Bu	MM	Ly	Ly	Bu	Bu	Ly	–	–	–	–	–	=	Di	MC
–	–	–	Bu	MC	–	–	–	–	–	Wo	Wo	Ly	Bu	Di	De	Wo	Wo	Ly	De
Bu	Di	Bu	–	MC	Bu	–	Bu	Bu	Di	Bu	Wo	Wo	Wo	Wo	Bu	MM	De	MM	Bu
Ly	Wo	MM	Wo	Bu	De	De	De	De	Ly	Wo	De	De	De	De	Wo	Bu	Di	De	Wo
MC	MC	Di	MC	Bu	Di	MC	MC	MC	Bu	MM	MM	MM	MC	Di	MM	Di	Bu	MC	Di
MM	MM	Ly	MM	Ly	Ly	Ly	Ly	Ly	Bu	MC	MC	MC	MC	MM	Ly	Ly	Ly	MM	Ly

Example 4(b)

STV thus produces a different ranking from both the preference score and majority number procedures (applied to candidates), namely:

STV	De	Wo	Ly	MM	Bu	MC	Di
preference score	Bu	De	Wo	Di	MM	MC	Ly
majority number	De	Wo	Bu	MM	Di	MC	Ly

The STV ranking has been obtained by setting the successful candidates above the unsuccessful ones, and ranking the former in the order in which they attained the quota, and the latter in the inverse order of their elimination. All three procedures agree in awarding a seat to both De and Wo. The preference score and majority number procedures also agree with each other in ranking Ly, to whom STV awards a seat, as the least deserving of the candidates, and in awarding a seat to Bu, who fails to get one under STV; while the majority number procedure agrees with STV in giving a seat to MM, the preference score procedure would give it instead to Di, the first to be eliminated under STV.

The disagreement between the preference score and majority number procedures over whether Di or MM is to be elected is not very significant, save to those candidates and their supporters, in that MM is the runner-up under the preference score procedure and Di the runner-up under the majority number procedure; if there had been only three seats, the two procedures would have produced the same overall outcome. We cannot tell exactly what would have happened under STV if there had been only three seats: the quota would have been 124, and the stages of the assessment process would have been markedly different, but, without making additional assumptions about which of the candidates were actually listed by the voters, we cannot precisely determine the redistributions. The probability is, however, that the assessment would have gone as follows:

	De	Wo	Bu	MM	Di	MC	Ly
stage 1	elected						
stage 2					elim.		
stage 3						elim.	
stage 4			elim.				
stage 5							elected
stage 6		elected					

De, Ly, and Wo would have been elected.

The principal anomalies of STV, as it operates in example 4, are its overvaluation of Ly, the weakest candidate either in terms of preference scores or of majority preferences, and its undervaluation of Bu, who has the highest preference score of any of the seven candidates. In general, STV takes account, selectively, of second and third preferences, but hardly ever of fourth or fifth preferences: the high degree of Ly's unpopularity with many of the voters, 220 of whom rate him the worst of the seven, is therefore not registered. Bu, on the other hand, suffers from the fact that the 84 supporters of Ly, who all rank Bu second, are represented by only 4 redistributed votes at stage 5, since only 5 of the votes for Ly are reassigned as surplus. Likewise, the 13 of Di's supporters who listed Ly second and Bu third are represented by only $\frac{5}{8}$ of a vote redistributed to Bu at stage 5: if Ly had happened to attain the quota before Di was eliminated, all 13 would have gone to Bu. The operation of STV is full of quirks of this kind, because it rests on no clear principle, but only on the woolly notion of the wasted vote, which has never been thought through. In particular, a candidate has a good chance of doing well under STV if he is the second choice of the supporters of a candidate who is eliminated at an early stage; he benefits little from being the second choice of the supporters of a candidate who at some stage only just scrapes a total in excess of the quota.

The rationale of STV rests on the concept of the wasted vote: but when is a vote wasted? In example 4, De was listed first by 175 voters, while the quota was only 99. The idea of redistributng the surplus votes of a successful candidate is that, if that were not done, some of the votes for him would have been wasted; for instance, 76 of those who listed De first. But, as Bogdanor remarks, 'we have no way of telling which of the ... votes are in fact surplus'.[1] He does not, of course, mean that there is some answer to the question which of the 175 votes are surplus and which necessary, but that we have, unfortunately, no means of discovering this answer. If he meant this, the difficulty would surely not be insuperable: the surplus votes might, for instance, be those of the 76 of De's supporters who arrived later at the polling station than the rest. Bogdanor means, rather, that it would be senseless to ask which of the 175 votes for De belonged to the surplus.

Now one might say that, if it made any clear sense to speak of any

---

[1] V. Bogdanor, *The People and the Party System*, p. 239.

of De's supporters as wasting their votes, it would have to be possible to say what would have to be true of any one of them for him to have done so. This is not quite fair, however. We earlier attempted to define a voter as wasting his vote if the situation was vulnerable to a set to which he belonged and to no proper subset of it. It might be that each of a number of voters belonged to some such set, although there was no set containing all of them. In such a case, all of those voters would, under the suggested definition, have wasted their votes: but there would be no outcome that they would all have preferred and that could have been obtained by their all voting differently. This does not show anything wrong with the suggested definition of a wasted vote: it shows only that, when a wasted vote is so defined, one cannot identify a wasted vote with a surplus vote. More exactly, there is no such thing as 'a surplus vote': there are only surpluses, which are numbers of votes, not particular sets of votes.

If our suggested characterization of a wasted vote is on the right lines, then, the aim of those who want to reduce the number of wasted votes is to offer a remedy for instability. Unfortunately, the remedy is simplistic. Since no measure is proposed of the degree of instability of a given situation under a particular procedure, let alone of the propensity of a given procedure to lead to unstable situations, no standard is provided whereby STV may be judged to be better, or not to be better, in this regard than other procedures in general. Rather, expressing the matter in terms of wasted votes allows us to compare STV only with certain specific other procedures: a vote that might have been wasted under some other procedure will not be wasted under STV. Thus the redistribution of votes from an eliminated candidate is justified by a tacit comparison with an extension of the relative majority procedure, under which each voter casts a vote for a single candidate, and those k candidates are elected who receive the greatest numbers of votes. Under this procedure, a voter who ranks X highest and Y second may waste his vote by voting for X instead of for Y; if under STV he lists X first and Y second, he will not have wasted his vote if Y is still live when X is eliminated, at least if Y is ultimately successful. We have already seen, from our study of the alternative vote procedure, that this ignores other relevant possibilities, for instance that Y is eliminated before X, but might have been saved from being so; the redistribution of votes from eliminated candidates does not guarantee that no voter who has listed the eliminated candidate first has wasted his vote. Likewise, the redistribution of votes from a candidate attaining the quota is justified by a tacit comparison with a procedure like STV but with redistribution of votes only from eliminated candidates. In fact, such redistributions do little to diminish instability: some of them will be unnecessary, some ineffective. In example 4, the 13 votes redistributed from De to MC did not save him: on the contrary, had there been redistributions only from eliminated candidates, MC would have been elected, because MM would have been eliminated at once and his 29 votes would have been transferred to MC. On the other hand, the redistribution of 15 votes from De to Wo was unnecessary, since Wo would have attained the quota by receiving 4 votes from Di when Di was eliminated.

STV is obviously a majority procedure; and under a majority procedure the situation is bound to be unstable unless there is an overall outcome that tops all the others, which there usually will not be. The best way to reduce instability, if that is one's object, is to employ the majority number procedure, applied to candidates rather than to outcomes for the sake of practicability, instead of engaging in complex schemes of redistributing votes. The terminology employed by advocates of STV is notably vague, and one might construe their aim as being, rather, to ensure that as many of the voters' preferences as possible go to determine the outcome. If so, the preference score procedure, again applied to candidates rather than to outcomes for the sake of practicability, achieves that in the optimum manner; there is still no point in arbitrary rules for taking certain preferences into account, but not others.

The best way to gain an insight into the arbitrary working of STV is to consider an example in which a small change in the ballot papers returned by a few voters will make a radical alteration in the overall outcome. In example 5, there are 1,000 voters, 4 seats to be filled, and 8 candidates, with a quota of 201. The assessment proceeds in the following stages:

	A	B	C	D	E	F	G	H
Stage 1	204	190	120	95	98	100	96	97
Stage 2	—	3	0	0	0	0	0	0
	—	193	120	(95)	98	100	96	97
Stage 3	—	47	48	—	0	0	0	0
	—	240	168	—	98	100	96	97

	A	B	C	D	E	F	G	H
Stage 4	—	—	39	—	0	0	0	0
	—	—	207	—	98	100	96	97
Stage 5	—	—	—	—	0	0	6	0
	—	—	—	—	98	100	102	(97)
Stage 6	—	—	—	—	2	48	47	—
	—	—	—	—	(100)	148	149	—
Stage 7	—	—	—	—	—	44	56	—
	—	—	—	—	—	192	205	—

Example 5(a)

The successful candidates are thus *A*, *B*, *C*, and *G*. The effect of transferring just ten of the initial votes from *A* to *D* may, however, be very considerable. Suppose that just ten voters have listed *A* first and *D* second. Since *A* has a surplus of only 3, they are too few to cause any of *A*'s redistributed surplus to go to *D*. If, however, they had listed *D* first and *A* second, the assessment might have gone as follows:

	A	B	C	D	E	F	G	H
Stage 1	194	190	120	105	98	100	(96)	97
Stage 2	0	0	0	24	24	23	—	25
	194	190	(120)	129	122	123	—	123
Stage 3	0	0	—	80	30	0	—	10
	194	190	—	209	152	123	—	133
Stage 4	3	2	—	—	1	1	—	1
	197	192	—	—	153	(124)	—	134
Stage 5	2	2	—	—	70	—	—	50
	199	194	—	—	223	—	—	184
Stage 6	1	2	—	—	—	—	—	19
	200	196	—	—	—	—	—	203
Stage 7	1	1	—	—	—	—	—	—
	201	197	—	—	—	—	—	—

Example 5(b)

This time the successful candidates are *A*, *D*, *E*, and *H*. The postponement of *A*'s eventual success has meant the elimination of *G* at stage 1, so that, instead of a very small number of *C*'s votes being redistributed to *G*, all 120 of them are divided among *D*, *E*, and *H*, conferring success upon these candidates at once or later. In example 5(a), *D* was eliminated, and 47 of his votes went to *B*; in 5(b), since *D* has attained the quota, *B* receives only 1 of his votes. There is no difficulty in constructing lists that will, with the necessary change in ten of them, fit both examples 5(a) and 5(b).

STV has, however, a great advantage in that respect discussed in the last chapter, the protection of minorities, in which the preference score and majority number procedures are exceptionally weak: instead of praising STV for those features in which those two procedures far outshine it, its advocates ought to concentrate on that feature in which it does excel all other procedures hitherto proposed. If the members of a minority M all list a certain candidate A first, he is certain to attain the quota at stage 1 provided that M exceeds, by however little, $1/(k+1)$ of the electorate (or, rather, of those actually voting). STV is thus as effective for this purpose as the cumulative vote procedure. In fact, it is much more effective, because it is unnecessary for the minority to agree to support a single candidate, as they must do under the cumulative vote procedure if they do not amount to $2/(k+1)$ of the electorate; and for this reason, it does not place anything like the high premium upon group organization that is conferred on it by the cumulative vote or limited vote procedure. All that is necessary, for a minority M forming more than $1/(k+1)$ of the electorate to be certain of electing at least one candidate favourable to it under STV, is that there should be some set of candidates, all favourable to M, to which each voter in M is solidly committed. Here a voter is understood as being *solidly committed* to a set of candidates if he includes every candidate in the set on his list, and ranks each of them higher than any candidate not in the set. M may comprise the supporters of some political party, and the set of candidates to which its members are solidly committed the candidates of that party; or M may be a racial minority, and the set of candidates those who themselves belong to that minority. Suppose, then, that the voters in M are solidly committed to j candidates $A_1, \ldots, A_j$: every member of M puts those j candidates, in some order or other, in the first j places on his list. Then, as soon as any one of these j candidates is eliminated, those of his votes which were cast by members of M will be redistributed to others of them: when sufficiently many of them—if necessary, all but one—have been eliminated, one of them will attain the quota, since by hypothesis there are more than $n/(k+1)$ members of M; since it is impossible for more than k candidates to attain the quota, there will at that stage be at least one seat as yet unfilled. Thus at least one of the candidates $A_1, \ldots, A_j$ is certain to be elected.

This effect may be generalized further: for this, the redistribution of the surplus votes of successful candidates, as well as of all the votes of those eliminated, is essential. Let q be the quota, and let h be any whole number less than or equal to k; suppose that M is any set of hq voters (not necessarily a minority) solidly committed to the candidates $A_1, \ldots, A_j$, where j is greater than or equal to h. Then at least h of these j candidates are certain to be elected. To see this, consider a specific example. Suppose that $k = 4$ and that 10,000 people vote: the quota q is therefore 2,001. Let M contain 6,050 voters, solidly committed to $A_1, \ldots, A_5$; thus $h = 3$ and $j = 5$. We have therefore to show that at least three of the candidates $A_1, \ldots, A_5$ will be elected. It obviously suffices to show this for the worst case possible, namely that none of the voters not in M includes any of the A candidates on his list. Let us call the candidates other than $A_1, \ldots, A_5$ 'B candidates': it makes no difference how many there are. By assumption, all the 6,050 voters in M put A candidates in the first five places on their lists: so at stage 1 there are 6,050 votes distributed between the A candidates, and the remaining 3,950 between the B candidates. This state of affairs continues until a stage of the assessment process is reached at which some candidate attains the quota: before that, if one of the A candidates is eliminated, his votes are distributed among the remaining A candidates, and, if one of the B candidates is eliminated, his votes are redistributed among the remaining B candidates. Suppose that the first candidate to attain the quota is a B candidate. If he has, say, 2,050 votes at that stage, his 49-vote surplus will be redistributed among the other surviving B candidates. There will therefore be altogether 1,949 votes distributed among the live B candidates, from which it is obvious that, whichever candidates are next eliminated, no B candidate can attain the quota of 2,001 before three A candidates have done so and all 4 seats are filled. When two of the A candidates have attained the quota, the redistribution of their surpluses will leave $6,050 - (2 \times 2,001) = 2,048$ votes distributed among the remaining A candidates, another of whom must therefore attain the quota before any votes can be transferred to B candidates from A candidates. Thus, as claimed, at least three of the four candidates elected will be from the set to which the members of M are solidly committed.

Most of the advantages advertised for STV are illusory; it is, for instance, even further from the truth than under the alternative vote procedure that a voter cannot lessen B's chances as against those of C by listing A first. Its disadvantages are great: it is complex for the tellers to operate, it is almost impossible to explain accurately, and its effects upon the outcome are often highly arbitrary. Its outstanding merit is the protection that it gives to minorities. This feature is so important a requirement of a just electoral system that any attempt to replace STV, where it is in force, by some procedure that lacks it, or to advocate the introduction of such a procedure rather than of STV, ought to be resisted.

It is better still to devise a procedure that shares this feature with STV, but lacks its arbitrariness. This can be done by grafting on to the preference score procedure, applied to candidates, an additional criterion of assessment, expressly designed to secure the required effect: the result may be called the QPS procedure (Q for 'quota' and PS for 'preference score'). As under STV, voters will be asked to list the candidates in order of preference, without bracketing; it would be possible to allow them to leave two or more candidates off their lists, but it is probably better to prohibit this unless it is found that a large number of ballot papers are then spoiled. The assessment will proceed by stages, all but the last of which may be called 'qualifying stages': it will of course terminate as soon as all k seats have been filled. We may first describe the assessment process for the case when k is 2 or 3. At stage 1, the tellers will determine whether there are any candidates listed first by more than $1/(k+1)$ of the total number n of voters: if so, they immediately qualify for election. If seats remain to be filled, the preference scores of all candidates not qualifying at stage 1 will then be calculated. At stage 2, the ballot papers will be scrutinized to see if there is any pair of candidates, neither of whom qualified at stage 1, to whom more than $n/(k+1)$ voters are solidly committed: if so, that member of the pair with the higher preference score now qualifies for election. If seats remain to be filled, the tellers will proceed to stage 3, at which they will consider sets of three candidates, none of whom has already qualified. If more than $n/(k+1)$ voters are solidly committed to any such trio, that one with the highest preference score qualifies for election. In general, at the qualifying stage i, the tellers determine whether, for any set of i candidates none of whom has so far qualified, there are more than $n/(k+1)$ voters solidly committed to those candidates; if so, the member of the set with the highest preference score qualifies for election at stage i. If there still remain seats to be filled after all the qualifying stages have been completed, they will be filled at the final stage by those candidates having the highest preference scores out of those who have not yet qualified.

There is room for slight variation in these rules. Suppose that there are 20,000 voters and 3 seats to be filled: at stage 3 it is found that 5,040 voters are solidly committed to A, B, and C, and 5,109 voters to A, D, and E; none of these has previously qualified. If A has a higher preference score than B or C, and D a higher preference score than A or E, then, under the rules as stated above, both A and D will qualify for election. If desired, the rules could easily be so framed that, in such a case, only A qualified; indeed, they could be modified further, so that only A qualified even if B had a higher preference score than A. The precise formulation of the rules governing qualification for election at a stage i at which there are overlapping sets of i candidates to whom more than $n/(k+1)$ voters are solidly committed is a matter of taste.

A more important question concerns larger solidly committed blocks of voters. We have seen that STV protects not only minorities but majorities: in the example given above, with 4 seats to be filled, a set of solidly committed voters numbering three times the quota, that is, just over three-fifths of the electorate, was guaranteed 3 out of the 4 seats. There seems no sufficient reason to retain this feature of STV: we are concerned to protect minorities, not to accord disproportionate representation to large blocks of opinion. When k is 2 or 3, therefore, we do not need to consider whether a solidly committed set numbers more than $2n/(k+1)$ voters, since this would make it a majority. When $k = 4$, however, it may be thought that a body of voters, amounting to more than two-fifths of the electorate and solidly committed to two or more candidates, is entitled to 2 of the 4 seats. To achieve this, the assessment process must be made a little more complex. Stage 1 will proceed as before, and, at stage 2, the same operation must be carried out as described above. Before proceeding to stage 3, however, the tellers must also consider every pair of candidates of whom one qualified at stage 1 and the other did not: if more than $2n/(k+1)$ voters are solidly committed to such a pair, that one who did not qualify at stage 1 qualifies at stage 2. (Note that, if more than $2n/(k+1)$ voters are solidly committed to two candidates, one of them must qualify at stage 1.) Likewise, at each qualifying stage i, the tellers must ask, of every set of i candidates of whom at most one has already qualified, whether more than $2n/(k+1)$ voters are solidly committed to those candidates. If so, and none of them has previously qualified, the two with the highest preference scores will now qualify; if one of them qualified at an earlier stage, that one, of the rest, who has the highest preference score will qualify at stage i.

In practice, k is unlikely to be greater than 5; unless it is, the foregoing description of the assessment process is complete. If k were, say, 7, however, it would be necessary for the tellers, at stage 3 and beyond, to consider sets of solidly committed voters amounting to more than three-eighths of the electorate, who would be entitled to 3 out of the 7 seats. In general, then, let j be the largest whole number less than $\frac{1}{2}(k + 1)$. If $i \leqslant j$, then, at stage i, the tellers must ask, of each set of voters solidly committed to i candidates, what multiple of $n/(k + 1)$ members it contains, up to $in/(k + 1)$. If it contains more than $n/(k + 1)$ voters, at least one of the i candidates will qualify for election; if it contains more than $2n/(k + 1)$, at least two will qualify; if $3 \leqslant i$ and it contains more than $3n/(k + 1)$, at least three will; and so on, up to the case in which it contains more than $in/(k + 1)$ voters, when all i candidates will qualify. If the tellers reach a qualifying stage i for which $i > j$, they need only go up to the case in which the set contains more than $jn/(k + 1)$ voters. Thus, if $k = 7, j = 3$; so if, when there are 7 seats to be filled, the tellers find, at stage 4, a set of voters solidly committed to four candidates, of whom at most two have previously qualified, and this set contains more than three-eighths of the total number of voters, they must ensure that three of those four candidates have qualified by the end of stage 4. It may be that this set of voters actually formed a majority; since this does not of itself entitle them to 4 of the 7 seats, there is no guarantee that all four of the candidates will qualify.

Through how many qualifying stages should the assessment process run? Each political party is likely to put up as many candidates as it can conceivably hope will be returned: the optimistic will put up k candidates each, and more modest parties fewer than k. If we were concerned only with the representation of minorities represented by political parties, it would therefore be unnecessary to carry the process beyond qualifying stage k, since no such minority would be solidly committed to more than k candidates. Suppose, however, that there are five political parties competing for four seats, and a racial or religious minority M amounting to just over one-fifth of the electorate. The voters in M may be determined that a candidate himself belonging to M be elected. If they are divided in opinion between the parties, however, and each party puts up one candidate belonging to M, then it may be that no set of voters larger than one-fifth of the total will be found to be solidly committed to any four of the minority candidates, even though every voter in M is solidly committed to the five of them. For this reason, the process must be carried beyond the qualifying stage k. It would in principle be possible for a minority consisting of just over $n/(k + 1)$ voters to be solidly committed to $r - k$ candidates (there being r candidates altogether), even though the remaining k candidates all had higher preference scores; in theory, therefore, the assessment should be carried to qualifying stage $r - k$. The labour of carrying it through so many stages would be great, however, and the need for it extremely rare. In practice, therefore, it would probably be sufficient to lay down that the assessment was to be carried to qualifying stage $k + 2$. Any minority divided between a greater number of candidates than this would have to develop a concerted strategy to ensure that it was represented; but this would very seldom happen.

Suppose that there is a set M of just more than $n/(k + 1)$ voters solidly committed to a trio of candidates, but divided over which of the three they most favour. Under both STV and QPS, one of the trio is bound to be elected. Under STV, this will tend to be the one most favoured by the members of M itself, although this will not be so when votes have been redistributed to one of them from other candidates. Under QPS, on the other hand, the candidate selected out of the three will be the one most acceptable to the voters in general. The principle is that any one of the three can be considered an adequate representative of M, but that, in selecting that representative, the preferences of other voters are entitled to be taken into account. Conversely, the preferences of members of M will count equally with those of all other voters in determining which other candidates are successful; by contrast, under STV, two or more candidates representative of a majority will often be selected principally or even wholly according to the wishes of that majority alone.

The fundamental idea of QPS is to superimpose, on the preference score procedure, applied to candidates, an overriding criterion designed to ensure minority representation. The detailed application of this fundamental idea could be varied considerably, according to the principles thought to be equitable. For instance, if it were wished, account could be taken of solidly committed majorities, simply by requiring the tellers to go up to the point of asking whether a solidly committed set contained more than $in/(k + 1)$

voters even when *i* exceeded *j*. Again, if it were thought more just, it would be possible, though more laborious, to consult only the wishes of a minority about the candidate chosen to represent it. Suppose that a set of voters, amounting to more than $n/(k + 1)$ in all, were solidly committed to a pair of candidates, neither of whom qualified at stage 1. It would be possible to compute the preference scores of those two candidates only over that set of voters, ignoring voters outside the set, the one having the higher of these restricted preference scores qualifying for election. I should personally not regard this as an improvement; but the matter is a delicate one, involving careful consideration of a difficult point of equity. QPS, being based on a clear fundamental idea, allows different principles concerning what would be just to be easily embodied in this or that variation of the procedure. STV, being based on an idea that corresponds in no direct or natural way with any coherent principle of justice, cannot readily be adapted to conform with one or another such principle.

QPS might seem at first difficult to explain to the voters. That would be so only to the extent that it involves conveying an unfamiliar idea; once that has been got across, there will be no difficulty. The complications of the foregoing discussion are due only to the possibility of varying the rules in one or another direction, and will not arise when any one specific version of the procedure is to be explained. The difficulties of explaining STV fully are, by contrast, almost insuperable, and it is usually not attempted. Equally, the task of the tellers is less arduous under QPS than under STV. STV violates the fundamental rule, that tellers should never have to do more than count and add: it forces them to multiply, and perhaps multiply repeatedly by ungainly fractions. (Of all other procedures mentioned in this book, only the composite score procedure requires the tellers to multiply.) If, under QPS, the tellers are supplied with $k + 3$ copies of the ballot papers, they can split into groups, each working on a different stage of the assessment process. One group can compute the preference scores; another, working on stage 1, can divide the ballot papers into piles, corresponding to the candidates listed first; that working on stage 2 can divide them into piles corresponding to the first two candidates listed, irrespective of order; and so on. In this way, no group of tellers will find itself faced with any inordinately difficult task.

QPS will make it easy for any voter to decide how to vote. No voting procedure can have the property, often claimed for STV, that, for any three candidates A, B, and C, no voter, by listing A first, can harm B's chances as against those of C: but QPS comes closer to having it than does STV. Under STV, the effect of listing A first may be to delay his elimination until after B has been eliminated; if B had been listed first, he might have survived to pick up other votes, some of them, perhaps, from A. Under QPS, there are no eliminations; there is therefore much less danger in listing B below A when A has poor chances of success. In particular, by listing A first and B second, a voter can have no effect on the number of voters solidly committed to A and B as a pair. A voter who supports a particular group of candidates to which it is likely that other voters will also be committed, whether they are those belonging to a political party or to a racial or religious minority, has little to fear under QPS from his choice of an order in which to list them. QPS thus gives little incentive for strategic voting. It does so in only one respect in which STV does not. Suppose that a voter supports a certain party, but strongly dislikes one of the candidates, C, standing for it: he would rather that no candidate of that party were elected than that C were. Under STV, he has no motive to list C at all; but under QPS he has a motive for listing him third, after two other candidates of the same party, because, by so doing, he might help to get one of the other two candidates elected at stage 3. This constitutes strategic voting in the strict sense that the voter is not recording his true order of preference: but it is voting of a kind for which the procedure specifically provides. In so voting, the voter is expressing a genuine feeling, namely his solidarity with the party: voters would need to know the value of doing this, under this procedure, whenever they felt such solidarity. It cannot be said, therefore, that the effect of voting in this manner will be to distort the outcome: the procedure is designed to give adequate representation to minorities, and this is the means it provides for minorities to achieve this; it has therefore worked as intended. QPS affords the voters a stronger incentive than does STV to draw up their ballot papers in accordance with their adhesion to blocks of opinion, which need not correspond to party labels; a block of voters concerned with a single issue on which the parties were divided, say nuclear disarmament or abortion, might be solidly committed to those candidates, of different parties, who shared their views. Since the point of both procedures is to guarantee representation for significant blocks of opinion or interest,

QPS has an advantage over STV in being more efficient for this purpose.

In some instances, QPS will produce a different outcome from STV, the candidates elected under QPS being just those with the highest preference scores. This will happen when the voters' preferences are scattered rather than being clumped, so that there are no sufficiently large sets of voters solidly committed to particular groups of candidates, but when the distribution of first and second preferences produces an anomalous outcome under STV. It will also happen in cases like example 4, when there are some solidly committed sets of voters, but QPS selects, to represent them, candidates with a high preference score and so more acceptable to the electorate at large, whereas STV selects those in greatest favour with the solidly committed minorities. Conversely, there will be cases when QPS and STV produce the same outcome, the candidates elected not being those with the highest preference scores or majority numbers: this will happen when the preferences are strongly clumped, so that there is only one way to secure representation for significant minorities within the electorate. We may illustrate QPS by an example in which it, STV, and the preference score and majority number procedures would all produce different outcomes.

There are 1,000 voters, 8 candidates, and 4 seats to be filled: the quota under STV is thus 201, and the critical size of minority under QPS 200. The preference scales, with corresponding numbers of voters, are as follows:

200	20	10	50	140	5	110	100	70	35	35	35	35	10	145
A	A	A	B	B	B	C	D	E	E	F	F	G	G	H
B	B	H	A	A	H	D	C	F	G	G	E	E	F	E
H	G	D	C	D	G	H	F	G	F	E	G	F	E	F
E	E	G	D	E	F	G	G	H	C	H	H	H	H	G
G	H	F	E	G	E	E	E	A	H	A	B	B	C	B
F	F	E	G	H	C	F	H	C	B	D	C	C	D	D
D	D	C	H	F	A	B	A	D	A	C	D	A	A	A
C	C	B	F	C	D	A	B	B	D	B	A	D	B	C

Example 6

The majority numbers and preference scores are:

A	B	C	D	E	F	G	H
2	3	0	1	7	4	6	5
3,305	3,600	2,125	3,015	4,505	3,395	3,965	4,090

Under the majority number procedure, the successful candidates are *E*, *F*, *G*, and *H*; under the preference score procedure, they are *B*, *E*, *G*, and *H*. The stages of the QPS assessment will run as follows:

Stage 1: *A* is ranked first by 230 voters, and qualifies for election.

Stage 2: 210 voters are solidly committed to the pair *C*, *D*; *D*, having the higher preference score of the two, qualifies for election. 410 voters are solidly committed to the pair *A*, *B*; *B* therefore qualifies for election.

Stage 3: 220 voters are solidly committed to the trio *E*, *F*, *G*; *E*, having the highest preference score of the three, qualifies for election. All four seats being now filled, the process terminates, and *A*, *B*, *D*, and *E* are declared elected.

Finally, the assessment process under STV will run as follows:

	A	B	C	D	E	F	G	H
Stage 1	230	195	110	100	105	70	45	145
Stage 2	—	28	0	0	0	0	0	1
	—	223	110	100	105	70	45	146
Stage 3	—	—	5	14	0	0	0	3
	—	—	115	114	105	70	(45)	149
Stage 4	—	—	0	0	35	10	—	0
	—	—	115	114	140	(80)	—	149
Stage 5	—	—	0	0	80	—	—	0
	—	—	115	114	220	—	—	149
Stage 6	—	—	3	0	—	—	—	16
	—	—	118	(114)	—	—	—	165
Stage 7	—	—	100	—	—	—	—	14
	—	—	218	—	—	—	—	179

The successful candidates are thus *A*, *B*, *C*, and *E*. This is an excellent example of the long-drawn-out character of the STV assessment process, with its tedious calculations of the votes to be redistributed from the surplus of each candidate, save the last, that attains the quota. In this example, QPS has produced much the same outcome as STV, and for essentially the same reasons. Between *C* and *D*, however, it has selected *D*, as more generally acceptable; under STV, *C* had a lead over *D* principally because, among the 210 voters solidly committed to these two candidates, very slightly more preferred *C*. Note that *C* not only has the lowest preference score, but also a majority number of 0; unlike the alternative vote procedure, STV does not prevent the election of a candidate with majority number 0.

When the preference score procedure would fail to accord representation to minorities, QPS will do so, and will then most often produce the same outcome as STV. When the minorities would gain adequate representation under the preference score procedure, QPS will usually produce the same outcome as it; it will in all cases avoid the haphazard effects sometimes resulting from STV. These haphazard effects are due to there being no clear principle underlying STV. If STV were simple to operate and to explain, the haphazard effects might be tolerated for the sake of that simplicity; it is in fact nearly as complex as a voting procedure could be. It is therefore a serious mistake to accept it as the best electoral method that could be devised. It has, however, the salient merit of giving as good protection to minorities as could be given by any procedure; that merit must be retained in any rival procedure proposed in its place. QPS retains it, and is in every other respect superior to STV: it is easier to operate and to explain, and, being based on two clear principles, will produce a fairer outcome whenever it diverges from STV.

QPS has here been advocated as superior to STV, but not necessarily as being the best electoral system. The question what is the best electoral system is of the greatest complexity, and does not belong exclusively to the theory of voting. It is hardly possible to discuss it adequately unless the fundamentals of the theory of voting have been grasped. That is why so much discussion of it is flawed; but it is beyond the scope of this book to discuss it comprehensively. Under most systems, a voter in a general election knows that his vote goes to determine two quite different things: who is to represent the constituency, and what is to be the composition of the next parliament. Should he be asked to vote only about the latter, as in Israel? Or should he be asked, as under the West German system, to cast two separate votes, one for one purpose and one for the other? In any case, how detailed a preference concerning the composition of parliament should he be allowed to express? Should he be confined to indicating which of the political parties he most favours? Or should he have the opportunity to show that he wants some second party to do comparatively well, or that he would prefer, or would strongly dislike, a coalition government? There are also important ancillary questions, such as whether the electorate should have a say, as in American primaries, in the selection of party candidates. Above all, there is a fundamental problem: given that a paraliament should be representative, what is the criterion for its being so? It was remarked in the Introduction that this question is seldom posed, although the answer is far from obvious. Even those who are most contemptuous of the relative majority procedure as a means of selecting a parliamentary representative take it for granted that whether or not a parliament is representative of the electorate as a whole depends only on the first preferences of the electors, as between the political parties. Any reader of this book will know that a party commanding the smallest number of first preferences may nevertheless top all other parties, that is, may be preferred by some majority to each of them: it then by no means stands to reason that it ought to have the smallest representation in parliament. The choice of an electoral system involves many very complex problems. No comprehensive treatment of it has therefore been attempted in this book, whose main purpose has been to explain the fundamentals of the theory of voting; without an understanding of these, the question of an electoral system cannot be properly tackled. All that has been argued in this chapter is that, given an electoral system with multi-member constituencies, the voting between the candidates would be better conducted by the QPS procedure here proposed, or some variant of it, than by any other known method.

Epilogue

This book has attempted to blend two traditions of enquiry into voting procedures, the practical and the theoretical. As remarked in the Introduction, there is now a whole body of theory, a rigorous and systematic mathematical theory of voting. In modern times, that is, in the post-war period, this was initiated by economists, in particular by Duncan Black and Kenneth Arrow, in about 1950, and has since largely remained in the hands of economists; a few professional philosophers have contributed to it, but not, so far, political scientists. The interest of economists in the theory is principally due, as it was for Arrow, to the possibility of viewing it in a more general context, that is, independently of the mechanism of decision-making, as a way of approaching welfare economics. To most of those concerned with the practical study of voting procedures, however, the mathematical theory of voting remains completely unknown. This unquestionably applies to those engaged in politics, at whatever level; and although some political scientists have recently begun to take an interest in the theory, it also still applies to the majority of academic researchers into the principles and workings of political and social institutions. From their side, there is a fairly substantial literature on electoral systems; but most of them seem unaware of the very existence of the mathematical theory built up, over more than three decades, by economists and others not professionally engaged in political studies. An excellent contribution to the literature on electoral systems is Vernon Bogdanor's *The People and the Party System*, which I have cited more than once; but its six-page bibliography reveals very vividly the astonishing divide between the theoretical and the practical traditions, the tradition of the economists and that of the politicians and political scientists. For this bibliography does not include a single one of the fundamental works in the theoretical tradition of the economists: not Duncan Black's *The Theory of Committees and Elections* of 1958, nor Kenneth Arrow's *Social Choice and Individual Values* of 1951, nor Robin Farquharson's *Theory of Voting* of 1969. Indeed, comparing Bogdanor's bibliography with the 26-page one appended to Professor Amartya Sen's 'Social Choice Theory', a comprehensive review of the whole existing body of mathematical theory on this subject, of which its author has kindly let me see a first draft, I have been able to find the name of only a single writer common to the two bibliographies, that of J. S. Mill. Nor does Bogdanor's index list any of the names of those precursors of the modern theory discussed by Duncan Black in the historical section of his book, Borda, Condorcet, Laplace, and C. L. Dodgson (Lewis Carroll). I think the neglect by the political scientists of the economists' contributions to fundamental theory less defensible than the converse: for the mathematical theorists may reasonably plead that the political scientists prove no theorems, whereas the political scientists cannot with reason claim that the mathematical theory has no bearing on their estimates of the effects and merits of rival voting procedures.

I have attempted in this book to construct a bridge between these two traditions. In the early chapters, the fundamental concepts of the mathematical theory of voting are explained; and throughout I have sought as far as possible to formulate propositions precisely and to give proofs of them, rather than to advance opinions or conjectures, or to employ unexplained and probably unexplainable concepts like that of the wasted vote. On the other hand, I have assumed no mathematical notions other than addition and multiplication, and have introduced none other than those directly required for discussing voting procedures: nothing more formidable than a linear equation occurs anywhere in the book. The discussion has been oriented from the start towards the practical question what voting procedure it is best to use; I have resisted the temptation to prove theorems not bearing directly on this question, and have taken feasibility as well as theoretical equity into account. Since the theory of voting offers no basis for a unique perfect answer to the question what is the most equitable voting procedure, the practitioners of the theory have often concentrated upon proving negative results; this might in part explain the neglect of their work by those with more practical concerns, save that there appears good reason to suppose that the latter have not in fact ever read it. In this book the non-existence of a single sharp criterion for a good voting procedure, and, in particular, of a procedure offering a straightforward strategy for every voter, has been squarely faced, without its being treated as a ground for refraining from recommending any one voting procedure in preference to any other. The merits of a known but relatively little-used method, the preference score procedure, have been canvassed; a modification of it—of practical, though not of theoretical, importance—was proposed for use when a choice is to be made between a large number of candidates for a post; and three new voting procedures have been presented. One was the majority number procedure, with its variant, the persistent majority number procedure, and its elaboration, the composite score procedure, for general use by committees. The second was the graded SV procedure, for use in the special but troublesome case when a committee may elect more than one, but need not elect any, from a set of candidates. The third was the QPS procedure, as an electoral method in multi-member constituencies. Both the majority number and QPS procedures appeal to a combination of criteria; each appeals to preferences scores and also to another criterion taken as overriding them. In the majority number procedure, the overriding criterion is that of majority preference; in QPS, it is a solid commitment by a sufficiently large minority. As an electoral method, QPS involves simpler computations than STV, which has nevertheless proved itself capable of practical use: the assessment process will involve fewer stages under QPS than under STV, and QPS avoids the need for the scaling down required under STV for the redistribution of the surplus votes of a candidate attaining the quota. Since QPS has all the advantages of STV without any of its sometimes bizarre consequences, I strongly hope that it will be seriously considered as a practical option. I am not very strongly disposed to advocate use of the majority number procedure, not having that belief in the rights of majorities needed to make it appear an improvement on the preference score procedure. Some have such a belief, however; moreover, the wording of a regulation or statute, by including a reference to 'a majority', will sometimes make the preference score procedure inadmissible. The interest of the majority number procedure lies principally in its highlighting the crux of the theory of voting. For a procedure to work satisfactorily, the voters must believe that it is fair. They will do so if they are under the illusion that the outcome it produces is always an expression of the general will. But the fact, which we have explored in this book, is that there is no one criterion for what is the general will: there are different criteria, which sometimes conflict. To understand voting requires a grasp of this fundamental fact. Even when it has been grasped in theory, however, it remains painful to become aware of such a conflict in an actual instance: whatever procedure is in use, it is essential to prevent the voters from becoming aware of the clash of criteria in a specific case. This may persuade some to adopt the preference score procedure, and pay no express attention to majorities. It may persuade others to use the unadorned majority number procedure, or its variant, but to take particular care that the tellers reveal no more than they are required to. It may possibly persuade others to settle for the complexities of the composite score procedure (which is still much less complicated than STV). However he decides, anyone who has faced this issue has become conscious, as he may well not have been before, of the difficulties of principle that face those concerned with the choice of a voting procedure. As for the graded SV procedure, it is devoid of complication, and invokes only one criterion. Although it is applicable only to a special case, the case is an important one, arising with awards of prizes, elections to fellowships, and the like. Those concerned with making such awards or elections are frequently perplexed how to proceed; I hope that they will be convinced of the merits of the graded SV procedure for this purpose.

I am well aware that anyone who builds a bridge runs the danger that no one on either side will want to cross to the other. Those engaged on the mathematical theory of voting may dismiss most of what is written in this book as lacking sufficient generality, or, in some cases, rigour, to count as a contribution to their subject. Political scientists and practical politicians may dismiss it as abstract theory remote from their down-to-earth concerns. It stands in danger of being too practical for the former and too theoretical for the latter. The former reaction on the part of the mathematical theorists I should wish to counter by saying: Your theory is hardly rich enough to be valuable as a piece of pure mathematics; of what use then is it if practical applications are not made of it? To those concerned with practical questions of politics who evince the latter reaction, I should like to say the following. Since this book is concerned with practical questions, and with questions the correct answer to which cannot be decided by any single criterion, it admittedly does not purport to demonstrate its eventual conclusions with strict logical cogency; there may therefore indeed be considerations which it overlooks and which would defeat some of those conclusions. It does, however, offer proofs of some propositions of direct relevance to the practical choice between alternative voting procedures; and it proposes a systematic approach to questions hitherto decided principally by appeal to intuitive guesses and speculations. Even if the solutions here proposed be rejected, the book will have served its purpose if those who reject them formulate their objections in at least as precise a manner as the grounds here offered for them; it will be found difficult to formulate them without appeal to the theoretical concepts here explained, and, perhaps, without devising further such concepts defined with equal rigour. But to reject in principle a systematic manner of thinking about a subject which of its nature manifestly allows of a systematic approach is to repudiate rationality itself: it is the equivalent of a remark recently made by an MP, 'Logic has nothing to do with real life.' To boast of thinking unlogically is to boast of not caring for the truth, since the laws of logic are the laws that we must follow if we wish to arrive at the truth. In some areas, it is sometimes legitimate to say, 'I cannot see what is wrong with that argument, and I can offer no counter-argument, but I shall hold fast to my conviction that its conclusion is false.' An extreme example is a paradox: only a fool would allow his inability to resolve Zeno's paradox to induce him to believe that Achilles really cannot overtake the tortoise; but even in such a case, that is no reason for not continuing to strive to discover where the argument leading to the paradoxical conclusion went astray. The theory of voting is not such an area, however. The so-called 'paradox of voting'—the non-transitivity of majority preference—is not a paradox at all, but an indisputable fact highly surprising to anyone when he first becomes aware of it. Mistakes in reasoning can of course be committed by anyone; but the subject-matter of the theory of voting is almost certainly too simple—more exactly expressed, too shallow—to allow of fallacious arguments the location of the fallacy in which is genuinely baffling. By speaking of the topic as 'shallow', I of course mean neither that it is unimportant—it is obviously of far-reaching practical importance—nor that the answers to its problems are obvious or even easily attained: it has been the contention of this book that the subject requires a systematic approach just because what seems at first sight obvious is often false; and some of the problems that arise in the theory of voting are far from easy to solve. I mean only that the subject does not involve deep concepts, like those of infinity or continuity, which present a danger of conceptual confusion and hence of fallacies not readily locatable. Because the subject is in this sense shallow, it is unlikely ever to be reasonable in connection with it to persist for any length of time in saying, 'I cannot see what is wrong with this argument, but I am sure that something must be wrong with it': the area is one in which systematic reasoning is a reliable guide, and intuition a treacherous one. Hence to reject in principle the application to this subject of a systematic approach, such as that attempted in this book, is to reveal oneself as not really caring what the truth about it is: and that means to forfeit the right to have opinions or make assertions about it altogether.

Bibliography

ESSENTIAL WORKS

Kenneth J. Arrow. *Social Choice and Individual Values*, Cowles Commission Monographs, no. 12, New York and London, 1951; second edition, 1963.
Duncan Black. *The Theory of Committees and Elections*, Cambridge, 1958.
Vernon Bogdanor. *The People and the Party System*, Cambridge, 1981.
C. L. Dodgson. *A Discussion of the Various Methods of Procedure in Conducting Elections*, Oxford, 1873.
——. *Suggestions as to the Best Method of Taking Votes, where more than two Issues are to be Voted on*, Oxford, 1874.
——. *A Method of Taking Votes on more than two Issues*, Oxford, 1876.
All three of these pamphlets are reprinted on pp. 214–34 of the book by D. Black listed above.
Robin Farquharson. *Theory of Voting*, New Haven, 1969.
P. K. Pattanaik. *Strategy and Group Choice*, Amsterdam, 1978.
Amartya Sen. *Collective Choice and Social Welfare*, San Francisco and Edinburgh, 1970.

OTHER WORKS

The following is a highly selective list. It includes everything cited in the text, and a number of other works of particular relevance. For more comprehensive bibliographies, see those in the book by Bogdanor cited above, and the survey 'Social Choice Theory' by Sen listed below.

G. E. M. Anscombe. 'Ursprung und Grenzen der staatlichen Autorität', in F. Inciarte and H. Thomas (eds.), *Globale Gesellschaft und Zivilisation*, Cologne, 1975, pp. 37–55.
K. J. Arrow. 'A Difficulty in the Concept of Social Welfare', *Journal of Political Economy*, vol. 58, 1950, pp. 328–46.
Duncan Black. 'On the Rationale of Group Decision Making', *Journal of Political Economy*, vol. 56, 1948, pp. 23–34.
——. 'The Decisions of a Committee using a Special Majority', *Econometrica*, vol. 16, 1948, pp. 245–61.
——. 'The Elasticity of Committee Decisions with an Altering Size of Majority', *Econometrica*, vol. 16, 1948, pp. 262–70.
——. 'Un approcio alla teoria delle decisioni di comitato', *Giornale degli Economisti e Annali di Economica*, vol. 7, n.s., 1948, pp. 262–84.
——. 'The Elasticity of Committee Decisions with Alterations in the Members' Preference Schedules', *South African Journal of Economics*, vol. 17, 1949, pp. 88–102.
——. 'The Theory of Elections in Single-Member Constituencies', *Canadian Journal of Economics and Political Science*, vol. 15, 1949, pp. 158–75.

BIBLIOGRAPHY

——. 'Some Theoretical Schemes of Proportional Representation', *Canadian Journal of Economics and Political Science*, vol. 15, 1949, pp. 334–43.
Duncan Black and R. A. Newing. *Committee Decisions with Complementary Valuation*, London, 1951.
J. H. Blau. 'The Existence of a Social Welfare Function', *Econometrica*, vol. 25, 1957, pp. 302–13.
——. 'Arrow's Theorem with Weak Independence', *Econometrica*, vol. 38, 1971, pp. 413–20.
——. 'A Direct Proof of Arrow's Theorem', *Econometrica*, vol. 40, 1972, pp. 61–7.
Vernon Bogdanor and David Butler (eds.). *Democracy and Elections: Electoral Systems and their Political Consequences*, Cambridge, 1983.
Jean-Charles de Borda. 'Mémoire sur les elections au scrutin', *Mémoires de l'Académie Royale des Sciences*, Paris, 1781, pp. 31–4 and 657–65; English trans. by A. de Grazia, *Isis*, 1944.
Steven J. Brams. *Game Theory and Politics*, New York, 1975.
Steven J. Brams and Peter C. Fishburn. 'Approval Voting', *American Political Science Review*, vol. 72, 1978, pp. 831–47.
——. *Approval Voting*, Cambridge, Mass., 1983.
Andrew McLaren Carstairs. *A Short History of Electoral Systems in Western Europe*, London, 1980.
Marquis de Condorcet. *Essai sur l'application de l'analyse à la probabilité des décisions rendues à la pluralité des voix*, Paris, 1785.
George Cunningham. Letter in *The Guardian*, 12 October 1981.
Michael Dummett and Robin Farquharson. 'Stability in Voting', *Econometrica*, vol. 29, 1961, pp. 33–43.
B. Dutta and P. K. Pattanaik. 'On Nicely Consistent Voting Systems', *Econometrica*, vol. 46, 1978, pp. 163–70.
Robin Farquharson. 'Sur une généralisation de la notion de l'équilibrium', *Comptes rendus de l'Académie des Sciences*, vol. 240, 1955, pp. 46–8.
——. 'Straightforwardness in Voting Procedures', *Oxford Economic Papers*, vol. 8, 1956, pp. 80–9.
——. 'Strategic Information in Games and in Voting', in Colin Cherry (ed.), *Information Theory*, London, 1956.
S. E. Finer (ed.). *Adversary Politics and Electoral Reform*, London, 1975.
P. C. Fishburn. *The Theory of Social Choice*, Princeton, 1973.
P. C. Fishburn and W. V. Gehrlein. 'Borda's Rule, Positional Voting and Condorcet's Simple Majority Principle', *Public Choice*, vol. 28, 1976, pp. 79–88.
P. Gardenfors. 'Manipulation of Social Choice Functions', *Journal of Economic Theory*, vol. 13, 1976, pp. 217–28.
M. Garman and M. Kamien. 'The Paradox of Voting: Probability Calculations', *Behavioral Science*, vol. 13, 1968, pp. 306–16.
W. V. Gehrlein and P. C. Fishburn. 'The Probability of the Paradox of Voting: a Computable Solution', *Journal of Economic Theory*, vol. 13, 1976, pp. 14–25.
A. Gibbard. 'Manipulation of Voting Schemes: A General Result', *Econometrica*, vol. 41, 1973, pp. 587–601.

———. 'Social Decision, Strategic Behavior and Best Outcomes', in Gottinger and Leinfellner, 1978 [see below].
H. W. Gottinger and W. Leinfellner (eds.). *Decision Theory and Social Ethics: Issues in Social Choice*, Dordrecht, 1978.
R. J. Gretlein. 'Dominance Solvable Voting Schemes: a Comment', *Econometrica*, vol. 50, 1982, pp. 527–8 [see H. Moulin].
Geoffrey Hand, Jacques Georgel, and Christophe Sasse. *European Electoral Systems Handbook*, London, 1979.
Thomas Hare. *The Machinery of Representation*, London, 1857.
———. *Treatise on the Election of Representatives, Parliamentary and Municipal*, London, 1859.
C. G. Hoag and G. H. Hallett. *Proportional Representation*, New York, 1926.
L. Hurwica and D. Schmeidler. 'Construction of Outcome Functions Guaranteeing Existence and Pareto Optimality of Nash Equilibria', *Econometrica*, vol. 46, 1978, pp. 1447–74.
Ken-ichi Inada. 'A Note on the Simple Majority Decision Rule', *Econometrica*, vol. 32, 1964, pp. 525–31.
———. 'On the Simple Majority Decision Rule', *Econometrica*, vol. 37, 1969, pp. 490–506.
S. K. Jain. 'Characterisation of Rationality Conditions in Terms of Minimal Decisive Sets', Indian Statistical Institute, Delhi, 1977.
Marquis de Laplace. 'Leçons de mathématiques, données à l'École Normale en 1795', *Journal de l'École Polytechnique*, vol. 2, 1812, 7th and 8th cahiers; included in *Essai philosophique sur les probabilités*, 1814, which forms the introduction to *Théorie analytique des probabilités*, second edition, 1814.
Bo Larsson. *Basic properties of majority rule*, Lund, 1983.
R. Duncan Luce and H. Raiff. *Games and Decisions*, New York, 1958.
R. D. McKelvey and R. C. Niemi. 'A Multi-Stage Game Representation of Sophisticated Voting for Binary Procedures', *Journal of Economic Theory*, vol. 18, 1978, pp. 1–22.
David McKie. 'Getting the M.P. you Want', *The Guardian*, 10 December 1981.
John Stuart Mill. *On Liberty*, London, 1859; reprinted in J. S. Mill, *Utilitarianism; On Liberty; Representative Government*, ed. A. D. Lindsay, 1910, re-ed. H. B. Acton, 1972, London, Everyman's Library, and in *On Liberty, Representative Government and the Subjection of Women*, ed. Millicent Garrett Fawcett, Oxford, 1912, World's Classics.
———. 'Recent Writers on Reform', 1859; reprinted in J. S. Mill, *Dissertations and Discussions*, vol. 3, London, 1867, pp. 47–96.
———. *Considerations on Representative Government*, London, 1861; reprinted in Everyman's Library and in World's Classics [see under *On Liberty*].
H. Moulin. 'Dominance Solvable Voting Schemes', *Econometrica*, vol. 47, 1979, pp. 1337–51 [see also R. J. Gretlein].
———. *The Strategy of Social Choice*, Amsterdam, 1983.
Y. Murakami. 'A Note on the General Possibility Theorem of the Social Welfare Function', *Econometrica*, vol. 29, 1961, pp. 244–6.
———. *Logic and Social Choice*, New York, 1968.
K. Nakamura. *Game Theory and Social Choice*, Tokyo, 1981.

J. F. Nash. 'Non-cooperative Games', *Annals of Mathematics*, vol. 54, 1951, pp. 286–95.
J. von Neumann and O. Morgenstern. *Theory of Games and Economic Behaviour*, Princeton, 1944.
Dieter Nohlen. *Wahlsysteme der Welt*, Munich, 1978.
Prasanta K. Pattanaik. 'On the Stability of Sincere Voting Situations', *Journal of Economic Theory*, vol. 6, 1973, pp. 558–74.
P. K. Pattanaik and M. Sengupta. 'Outcomes of Admissible Nash Equilibria and Sophisticated Voting when Decisions are based on Pairwise Comparisons', *Mathematical Social Sciences*, vol. 2, 1982, pp. 39–54.
P. K. Pattanaik and Maurice Salles (eds.). *Social Choice and Welfare*, Amsterdam, 1983.
B. Peleg. 'Consistent Voting Systems', *Econometrica*, vol. 46, 1978, pp. 153–62.
——. *Game-Theoretic Analysis of Voting in Committees*, Cambridge, forthcoming.
C. R. Plott. 'Recent Results in the Theory of Voting', in M. Intriligator (ed.), *Frontiers of Quantitative Economics*, Amsterdam, 1971.
Stein Rokkan. *Citizens, Elections, Parties*, Oslo, 1970.
Jean-Jacques Rousseau. *Du Contrat social, ou Principes du droit politique*, Amsterdam, 1762; English trans. by G. D. H. Cole in *The Social Contract and Discourses*, London, 1913, Everyman's Library.
Christophe Sasse (ed.). *The European Parliament: towards a Uniform Procedure for Direct Elections*, Florence, 1981 [distributed by HMSO].
M. A. Satterthwaite. 'Strategy-proofness and Arrow's Conditions: Existence and Correspondence Theorems for Voting Procedures and Social Welfare Functions', *Journal of Economic Theory*, vol. 10, 1975, pp. 187–217.
D. Schmeidler and H. Sonnenschein. 'Two Proofs of the Gibbard-Satterthwaite Theorem on the Possibility of a Strategy-proof Social Choice Function', in Gottinger and Leinfellner, 1978 [q.v.].
Amartya K. Sen. 'A Possibility Theorem on Majority Decisions', *Econometrica*, vol. 34, 1966, pp. 75–9.
——. 'Quasi-Transitivity, Rational Choice and Collective Decisions', *Review of Economic Studies*, vol. 36, 1969, pp. 381–93.
——. *Choice, Welfare and Measurement*, Oxford, 1982.
——. 'Social Choice Theory', to be included in K. J. Arrow and M. Intriligator (eds.), *Handbook of Mathematical Economics*, vol. 3, forthcoming 1984.
A. K. Sen and P. K. Pattanaik. 'Necessary and Sufficient Conditions for Rational Choice under Majority Decision', *Journal of Economic Theory*, vol. 1, 1969, pp. 178–202.
K. Suzumura. *Rational Choice, Collective Decisions and Social Welfare*, Cambridge, 1984.
W. Vickrey. 'Utility, Stategy and Social Decision Rules', *Quarterly Journal of Economics*, vol. 74, 1960, pp. 507–35.
B. Ward. 'Majority Voting and Alternative Forms of Public Enterprise', in J. Margolis (ed.), *The Public Economy of Urban Communities*, Baltimore, 1965.
Philip Williams. 'Labour and the Alternative Vote', *The Guardian*, 11th March, 1974.

Index

abstention, 27
admissible contingency, *see* contingency
admissible strategy, 46, 65, 78, 80–1, 90–1, 98, 224, 231–3; *see also* secondarily admissible strategy, ultimately admissible strategy
admissible situation, *see* situation
alliance, *see* collusion
alternative vote procedure, *see* voting procedures, types of
amendment procedure, *see* voting procedures, types of
ancillary criterion for a fair outcome, 130
announcement of results of voting, 179–80, 182–3, 194
Anscombe, Elizabeth, 15, 26
appointments, 243–54
Arrow, Kenneth, 4, 11, 118–19, 142n., 294
Arrow's possibility theorem, 50–4, 85, 210–11, 219n.
asymmetric relation, 32

ballots, 40, 57, 80
beats another, one strategy, 45
Benn, Tony, 2–3
binary procedures, *see* voting procedures, types of
Birmingham Liberal Association, 229, 265
Black, Duncan, 4, 133n., 169n., 294–5
Bógdanor, Vernon, 229, 261n., 264n., 265, 278, 294–5
Borda, Jean-Charles de, 4, 133n., 176, 295
bracketing, 155–6, 169, 176, 180, 186, 187, 245

Carroll, Lewis, *see* Dodgson, Charles Lutwidge
casting vote, 47, 82, 102n., 166
chairman, 47, 59, 82, 88, 102n.
collusion, 15–25, 80–1, 91, 99, 104, 211–12, 228–9
complete list mechanism, 155–67, 169, 175, 210, 247–8

desirable properties for procedure using, 215–23
composite outcome, *see* outcome, composite
composite score of an outcome, 184–9
adjusted, 188–9
raw, 188
composite score procedure, *see* voting procedures, types of
conditional preferences, 57–9, 71
Condorcet, Marquis de, 4, 84n., 113n., 295
connected relation, 31, 82–3
contingency, 45, 47–9, 80–1
admissible, 99
n-admissible, 103
critical member of decisive set, 207
critical ratio, 261–4
cumulative vote procedure, *see* voting procedures, types of
Cunningham, George, 2–3
cyclic triad, 85, 100–1, 115–17, 146–51

decisive set of voters, 53, 207–9
critically decisive set, 207
minimally decisive set, 207–8
decomposition, 72–6
consistent with preference scale, 73
corresponds to split procedure, 74
deputy leadership of Labour party, 1981
election to, 1–3, 27
determinate procedure, *see* fully determinate procedure, secondarily determinate procedure, ultimately determinate procedure
determines outcome outright, procedure, 90, 202
Dodgson, Charles Lutwidge, 4–5, 169, 295
dominates another, one strategy, 45–6, 80
dominance a transitive relation, 46
Droop quota, 269–74

electoral reform, 5–10, 292–3
electoral systems, 9–10, 255–93

electoral systems—*cont.*
  Eire, 268
  India, under British Raj, 260
  Israel, 9, 292
  Malta, 268
  Northern Ireland, 268, 273–4
  U.K., 9, 171, 259–60, 261
  U.S.A., 9, 171, 259–60, 292
  West Germany, 9, 292
  Zimbabwe, 260
elimination procedures, *see* voting procedures, types of
empirical studies, low value of, 29–30
equivalent strategies, 153
expected satisfaction, 48

fair outcome, 51, 55–7
  clash of criteria for, 129, 142, 176, 179–84, 194
  principles governing criterion for a fair outcome: (1) 83; (2) 84; (2') 84; (3) 84; (4) 84, 114, 121–2, 125, 126, 127, 130, 140, 171; (5) 87, 114, 118, 122; (6) 115, 117–20, 124–5, 127–8, 134, 141; (7) 120, 122, 124–5, 127–8, 130, 180; (8) 122, 124–5, 126–8, 130; (9) 125, 126–8, 130; (10) 130; (11) 130, 132–3; (12) 132–3; (13) 134, 140–1, 171, 176; (14) 134; (15) 141
fair voting procedure, 29, 50, 81–2, 114–42
  fair to outcomes or to voters, 173–4, 255–6
family visit to theatre, 38–9, 50, 54–5, 81–2, 129
Farquharson, Robin, 4n., 23–6, 60, 84n., 111–13, 202n., 294
fully determinate procedure (relatively to given preference scales), 90, 95, 98, 202

Gardenfors, P., 202n.
general will, voting as expressing the, 181, 296–7
Gibbard, Allan, 202n.
globally hypersensitive criterion for a fair outcome, 126
globally sensitive criterion for a fair outcome, 125–6, 129–30
graded SV procedure, *see* voting procedures, types of

Hallett, G. H., 216, 222
Healey, Denis, 2–3
height of a ballot (in multiple-ballot procedure), 93
height of multiple-ballot procedure, 100, 104
Hoag, C. G., 216, 222

Inada, Ken-ichi, 4n.
inadmissible stretegy, 80, 90–1
inadmissible result of ballot, 95
independence of irrelevant alternatives, 52–6, 118–19, 142n., 210–11, 219n.
indifference, 31, 32, 35, 36, 50, 66, 70
induction, argument by, 93
insecure outcome, *see* secure outcome

Jain, S. K., 202n.

knock-out procedure, *see* voting procedures, types of

Laplace, Marquis de, 4, 295
leading criterion for a fair outcome, 130
Lehrer, Keith, 33
Lincoln, Abraham, 1
limited vote procedure, *see* voting procedures, types of
live candidate (after stage), 269
live outcome (after ballot or stage), 94, 98
Lords, House of, 260
Lotze, Hermann, 4
Lowe, Robert, 264
lower bound for desirable number of strategies, 152–3; *see also* upper bound

majority, 14–22, 296; *see also* special majority
majority number of an outcome, 115
majority number procedure, *see* voting procedures, types of
majority preference, 54, 81–5, 114–28, 129, 142, 256, 296
  not always transitive, 85–6
majority procedure, 17, 88, 93, 177–8, 280
majority score of an outcome, 121, 128
Marshall, J. G., 263–4
McKie, David, 273

INDEX

method of assessment, 27, 30, 56–7, 78, 152, 156, 168, 210; *see also* simulation
Mill, John Stuart, 295
minorities, guaranteeing representation for, 256–65, 282–93
multi-member constituencies, 260–92
mystique of the majority, 142, 178

n-admissible strategy, 103
naive vote (strategy), 98, 162, 164, 169
n-determinate procedure, 104
n-determines an outcome, procedure, 104
n-dominates another, one strategy, 103
'no election', 250–4
notional votes, 270–2
n-rivals another, one strategy, 103

open ballot, 27
optimal strategy, 224
ordering relation, 36; *see also* weak ordering
outcome, 31, 50, 60; *see also* secure outcome, stable outcome
   at acute risk from a voter on a ballot in an elimination procedure, 106, 217
   at risk from a voter on a ballot in an elimination procedure, 106, 217
   best attainable, 224
   composite, 64, 71, 87
   doomed on a ballot in an elimination procedure, 107, 217
   overall, 39–40
   produced by a situation, 45, 78
   secure from a voter, 217

paradox of voting, 11, 54, 85, 114, 298
party lists, 268
Pattanaik, Prasanta, 4n., 202n.
persistent majority number procedure, *see* voting procedures, types of
persistently has the highest majority number, outcome, 120
political parties, 24–5, 228–9, 264–5, 268, 282, 286–7, 289
possible outcome, *see* outcome
possible winner, 224
preference relation, 31
   connected, 31–2
   transitive, 32–5, 46

preference scale, 36, 39–40, 50, 57–8, 78; *see also* strong preference scale, weak preference scale
preference score of an outcome, 133–51
   maximum and minimum for given majority score, 135–40, 144–51
preference score procedure, *see* voting procedures, types of
preference, strength of, *see* strength of preference
preference, strict, 31, 32, 35
preference table, 84
preferences, scattered or clumped, 290
preponderance of voters, 123
preponderance score of outcome, 124, 128
proportional representation, 6, 259, 268
psychology of voting, 212–13

qualifying stages (under QPS), 284–7
quota, 268–74, 277–8, 280–3, 284
QPS procedure, *see* voting procedures, types of

random process, 209
redistribution of votes, 269–72, 274–83, 289, 291
reduction number, 106
regular strategy (in alternative vote), 224
regular strategy (in preference score procedure), 233
relative majority procedure, *see* voting procedures, types of
representative parliaments, 6–8, 255–6, 292–3
residual outcome (under amendment procedure), 62
result of a ballot, 60, 65–6
rivals another, one strategy, 45
R_{maj} diagram, 100
Rousseau, Jean-Jacques, 23–5
   objections to political parties, 24–5

satisfaction value, 14–25, 37, 39–40, 46, 48–9, 253; *see also* expected satisfaction
Satterthwaite, M. A., 202n.
Schmeidler, D., 202n.
school boards, election of, 264
secret ballot, 27
Second Reform Act, 261, 264

secondarily admissible (2-admissible) strategy, 99, 215
secondarily determinate (2-determinate) procedure, 100
secondarily determines (2-determines) an outcome, procedure, 100
secondarily dominates (2-dominates), 99
secondarily rivals (2-rivals), 99
secure outcome, 82, 87, 89
semi-regular strategy (in preference score procedure), 233
Sen, Amartya, 4n., 294–5
short list, 244–7, 251
simulation of a voting procedure by a method using the complete list mechanism, 156–64, 169
sincere voting, 14, 16, 21, 25, 26, 30, 41–2, 44, 56, 78–80, 98, 168, 211
single-issue voters, 289
single-peakedness, 4n.
situation, 44–5, 78; *see also* vulnerable situation
  admissible, 90, 98
  as point in space, 205
  n-admissible, 103
  secondarily admissible (2-admissible), 100
  sincere, 212, 222
  surest situation for an outcome under a majority procedure, 88
smooth strategy (in alternative vote), 224
social choice function, 51
social choice theory, 54
social ordering, 51–2, 85
social welfare function, 51–2, 56, 210
solidly committed voters, 282–91, 296
Sonnenschein, H., 202n.
space of situations, 205–8
  boundary between regions, 205–6
  contiguous points, 205
  path, 205–7
  region, 205–6
special majority, 22–3, 27
split binary procedure, *see* voting procedures, types of
stable outcome, 87, 88–9, 280
stable situation, 87, 89–90
straightforward strategy, 41–4, 65–70, 74–5, 76, 78, 80, 81, 98
straightforward procedure, 202–9, 211
strategic voting, 17, 21, 25–6, 210–42
strategy, *see* voting strategy
strength of preference, 37–40
distance on preference scale as surrogate for, 38–9, 54–5, 57, 71, 210
strong preference scale, 66, 84, 100
STV procedure, *see* voting procedures, types of
superfluous strategy, 153, 157–8, 160
surplus of votes, 270–1, 274, 278–9, 282–3, 291
symmetric relation, 32
symmetrical elimination procedure, *see* voting procedures, types of
symmetry of procedure with respect to outcomes, 203, 219
symmetry of procedure with respect to voters, 202n., 204

Thatcher, Margaret, 260
theory of voting, 4–5, 11–12, 294–5, 297
  dynamic, 14–26, 28, 40–1, 57–9, 71–2
  static, 14, 26–8, 40–1, 57–9, 71
tie, 27, 82, 165–6; *see also* casting vote
top, 4n., 84, 293
transitive relation, 32, 46, 85
tree diagram, 60

ultimately admissible strategy, 105
ultimately determinate procedure, 105–6
unlikelihood of examples, 7–8, 131–2, 169
unstable outcome, *see* stable outcome
unstable situation, *see* stable situation
upper bound for desirable number of strategies, 153–5

voting as expression of personal taste, 170
voting as expression of judgement, 170
voting mechanism, 27, 30, 78, 152–67
voting procedure, criteria for a good, 29, 50, 81, 131, 168
voting procedure, principally determined by voting mechanism and method of assessment, 27, 78; *see also* announcement of results
voting procedures, types of:
  alternative vote, 156–7, 160–1, 163–4, 172–5, 176, 214–30, 241, 255, 266–8, 279
  amendment, 29–30, 41–2, 61, 62, 66, 96–7, 98, 100–1, 169, 203–4; simulated, 157–8, 169, 171–2
  binary, 60–77, 93–5, 157, 202–3
  binary elimination, 62, 67–8

INDEX

composite score, 183–201, 296, 297
cumulative vote, 263–5
elimination, 62
impure binary, 76–7
individual PS (preference score), 252
individual SV (satisfaction value): graded, 252–4, 296, 297; straight, 252
knock-out, 43–4, 60, 62, 65, 66, 67, 95–6, 98–9, 101, 102, 164; simulated, 158–60, 171
limited vote, 261–3; simply, 261–3, 265; strictly, 261–2
majority number, 178–80, 181–3, 194, 216, 237–42, 251, 277, 280, 282, 290–1, 296
mixed binary, 62, 64
multiple-ballot, 40, 57
multiple vote, 256–9
persistent majority number, 180, 194, 296
preference score, 176–8, 182, 216, 231–7, 241–2, 250, 259, 267–8, 296, 297; curtailed, 244–6, 259, 296; candidates', 247–8, 263, 277, 280, 282, 290–2
pure binary, 61–2, 76
QPS (quota preference score), 284–93, 296
relative majority, 29, 47, 102n., 165, 172, 215, 241, 279; modified, 165–6, 171, 216; simulated, 166, 171

separate, for equal posts, 248–50
single-ballot, 165–6
split, 63, 67, 70–6, 78–9, 81, 87–8, 97, 101
STV (single transferable vote), 268–84, 285, 288–92, 296, 297
symmetrical elimination procedure, 106, 156, 164; with positive voting, 106, 107, 110–11, 156, 160–1, 162–3; simulated, *see* alternative vote; with negative voting, 106, 107–10, 156, 160; simulated, 156–7, 160, 175, 176
voting strategy, 41, 44–6; *see also* admissible strategy, beats, dominates, equivalent strategies, n-admissible strategy, naive vote, n-dominates, n-rivals, optimal strategy, rivals, secondarily admissible strategy, secondarily dominates, secondarily rivals, sincere voting, straightforward strategy, superfluous strategy, ultimately admissible strategy
vulnerable situation, 25, 45, 87, 90–1, 222

wasted vote, 30, 214–15, 229–30, 266, 269, 278–80
weak ordering, 36, 51
weak preference scale, 66–7
weighted preferences, *see* satisfaction value, strength of preference
West Belfast, 273–4